# THE AUTOBIOGRA[

OF

# ROBERT STANDISH SIEVIER.

1906.

LONDON :
THE WINNING POST (1906) LIMITED, 15, ESSEX STREET,
STRAND, LONDON, W.C.

Printed by
Walbrook & Co., Ltd., 13–15, Whitefriars Street,
London, E.C.

Yours very truly

R. S. Sievier

# CONTENTS.

# THE AUTOBIOGRAPHY

OF

# ROBERT STANDISH SIEVIER.

## CHAPTER I.

### EARLY DAYS.

 WAS born in a hansom cab, and have been going on ever since. Making a premature entrance into the world on the 30th of May, 1860, it may fairly be stated that the whole of my natal surroundings were most unorthodox.

Before I dive into the depths of the adventurous and travelled life I have led, I feel it would put my readers more on a par with my friends to let them know something of my progenitors.

My father was Robert Moore Sievier, the eldest son of Robert William Sievier, a Fellow of the Royal Society and the premier sculptor of his day. Besides exhibiting in the Royal Academy, he had the honour of staying at Windsor Castle, when he made a bust of the late Prince Consort, and the "Court Circular" of this period reads as follows:—"Mr. Sievier, the sculptor, was honoured this morning by Prince Albert with a sitting for a bust of His Royal Highness." Amongst other works of art which he executed was a very large marble statue of Lord Harcourt, now in St. George's Chapel, Windsor, and it so happened that Lady Mary Harcourt was godmother to all his daughters, my aunts.

A similar work, representing Sir William Jenner, is in Gloucester Cathedral; a bust of Sir Thomas Lawrence, R.A., is now in the Soane Museum, Lincoln's Inn Fields; a very fine statue of Dibdin, the author of "Tom Bowling," to-day adorns the library at Greenwich; and other works are entailed with the Chatsworth property, inherited by the present Duke of Devonshire.

Having reached the zenith of his fame as a sculptor, my grandfather turned his attention to science, and "Redgrave's Dictionary of British Artists" and another volume called "Men of the Reign" (Victoria) give a lengthy account of his different successes and his extraordinary scientific and general attainments. Authorities on science and telegraphy during the early Victorian era refer to his name, and he is mentioned by them as being one who successfully perfected telegraphy up to the time in which he lived. He was a close friend of *the* Lord Brougham, and took a plaster cast of his face to save the time of sitting, and the bust is one of his best works. I have in my possession a bust of my father executed by him.

It was because of his achievements in science in general, and telegraphy in particular, that he was made a Fellow of the Royal Society at a very early age, and at a time when such honours were not conferred so lavishly as they are to-day. He also received the Freedom of the City of London.

He married Anne Eliza Horne, whose grandfather, Jacob Wilkinson, was a member of Parliament. Her father died soon after her birth, and her mother being killed while hunting, she was made a ward in Chancery. The late Archdeacon Brymer was her cousin.

Of marvellous versatility, discarding art, no sooner did he master one branch of science than he turned his attention to another, or, by way of a change, to something of an inventive nature, which had little or no connection with his previous experiments. Amongst other things, he invented a loom, which the late Jacob, John, and William Bright took up; but no sooner was this successful, than, after a long course of experiments carried on in Belgium, he discovered a new method of smelting iron, which produced great results, both from a mechanical and economical point of view; while a few months later Mr. Brockton, when lecturing at the Royal Institute upon indiarubber, the use of which was only understood in those days to the extent of erasing pencil marks from paper, concluded his discourse with the following words: "For the perfecting of indiarubber and bringing its greater use before the public, the machinery and solution were the invention of Mr. Sievier, the sculptor."

A part of the notice of his obituary, which appeared in the "Times" in 1865, and which I have before me at the time of writing, runs as follows:—"He (R. W. Sievier, F.R.S.) also studied surgery and anatomy, and, as if this were not enough for an ever-active, enterprising mind, to mechanics his talents were afterwards directed, and here his triumphs were extraordinary. It would fill a volume to describe all his achievements and projects—some of the latter, it is feared, may be lost from the absence of the mind in which they originated," &c. He was the son of John Sievier, a solicitor of the High Court who did not practise, but lived some hundred years ago in Russell Square, which in those times would be on a par with Berkeley Square of to-day.

My father, who was born in this house, was never engaged in any business or profession, and died at the early age of thirty-nine, when I was five years of age and my sister three, leaving my mother in anything but affluent circumstances. My mother's maiden name was Alicia Maria Sutton, and she was born at Fyfield Manor House, her father, Henry Stephen Sutton, holding a commission in the service, and his only brother was an officer in the navy. The rest of the particulars of my family can be found at the Heralds' College. My mother in her day was an excellent horsewoman, and the late

Assheton Smith, Master of Foxhounds, bestowed upon her the name of " His Diana."

If I have been somewhat lengthy in explaining these family matters, I crave the indulgence of my readers on the ground that there have been so many rumours and stories in connection with me that I feel it better, once and for all, to set at rest the question of whence I came.

So here I am, just the ordinary individual, more or less connected in the ordinary way ; and except for inheriting my grandfather's volatile characteristics I am nothing out of the common. The romances surrounding adventures, the learning travel instils in us, the glorious uncertainty of sport, the throes of racing, all these experiences are at anyone's command, but it is the degree of success or failure attending them which creates the interest or loses it. What success or failure has been my share in perhaps one of the most varied careers of any man alive to-day, I will leave my readers to judge ; but I preface my autobiography by saying, that except for one or two instances, which rather touch the heart than the conscience, I would willingly live my time over again. Taking my life from the standpoint of a man of the world— that Bohemian world which never encouraged angelic opinions or the views of an extremist—I feel I have no more to reproach myself with than has any other ordinary sinner, while I may at once say that if I were asked which I would sooner be, an angel or a devil, from the accepted standpoint as understood on this earth, I would at once declare myself a devil, for I should then at least escape that greatest of all insidious evils in man—hypocrisy. The man who has no devil in him should have been born a woman, just as much as a woman without love should have been a statue—Galatea reversed.

I do not wish to be in any way misunderstood, or to create a false impression. It is not my intention to plead for any one line of life, my own included, but what I wish to point out is that as every man possessing an ounce of character has his own code of honour, so has every man his own views of right and wrong, from the particular ground upon which fate has placed him to judge. By dissenters from the ordinary usages of Bohemian life I have no doubt I should be pronounced a very naughty boy, but some reminiscences are so pleasant to me that if I have any regret in connection with them it is that I have not been worse.

I merely make these observations, emphasising those facts of my life which have gone to make up these convictions, that I may better introduce myself, and that I may be thoroughly understood in this, my endeavour faithfully to chronicle episodes and experiences of my travels, without in any way misleading my reader or attempting to pose as a saint in the hope that when my autobiography, in the fulness of time, fades into an obituary. my likeness may be transferred to a stained glass window. I should resent any such proposal as a malicious libel on myself. Such likenesses are invariably unfaithful, and the colouring is shocking!

I have already stated that on the death of my father, when I was but five years old, my mother was left with only my sister and myself as a legacy. She had very small means, and my uncles on both sides all, save one, died early, which left me the one bright male star in a firmament of married and maiden aunts. Like Topsy, I grew, and puerile inspirations increased as I sucked sweets. My mother was an exceptional pianist, and had played duets with the late Arabella Goddard at charity concerts. I believe my greatest enjoyment, certainly my greatest solace, is to hear her play to-day those pieces which recall my childhood. She was a most intimate friend of Miss Kate Loder, afterwards Lady Thompson, a friendship which remained undisturbed until that lady's recent decease, while the late Sir Henry Thompson more than once defrayed my school bill, which I am only too pleased to have this opportunity of gratefully acknowledging. During the holidays, my aunts would meet and discuss what was to become of me, but each had her own opinion, one leaning to medicine, another inclining to the law, while, through a personal acquaintance with the late Admiral King-Hall, my mother wanted to make me a sailor. The different views and opinions of these good ladies, whose memories I revere, were expressed with reasons pro and con., but an agreement could never be come to among them, and the diversity of views which existed at their first meeting lasted until the climax, which I myself brought about. My good-natured mother was the first to give way, and I must admit that, fond as I am of our sailors, the sight of the horizon day after day would not have satisfied my restless nature, and a life on the ocean wave would soon have lost any attraction for me, and drowned whatever ambition I might have possessed in that direction.

Adverse circumstances affected my mother in their severest sense, and these vicissitudes are the more acute when they attack a lady reared in affluent surroundings, but of a family which had slowly fallen into pecuniary decay, only to become a derelict among many others, except in name and blood. Inexperienced in the reverses of the world as my mother was, and without the protection of a man, these circumstances were the cause of my school being shifted more than once, and thus early I was, as it were, a fledgling of passage. Scylla and Charybdis instil no fears compared with those which beset a loving, hopeful woman suddenly stranded in the midst of adversity, her only anchorage two young children, her haven the universe. As I write here to-day, about to relate many hardships and reckless adventures which I have gone through, I feel how much greater were my mother's silent trials in those days, brought about by my father's death, and borne by her with uncomplaining resignation and patience. We men who have played our parts in the wars of countries and of life, we who have survived shipwreck and those storms manhood was born to resist, can never fathom that inestimable, uncomplaining nature of a good, brave woman whose thoughts are her only confidant.

Although but a youth, having been cast among those older than myself, I was in many respects older than my actual years. My holidays had been passed at different houses and places, and at the age of sixteen I perhaps "knew" more of the world and less of my studies than I should.

The first races I ever attended, or can recollect, were those which were once held at West Drayton. Living at the time at Iver, I used to fish the stream which skirted the racecourse, and one day, not altogether to my surprise, when bent on the sober piscatorial sport, I heard that a race meeting was about to take place so conveniently at hand. I discarded my rod and line, hiding it in the rushes, and quickly found myself one of the outside spectators. I frankly admit that my first impressions, except for the infatuation I always had for horses, were anything but favourable. I think even the pedant would have pronounced me reasonably innocent at this period, and for the first time in my life I saw before me the most repugnant class of men, and in instances women, I could possibly have imagined to exist.

My feelings were those of curiosity combined with disgust. I was in their midst, not lost, not afraid, but no less in a state of wonderment. The racecourse in those days was the resort of all sorts and conditions of criminals, and I could recognise in the majority of the faces which I looked on the impress of crime. I saw one race, retraced my footsteps, and, finding my rod, wended my way home to the sleepy village of Iver. If anyone had then ventured to prophesy that I should one day become a prominent owner of racehorses, and that a mare such as Sceptre would carry my colours, I believe I should have resented the statement with some warmth.

A few years passed, and with them the West Drayton impressions. Staying in the vicinity of Ascot during the race week, I felt once more a growing inclination to pay a visit to a racecourse, and telling my aunt a story that I should like to see Windsor Castle, I found myself stepping out not in that direction; on the contrary, my footsteps led me with

all possible speed to the Royal Heath. I remember the
timidity with which I approached the course. for fear someone might recognise me! I do not suppose there was a soul
present who would have known me if I had been paraded
before the whole company! I found myself amongst the
coaches. By degrees, when I discovered there was no charge
made, I crossed the course, and the contrast was indeed
great. Again I found myself in a den of offensive-looking
characters, not so deplorable as those I had seen at West
Drayton, but, nevertheless a most repulsive mob. I quickly
retraced my steps towards the coaches, and saw Verneuil win
the Gold Cup, while to this day I carry in my mind's eye the
photograph of the man who welshed me.

By this time I had made some friends, whom, as they were
some years my senior, I naturally found most entertaining.
I had visited the old Pavilion Music Hall, when my dear,
good-natured mother believed I was attending a sick friend,
and the Alhambra and Pertoldi also had attractions for me.
I had once, or perhaps twice, slipped into the Duke's, and
had made the excursion to Cremorne. It was the latter place
which was to bring me to grief, and was to lay bare my
precocious conduct to my mother, not to mention the aunts.
It was the day of the Oxford and Cambridge boat-race, and,
as was customary, a fancy-dress ball was to take place at
Cremorne that evening. A friend of mine—it always is a
friend who is the delinquent—persuaded, or shall I say asked
me how I should like to accompany him to the ball that
evening. I felt paradise had opened its gates, and when he
added that I could go in fancy costume, and that he would
get me a dress, I felt he was quite the best fellow in the
world. I went with him to choose my costume. Always a
student of Shakespeare, I decided upon going as Hamlet!
Cremorne and Hamlet! What better double could be
suggested to a youth about to enter his sixteenth year! To
relate how I got into the costume, how I admired, with the
aid of a long cheval glass, my dress, and more particularly

myself in it, would touch the conceit of the vain. The chic red feather in the black bonnet, the sparkling buckles, the sword hanging by my side—there was nothing of the fretful Dane about me. The too, too solid flesh had no desire to melt, and Cremorne was reached by the aid of a hansom. Hamlet! There was almost a little buzz of excitement among the ladies—at least, so I fancied. The ghost had no fears for me, and all I saw before me was a bevy of Ophelias! As time went on I found my sword became a refractory nuisance ; but things went merrily, ever so merrily. Time passed, as time must, and it was not until eleven o'clock the next morning that I began to realise the situation. Suffice it to say that at midday Hamlet was being driven through Piccadilly in a hansom—a part of the play Sir Henry Irving has rigidly " cut," but one which I rehearsed with no small degree of success and amusement.

The aunts met in solemn conclave.

I had made the acquaintance, which quickly ripened into friendship, of Thomas Rodber Busby, who had left school and was some three years my senior. Like myself, he was fatherless, a circumstance which doubtless linked us together with a bond of natural sympathy. Busby was a good all-round fellow, well-known at the German Gymnasium as an athlete of no mean standard, and though I was his superior at billiards he towered above me in all other games except that we were an equal match with the gloves.

About this time considerable recruiting was going on in England for the Frontier Armed and Mounted Police of South Africa, since absorbed in the Cape Mounted Rifles. The advantages of joining this force were eulogistically described in the Press, holding out a tempting bait, and rousing the adventurous spirit of youth. One afternoon my friend Tom Busby, after recounting, not without a tinge of romance, tales of the fortunes which had been made " across the blue sea," concluded his observations by informing me he had that day enlisted in the Frontier Armed and Mounted Police, with another acquaintance of ours, by the name of Bloxham. I was bursting to go, too, and I believe this was the first time in my life I ever felt envious of anybody. It was September of 1876, and I was therefore sixteen years of age. Building castles in the air, my youthful imagination lent itself to all kinds of possibilities, and infused with the militant spirit, I carried myself with a military bearing worthy of a captain in the Guards. We discussed this and that, that and this, until our imaginations painted an impregnable fortress surrounded by adventure and romance worthy of Ouida herself to be stormed and captured. They were due to sail within forty-eight hours when Busby and I called on Bloxham.

Arriving at the house, we passed through the hall and entered one of those small, dull, square back rooms to be found in the majority of London houses, overlooking a strip of garden or a back yard. The three of us discussed the situation, and I noticed in Bloxham anything but that esprit so pronounced in Tom Busby, which I shared, and, as I have stated, envied. At last Bloxham found the opening he had evidently been waiting for, and asked Busby if he would think very ill of him if he, by some means, did not go, though he had already enlisted. At this moment his mother entered the room, and her troubled features disclosed her feelings.

After paying our respects we all remained standing, and a silence fell upon the dull little room. Mrs. Bloxham cast her sad, moist eyes with one steadfast look at her son, and turning to Busby, asked, " Is there no way out of this, Mr. Busby ; cannot something be done? " No one answered her appeal, and her feelings overcoming her she burst into tears. This was my opportunity.

"Your son need not go, Mrs. Bloxham."

" How?—tell me how? "

" I will go in his place."

And I went.

## CHAPTER II.

## MY FIRST VOYAGE.

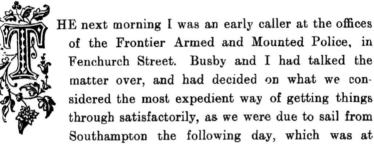HE next morning I was an early caller at the offices of the Frontier Armed and Mounted Police, in Fenchurch Street. Busby and I had talked the matter over, and had decided on what we considered the most expedient way of getting things through satisfactorily, as we were due to sail from Southampton the following day, which was at least cutting it a little fine. I interviewed Mr. Fuller, the manager, an old gentleman with a flowing grey beard—I, a young stripling of sixteen, my blood pulsating for adventure, and my spirit bold, "e'en to the cannon's mouth." I had screwed myself up to tell my first real big lie. Seated in this old gentleman's office, I explained that I had enlisted in the name of Bloxham, but that my real name was Sievier. To my delight he congratulated me upon coming to see him to set things right before sailing, crossed out the name of Bloxham on the papers, substituting mine in its place. In a second I felt quite at my ease, and if I had uttered an untruth it was of such a nature that it did no one any harm, and made at least one home happier— Bloxham's. We all have our own definitions of a lie ; mine is that it is a false statement which does some one harm, but where no ill is done, and good results, then it is no lie. Good cannot come out of a lie, hence where good grows a lie could

not have been sown. Thus, from my own standpoint, I had a clear conscience, and on September 22, 1876, I sailed on the R.M.S. Anglian, of the Union Line, for the Cape of Good Hope. This is the word we all foster in the early adventures of life—Hope. It tingled in me to the tips of my fingers; my thoughts were imbued with it, and my sight was spectacled in its golden rim.

Among the men and youths of our party were all sorts and conditions, and we boasted a son of a late Colonel of the Guards, a clergyman's son who belied his breeding, an Admiral's son, those of shopkeepers and others, all more or less respectable or disreputable, as you will. Whatever we were, good-fellowship reigned, and we messed together happily. The world and its cares were yonder, beyond the horizon; while the little floating world upon which we lived had its full complement of all we wanted, and there was no room for the petty worries of life on shore.

A sea voyage may be best described as a gliding indolence, and as I write of those days of careless, thoughtless luxury— I can look back upon them as nothing else—I feel I can appreciate what a great asset is contentment. Sea-sick? Bah! There was poetic rhythm in the motion! Rough? What so exhilarating! Smooth? What so leisurely lazy! At sixteen, healthy, strong, and vigorous, one is a philosopher—then or never.

In due course we reached that garden of the ocean called Madeira. To the enthusiastic youth, it was looking from Neptune's castle on a huge evergreen of many tints, rising to the cloudless sky, encircled by a gold-tinged ring of sand, encompassed by a liquid blue. A living lullaby. This was my early impression of my first experience of travel. As life runs on those impressions change. Novelty wears off and gets tarnished. Our maiden experiences are invariably of something we remember fondly, but time and use call for a lot of garnishing and burnishing to keep up these traditions. But I am digressing. The boatmen, as at all such ports of call, flocked round our vessel with their wares, principally fruit and the small filigree industries of the island. Its principal imports are consumptives, and we brought a consignment of two. Making use of the few hours allotted to passengers, we went ashore, visiting different places according to our inclinations. Not one of our recruits paid homage to the convent, a large white building standing prominently out among the foliage half-way up the slope. though most, if not all, became converts to the handsome, dark-eyed Portuguese girls.

The time ashore was all too short, except to the man of business, who cared for nothing except reaching his destination. Soon after noon we weighed anchor and sailed. We crossed the line in traditional fashion, and that good old rollicking fun prevailed which of late years has faded and faded away, until, like many other good customs on shore, it is to-day almost forgotten, or only remembered in a lukewarm spirit. There were concerts and dances, and conviviality reigned supreme. At one of the former functions I sang "John Peel" and recited, but those days are gone, and I wish to give my friends the intimation that I am not now taking any encores.

Nautical games were the order of the day, and "Nap" was the ruling game of cards. a rubber of whist being much too dry for us youngsters, it being a game we all then associated with our dear old grandmothers, who played it in those days. Zooks! if those courtly old ladies of our childhood, in their black brocades, crinolines, and long curls, could step down on to this world and see the "Bridge" girl of the ladies' clubs to-day, what a shock it would be for them!

By the time we reached Cape Town—we did not touch at St. Helena—my silver watch and telescope had gone in a raffle, the latter being twice put up, I having won it myself on the first occasion, and the proceeds, together with all my cash and available assets, had been absorbed by "Napoleon," which seemed hard lines on a British subject, considering we

were so close to St. Helena! I stood watching our approach
to the Cape of Good Hope without a coin of the realm to
call my own. Table Mountain, mantled in mist, loomed in the
distance, with the white houses of Cape Town sleeping at its
foot. Yet a feeling of confidence pervaded me. I was young,
my English birthright gave me a feeling of superiority as I
looked upon the shores of one of our colonies, and my state of
indigence caused me no anxiety. Our destination was East
London, but we had a few days to put in at Cape Town, for
the Anglian to unload cargo.

During the voyage Busby and I had chummed in with
two other recruits, named Gauntlet and Boxer. All we could
muster between us was four shillings and sixpence, not a
Johannesburg amount to keep four youngsters going for two
days! Nevertheless, we set foot in the colony with hearts
as light as our pockets, and with the natural instincts of the
New Chum, made tracks for the best hotel, then called the
Royal. On arriving we entered the billiard-room with regal
demeanour, befitting the sign of the hostelry, and found a
game of pool was in progress. I was a fair billiard player,
and after holding a council of war it was decided that I should
enter the ranks of the players, armed with the four shillings
and sixpence and whatever skill I possessed. I felt a great
responsibility was placed upon me, and it has been in such
tight corners that I have buckled on my energy and nerve, which
have enabled me to preserve my presence of mind, and it has
not often deserted me. Failure to achieve my object meant so
much to my friends, apart from myself, that such a result never
seriously entered my mind, and I chose a cue from the rack
with a dogmatic decision which must have inspired confidence
in my three chums. The balls were rolled out of the basket,
and had I been a superstitious youngster I might have deemed
it a bad omen when I received the symbolic green as my
ball. Had it been prismatic, with kaleidoscope changes, it
would not have shaken my set determination. The three
privates sat on the leather seat, dressed in line, while the

juvenile general went to the table to make his first stroke. "Green on yellow, player in hand," cried the marker. I can see myself again to-day, as plainly as though Father Time had set back his annual clock to 1876 ; the billiard-room, its oilcloth floor, everything is vivid before me. The position of the yellow ball afforded the opportunity of a fine cut into the end pocket. I made my stroke, and the yellow dropped. It was a good stroke, followed by the expressed appreciation of the onlookers, but there was still something more to follow. My ball, the ominous green, rolled on, hung in the jaws of the bottom pocket, wobbled, and disappeared. I put a shilling on the table to pay for the life I, or rather the green, had lost. " It is half a crown a life," said the yellow. Nothing daunted, I placed eighteen pence more on the table, which left me capitalised to the extent of two shillings in all, remarking that I understood it was a half-crown pool, not half-crown lives. " No, sir," replied the marker, in his most urbane manner ; " the lives are half a crown, the pool is seven and six." I slowly wended my way to where Busby, Boxer, and Gauntlet were sitting, and quietly inquired of them if they could raise sixpence more between them, as I had only two shillings left should I unluckily lose the next life. They could not collect it among them, even in coppers! My turn to play arrived, and my capital depended upon my hazard. I had a fairly easy shot, which I accomplished successfully, and taking two more lives and leaving myself reasonably safe, I saw an expression of satisfaction, I might almost say of jubilation, upon the faces of my three friends.

I believe I was as good a player then as I am now, which is not saying much, but billiards in the Colonies in 1876 was not what billiards is in England in 1906. I ultimately divided the pool, and before the afternoon was over had netted some £6 odd, and we left the smoking-room of the Royal Hotel merry men. We spent the evening at the theatre, then managed by Captain Disney Roebuck, and after various exploits, which I need not graphically describe, returned to the ship somewhat late, sleeping soundly in spite of the donkey engines and shifting of cargo. I am afraid we knocked an injudicious hole in the £6, and the following morning we were not overburdened with loose cash. Deeming we had not sufficient funds to carry us to the end of the evening in that luxury which we had enjoyed the previous day, I proposed I should go to the bank and cash a cheque, and my three friends' curiosity was not appeased until I again led them into the billiard-room of the Royal Hotel—our bankers! There was a gentleman knocking the balls about, Mr. W. Stanley Cook, who is a friend of mine to-day, and he asked me to play a game of skittle-pool. I had never seen the game played, nor do I believe it was known in England at the time, except in rare instances. This venture, even to my sanguine nature, appeared a little too risky, and so we agreed upon a game of pyramids. We started playing at one shilling a ball, and, I think, five shillings on the game. I am not quite certain of the latter, but I am certain that we finished by playing £1 a ball and £5 on the game, and that I received at the end of the play an open cheque for £50 and £30 in gold. That night four young men, due to sail the next morning to join the ranks of the Frontier Armed and Mounted Police as troopers, each with £20 in his pocket, painted Cape Town red! Judging from the coloured stars and blurs we saw the next morning I am inclined to think we had done so effectually.

The weather was too rough to permit our landing at Port Elizabeth, and on our arrival at East London we were taken ashore in surf boats. The railway to King Williamstown, the headquarters of the F.A.M.P., was not then completed, and the greater part of the journey was accomplished by the aid of a coach. As we got more inland, the country began to pall on me. There was a monotonous sameness about it, an uncared-for, God-forsaken plain of scrub, devoid of anything restful to the eye, one long continuation of the same scene in its front and rear aspect, not a barren patch different— to sleep for twenty miles was apparently to wake up in the same place. Yet there was something which atoned for this melancholy outlook—there was a zest in this complete change of scene, of country and of men—the zest of youth and adventure.

## CHAPTER III.

## CAPE COLONY.

T King Williamstown we reported ourselves, and the unenviable life of a cavalry recruit, or its Colonial equivalent, began. In England I had hunted whenever, and on whatever, opportunity had afforded, hence I passed the riding-school, which was the open veldt, almost at once, and with only forming two's and four's and skirmishing drill to get through, I soon became proficient in these preliminaries, and was one of the first batch to be sent up country, my station being Grey Town.

Grey Town consisted of the barracks, which stood on rising ground, overlooking the roadside hotel, opposite to which was the Kaffir Store, which also supplied the men with rations. Every man kept himself, receiving extra pay as a consideration.

The work of the Frontier Armed and Mounted Police consisted in patrolling the country and keeping down native raids, which were of frequent occurrence ; while sheep and cattle stealing among the Kaffirs might be termed a religion, and some of them were most devout in this respect. Rations were carried for four days in saddle bags, without the aid of a pack horse : flour. tea. sugar, and biltong being the chief provisions, as the fresh meat, which might be carried, always ran out the first day. The patrol tents were little else but full-sized sheets, with a small stick at either end and a rope running along the top as supports. When pegged out, the tent gave just enough room to crawl into.

Four days patrol in incessant rain was not a thing of joy, but at that age, what did it matter? What the old hands might have called work, the young ones were only too eager to do, and adding to this the chances and risks which surrounded all patrols, there was a charm about these excursions which gave to them a ring of adventure. Beyond this, there was little of interest in our everyday life, and after being promoted to the distinguished rank of corporal, I was transferred to Dordrecht, a township which played a very prominent part in the recent war, and to which I shall refer later on. Here I found the romance which I had built up was beginning to fade. In fact, with nothing but an exchange of courtesies with a Kaffir or a Dutch prisoner coming my way, I was already getting a little sick of my position. Nevertheless, with the exception of the monotony which an active nature feels so keenly, I was to all intents and purposes quite contented. The barracks at Dordrecht were not quite what one would style palatial, as they consisted solely of sod walls, a thatched roof, which birds and rats had well gleaned, and mother earth for a flooring. I had made a few friends in the town, and with the magistrate and Dr. Foster, who was the medical practitioner of the district, played pool every afternoon at a small hotel just off what one might call the main street, that is to say, the coach road.

It transpired that Dr. Foster had known my father in England, and I spent a good deal of my time in his house ; and having more than once expressed "the cooling of my zeal" for further adventures under the auspices of the Frontier Armed and Mounted Police, the warmth of his heart extended to me, and by his influence I procured my discharge. I was then seventeen years of age. I helped to dispense the medicine with Dr. Foster, and with more confidence than experience I became his assistant. His dispensary was not of a magnitude that could vie with Savory and Moore in Bond Street; in fact, Dordrecht all round was a very small place.

Compared with the arduous, if brief, work I had done in the force, this fresh life was an indolent if not a luxurious one; but one day, whether I had learned my new profession too quickly or not, it was only by a miracle that I escaped being the cause of a terrible tragedy in a Boer family.

In making up a prescription for a baby, in which was to be mixed an ounce of sulphate of magnesia, I had, through some stupid blunder, mixed an ounce of sulphate of zinc, and the Boer had taken this away in his pocket, and was already some six miles on his road home, when the mistake began to dawn upon me. What made my dilemma still greater, was that the instructions on the bottle were that the medicine was to be taken at once. I upsaddled immediately, and rode out in the direction of the man's farm, having nothing but a Kaffir path to direct me the last three miles. What passed through my mind as I urged on my horse, I won't say, except that if ever man felt that he had made an egregious ass of himself, I was that individual.

It is an everyday trite saying that the head of a house does not want any children, or that he already has enough in the family; but once let the intruder appear, and nothing is good enough for him. Adding to this that the father of this innocent little babe, for whom I had dispensed one ounce of sulphate of zinc, was a man standing some 6ft 3in, and pro- portionately built, it may be imagined that I had not quite reached that happy state which I had pictured to myself when leaving Southampton Water in September.

Men who have travelled, and whose destination has been the end of an almost unknown path, will understand how, if a man never hesitates and goes on instinctively as it were, he seldom, if ever, loses his way. But let him once halt and take a survey of his surroundings, and he will do nothing else until he reaches some place—anywhere, except the one he started for. I had not hesitated a second on this journey of life and death ; for, apart from the baby's life, there was possibly my own thrown into the consideration, and reaching the farm I dismounted, opened the door, and entered without giving any other notice of my arrival. There was the mother seated on a chair—the hope of her life in her lap. The father stood with the phial in his hand, and between them they were trying to coax the child to swallow the dose. I was just in time. I told the man the truth, and expected him to tell me I was a fool. I was, but both of them thanked me —the woman with tears in her eyes, saying how " thoughtful " it was that I had been so good as to arrive just in time ! I have often wondered whether that babe I saved from the result of my own error, ever shot any of my countrymen in the recent Boer War, the district being one of the hotbeds of Cape Colony, and only a little south of Aliwal North.

After this episode I concluded medicine was not my forte, and, having explained the circumstances to Dr. Foster, expressed the opinion that I thought I had better seek some other occupation, so I left soon after with a few pounds in my pocket, and started for the Free State. I could not afford a passage by the mail cart, so I walked to Aliwal North, where I picked up a Kaffir pony, and continued my journey. There was no bridge across the Orange River in those days.

I had a letter of introduction to Dr. Bird, of Rouxville, and was immediately impressed with the good nature and feelings with which the English settler greeted all newcomers from the old country. Both Dr. Bird and his wife extended to me every hospitality, and though his practice was a small one, and possibly did not bring in much more than was sufficient to support life from day to day, everything his house could afford was offered to me.

Whatever may have been the racial feelings of the Dutch between twenty and thirty years ago, they were only too anxious to imitate the English, more especially the women folk ; and in Boer houses, where not one of them could speak

English, home papers containing young ladies' fashion plates were to be found.

Dr. Bird one day asked me how I would like to accept a position in the house of one of these Boer farmers named Palm—pronounced Polom—to teach one of his sons and two of his daughters English. I readily agreed, only too glad to relieve my hospitable host of his incubus. I was not over-burdened with luggage, and required no Saratoga trunk for my belongings, the Kaffir pony being sufficient to carry me "all in" to the farm, which was situated some six miles out of Rouxville.

Imagine my astonishment when I arrived to find the household got up in their Sunday best; the two daughters and son that I was to teach grown up, the youngest of them about twenty.

The amusement the situation caused me I have never forgotten. The man was dressed in what I have always dubbed "Cad's black," a kind of shiny cloth, while the young ladies of the family had on creations of green velvet, embellished with rabbit skins, in imitation of the fur they had seen on dresses in the fashion plates which came from England.

The well-to-do Boer girls were nothing if they were not dressed. Do not misunderstand me. Perhaps I should have said overdressed with material, as one might describe the evening gowned lady of to-day as underdressed—but that is immaterial. The dress of the latter is as charming as that of the former was ponderous.

The younger sister was good looking and already spoke a broken English, and was capable of reading easy words. I had been there some two or three days when she explained to me that what she wanted particularly to learn was the English accent, and as she became more advanced, I found the lessons I gave her more pleasant. The elder sister, prosy and much older, soon gave up her studies, which afforded me more time with the younger one, whom, I do not hesitate to say, I began to like very much, which, in a tutor, perhaps, is as big a mistake as sulphate of zinc for sulphate of magnesia is in the dispensary.

The study soon developed into a rendezvous on the banks of the Orange River, and finding the young lady a most apt pupil, I can say, without fear of contradiction, that she was thoroughly acquainted with English in a very short time. But now the feud between the English and the Kaffirs broke out, and it was with great reluctance and shedding of family tears, that I left the Boer family to retrace my steps to Dordrecht. From thence I went further and reached Queenstown, the war having then already broken out. I immediately presented myself to the resident magistrate, Mr. Hemming, and made a public proposal to him in the Court House, that Queenstown should enroll volunteers for the front, and that he should telegraph to the Minister at Cape Town for his sanction for authority to carry my proposal into effect.

A more able and courteous gentleman I have never met in all my travels, and he is to-day High Commissioner for Grahamstown. The reply came agreeing to the proposal Mr. Hemming had made, and a meeting was held the next day in the town hall for the purpose.

Volunteers rolled up bravely, and in fair numbers, and it was proposed by Mr. Hemming, taking into consideration the experience I had had with the Frontier Armed and Mounted Police, that I should hold a commission in the force as a lieutenant. and this was publicly proposed and carried, I may add without being egotistical, unanimously.

Being only seventeen years of age, I hardly felt that I was a leader of men, and, in a short speech, I informed the townspeople assembled that I considered an older man than myself should accept the commission, and that I would be only too willing to go to the front as a sergeant, in which position I thought I could be of much more use. I formed a corps of Queenstown Volunteers, and with Captain A. N. Ella took them to the front, and we reached Ibeka the day after the first shot had been fired.

## CHAPTER IV.

### THE KAFFIR WAR, 1877-8.

HIS war was brought upon us through the Kaffir chief Kreli taking up arms against the friendly Fingoes.

The latter tribe had, in previous campaigns. always been loyal to the English, and in return for these services we had pledged ourselves to assist the Fingoes and protect them against all unlawful acts. Hence when the dispute between these tribes reached the culminating point, and the Kaffirs fired upon the Fingoes, England was compelled to step into the breach.

This was only the forerunner of the Basuto and Zulu wars, followed by the fight with the Boers at Majuba Hill, which was so ingloriously succeeded by the craven submission of Gladstone.

I need not hesitate to say that it was I who got the Queens-town Volunteers together and supervised their equipment; and, unhampered by red tape, having only the main object in view, I venture to assert that the expedition in the despatch of our corps might well be held up as an example compared with the late methods in which the Imperial Yeomanry were scrambled out to South Africa in the last Boer War; but as I shall have to deal with the Imperial Yeomanry more fully as my autobiography progresses, I will not break away from my present subject.

Leaving Queenstown early one morning—the day and date I cannot remember—some armed with Snider carbines and others with two-ringed Enfield-Snider rifles, we started on active service in the same spirits as a boy returns from school for his holidays.

Marching was one continual sing-song, for every man in the troop assumed he had a voice, and each in turn did his duty as a chorister. Their efforts varied from "The Elephant Walked Around" to "God Save the Queen."

In our ranks was a man called Pink, who sang many of George Leybourne's songs, and one of the choruses, stupid though it may read in words, was set to an air which gave it an "all-round fillip." The words ran :

> "My Maria's a fairy queen,
> Such a fairy ne'er was seen.
> Round she goes on her darling toes,
> Round on her tootsy wootsies.

> "She's the girl that I adore,
> You should hear 'em cry 'encore.'
> My love she's honest, although she's poor,
> And she's all the world to me."

While another ran :

> "Cerulia she was beautiful, Cerulia she was fair,
> And she lived with her mother in Gooseberry Square.
> She was my humpty-doodle-dee ; but oh! alas! she
> Played snicky snacky snooky snum,
> With a man in the Royal Artillery.

Hardly worth quoting to the present generation, but, ridiculous as the verses are, they may bring back to not a few, memories of the good old rollicking days now departed, killed by the lack of fun of the age in which we now live. What has turned times so topsy-turvy in the course of two or three decades? I cannot suggest, unless it be the many different responsibilities that women have taken upon their shoulders, which have made them "independent" of man. In my humble opinion, when woman becomes independent of man, or man independent of woman, Nature is insulted, and a crime against heaven is committed.

The Queenstown Volunteers were of the type of the time, and composed mostly of English-born men. We were the first volunteers in the field, and reached Ibeka just in time to relieve the Frontier Armed and Mounted Police, who were in charge. The battle of Ibeka, where, as I have said, the first shot was fired by the English, was of considerable strategic importance to the Colony, for had the Kaffirs been successful an unprotected country lay before them to raid and plunder, apart from the incursions they could have made into the small townships, which would have meant the wholesale slaughter of every white in the place.

Ibeka consisted of a native store, a square house of about four rooms, with corrugated iron roofing and mud floors, one of the rooms being set aside as a shop or store. Drop this in the midst of the scrub of a desolate-looking country, and you have the picture, the Kaffirs coming from far and near to purchase what European merchandise they might require, principally beads and tin pots. Surrounding the trader's house was a mud wall, and this, with the waggons, made a strong laager.

The first shot which had been fired the previous day was the harbinger of the conflict which was to take place on the morrow, and at the first sound of cannon, being aware that two companies of police artillery were already on the scene of action, I gave the order to trot, which was soon increased into a gallop, without consulting my superior officer, Captain A. N. Ella; in fact, he rather obeyed my command, and trotted and galloped with us. As we drew nearer, the firing became more general, and reaching the summit of the high land we saw before us, some mile ahead, the Ibeka laager, which was occupied by not more than 250 Frontier Armed and Mounted Police, partly surrounded on two sides by the enemy, with a third severely threatened. We halted for less than a minute. The Kaffirs were within a hundred paces of two sides of the mud walls, and their numbers might have been estimated in thousands.

Our appearance diverted the attention of the besieging enemy, and, first at a gallop, then at the charge, we made for the side of the square which was open to us. This we gained with only one man slightly wounded. In a second we dismounted, and two out of every three of us, covered by the mud wall, helped to defend the laager, without a thought of anything except the work that lay before us. Each third man held the horses.

There was no such thing as reporting ourselves to the commanding officer ; nor did he even know who we were, except that we were whites. Each man threw himself under the best cover of the wall he could find, and here the fighting was fiercest. The friendly Fingoes inside the laager took charge of the horses, which relieved the remaining third of our troop, who immediately joined us, rifles in hand, and plugged away. So near and so thick was the fight that when the nine-pounder of the artillery was fired it made a lane through the black mass, which was quickly closed up again by the survivors, and be it said of them, the Kaffirs filled up each gap cheering.

The battle had commenced about ten o'clock in the morning, and the whites had retired slowly, until the engagement reached the point I have described at the moment of our arrival.

The overwhelming numbers more than once looked like enveloping us, but there was just that hesitation in their final rush which held them back. It lacked that fanatic and inflexible resolution characteristic of the North-Eastern African.

From the elevation, looking down upon the mass of bronzed shoulders, with not a blade of grass to be seen, the eye met a scene almost incapable of description.

I do not know what feelings possess most men in the initial flush of battle; but with me, so long as the battle of Ibeka lasted, no thought was in my mind except the desire to kill. Whether it was my youth (I was only seventeen), or what, I cannot recall; but whatever order had been given, there is nothing on that day I would have hesitated to attempt to carry out, nor a task that I would not have felt I could have succeeded in performing. Now. in my maturer years, I put those feelings down as the result of the free, open life I had led, short though it had been at this period, and to those escapades in which the young man of those days indulged so freely. There was nothing subtle about the youth of that period—that, perhaps, was his sin.

Our opportune arrival was telling its tale, and the front rank of the Kaffirs was already diminishing and retiring, while, on the other hand, their rear rank was still pressing forward, the result of want of discipline and command. Immediately this weakness showed itself we poured volley after volley into them with marvellous effect, for they fell in such numbers as to cause consternation among them, and at last they turned and fled, while we, the Volunteers, comparatively fresh, followed them; but being wary of the hills and creeks and their numbers, we did not inflict much damage upon our flying enemy.

Retracing our steps with the setting sun, we met some of the hospital corps, and I learned the police had lost seven men in retiring on the laager earlier in the fight, and before our arrival. The bodies had been mutilated in a manner too fearful for words, too terrible for the ear, too disgusting to the eye.

Some two hundred yards before me, huddled under a bush, I saw the body of a man, and taking two men with me I went towards the spot. There lay the poor fellow, with his feet and hands hacked off, his eyes gouged out, his body hideously mutilated. We threw it across my saddle, and a trooper either side held it in position—our blood boiling with horror and hatred, we made our way towards the camp in silence.

The corpse I had brought into camp, unrecognised by me, unrecognisable by man, except for the uniform he wore, was one of my four Cape Town friends, Boxer, who had come out with me on the Anglian.

A few hours earlier I had felt I was hard enough to withstand anything that might happen in warfare; but on the news being broken to me that the terribly mutilated corpse was that of my friend Boxer, I am not ashamed to own that a tear rolled down my cheek, and I felt how weak I really was.

The burial of our dead and those of the enemy required a greater effort—if possible greater courage—than the fight itself demanded, and long before all the bodies could be consigned to mother earth, the aasvogels hovered, lighted, and fed upon the dead, adding to the horrors which a man must go through without flinching, or he would be better back at home at the fireside of his family.

If the truth is terrible to relate, the reader must remember how much more terrible it is to experience. As the burial party neared the corpses, the carrion rose with flapping wings, bearing away gruesome lumps of flesh, or draggling entrails, as it slowly made its flight.

So much for Ibeka, my first experience of an engagement.

Two days later Captain Ella sent me to fetch the rest of our Volunteers, who were concentrating at Queenstown from different outlying places, and taking a couple of Fingoes and a trooper with me, I started to retrace my steps. Soon after arriving at Queenstown, Mr. Hemming handed me the keys of the magazine, and I was treated like a little Commander-in-Chief of a garrison without any barracks, and, I might add, without the jack-boots and spurs typical of the post entrusted to me.

Naturally, I was besieged for news—and by photographers!

As the men came in, I imparted to them that crude knowledge of skirmishing which I had gained from the South African Force, and which formed the extent of my military acquirements.

Queenstown in those days was a pretty little place compared with its sister townships, being well planted with trees, and its octagon-shaped market-place reminded one to some extent of our provincial towns at home.

About this time Captain Ella was transferred to the charge of the commissariat, and Commandant Hay, a resident of Queenstown, took over our contingent. The camp at Ibeka was struck, and our troop was sent to a station called by the Kaffirs the Bolo River. The place was a deserted missionary house, and I left Queenstown for the second time with the remainder of the contingent to join them there.

On the march a rather funny episode happened towards sundown. There is no twilight in this country; the sun rather falls than sets. We were marching along the edge of a precipice—I always kept on the high ground, having only an advance guard of two—when a fusillade suddenly burst out in the valley below. We could see nothing, nor could we descend. At this moment a trooper, by name Cherry, a man of about fifty years of age, charged me with having brought them by too dangerous a way, and said that if anything happened, as he was a married man with a family at home, I should be the first one shot! That would have been an inglorious end to my career, and a risk which after those I had run I did not feel justified in incurring.

I need scarcely say that there was not that military discipline about us which would be looked for on the Horse Guards' Parade, and knowing that a threat under such circumstances, and in those unsettled South African days, was not always an idle one, I promptly knocked Trooper Cherry out of the saddle, and a brother trooper was on top of him before he had quite realised what had happened, and I made him a prisoner. On reaching the summit, at a point which secured us from attack except on one side only, the way we had come, we off-saddled, and every man slept under arms. I took charge of the guard, keeping watch throughout the night. At daybreak not a sound was to be heard nor any sign of the enemy ; and, making a hasty meal of coffee and cookies (flour mixed with water and fried in fat, the result being an omelette of indiarubber), we renewed our march, and Trooper Cherry having regained his confidence, his arms were restored to him, and his insubordination was forgiven.

With the exception of this incident, we reached the Bolo River without anything to record, and, reporting myself, I handed over the troops to Commandant Hay. We were surrounded by small groups of Kaffirs, and they appeared at intervals, at a distance out of range, shouting uncomplimentary epithets into the camp ; and it is extraordinary how they could make themselves distinctly heard at such a distance. This is done by the echo and re-echo, through a natural gift of pitching their voices at certain angles against the hills.

Night alarms were continuous at the missionary station, the Bolo River being nothing but a creek, the bed of which consisted of large boulders, and like many another colonial river it had no water, and therefore had to be vigilantly guarded.

Some seven days after being stationed here, despatches arrived with the news that the enemy was concentrating with a view to attack Queenstown. There were no direct means of communicating with that town to forewarn them. A council was held, and it was suggested that the men should be mustered and volunteers called for, but in a private conversation with Lieutenant Heinemann (who was subsequently shot) and Lieutenant Tripp, it was arranged that I should attempt to reach Queenstown with despatches.

Taking two horses, a couple of revolvers, and some fried meat, I set out on my journey, a distance of some seventy-four miles. Starting that night, I kept to the Kaffir path which had brought us from Ibeka, and alternately trippling and cantering—the South African tripple being a kind of ambling trot—I passed the late battle-field, now covered with the silent graves.

At daybreak groups of three or four Kaffirs together were here and there discernible on the different hill-tops, causing me to change my course from time to time, my signposts being the landmarks Nature had placed to guide its travellers. These and determination were the compass for my course. Leaving the path, I would get back to it, follow it for a distance, then leave it again, always keeping in view some kopje, hill, or tree as my guide.

Odd Kaffirs had followed me mounted on their ponies, but I was better served with horseflesh. I changed horses more than once, avoiding all bushes and anything that approached the nature of cover.

I had got, as well as I could estimate, to within twenty miles from Queenstown unmolested, though I had been chased; but here the Kaffirs were more concentrated. Every kraal (a Kaffir homestead or village) I passed was deserted. As I rode on with the Kaffirs in front and on all sides, I made full use of all possible cover and stuck to the low ground. I now continually rode one horse, saving the other for a final effort if necessary. It is difficult to write of one's self under these circumstances and to recount facts —not that I do not remember them. Suffice it to say that I reached Queenstown, riding bare-back, with three cartridges in my revolver still undischarged, and delivered my papers safely just inside twenty-four hours of my starting.

The town was already to some extent on the alert, and a guard had been formed for night watch. On my arrival every man was called out, and the women and children sought refuge in the gaol. Planks were fastened from house to house, as a mode of communication if necessary; or, in the event of the building being fired, as a primitive means of passing from one to the other. That night Queenstown was attacked, but, being forewarned, was prepared, and in due course the attack was repulsed.

All our men were good shots. In those days every man in Africa could use his rifle with skill. How close the fight was that night has been told by other pens, and I may conclude this episode by saying, that I received later in life an illuminated address from the inhabitants, signed by many of the leading men in the Colony, which I still have in my possession.

Before returning to the Bolo River. I took despatches to Tyldens Post, then occupied by the 88th Regiment, the Connaught Rangers, and on the road I shot two chickens and a peacock, which we had in the officers' mess as a luxury that evening. I remember Captain Mann, but the rest of the names I cannot recall. To show the friendly feeling which existed at the time. though I was a non-commissioned officer of the volunteers, I was put up that night in the officers' quarters and messed with them up to the time of my returning to Queenstown the next day. Red tape was not hung up in the officers' mess of the 88th Regiment in those days.

I took part in several actions with the Queenstown Volunteers up to the capture of Kreli, the chief, which virtually ended the Kaffir War of 1877-8.

That I do not recall all the adventures which I went through during that campaign, the reader may, if he please, attribute to my innate modesty ; but, from an anecdotal point of view, I will mention a few incidents which may be interesting.

In our contingent was a Boer with one arm, and a very good fellow he was. He was an excellent shot, and lying on his back would rest his rifle on his knees, and from this peculiar position never missed his mark. The Enfield was then sighted up to 1,650 yards. One day on the march, three Kaffirs, standing on a ridge on the opposite side to where we were marching—a wide chasm yawned between us—shouted insulting epithets at the white men. This man jumped from his horse, and taking his sight at 1,650 yards took aim, fired, and one of the three Kaffirs standing on the edge toppled over into the abyss below.

On another occasion, when marching through some scrub with a scouting party, a shot was fired from some 300 yards away and my horse fell under me, and though we searched everywhere for the man we found nothing but his rifle, nor was he ever seen by one of us. This is the more extraordinary as the bush was very scattered, and only growing in bunches here and there.

One of the most important events in my life occurred at Dordrecht, as it was here I became possessed of my first racehorse, named Snowdrop. I have since owned another of the same name, recently dead. The South African Snowdrop was a dun with black points, and it is seldom we see a racer of that colour. She ran against a horse called Mail Train, at the primitive races held there, and was beaten pretty easily, and, there being only two runners, though last, I had the consolation of getting second money. which, if I remember rightly, was a fiver. Thus at an early age, apart from my truant experiences at home, I took an early and active part in racing, racehorses and ownership.

The impression this campaign left on me (and one which in all my travels has not been modified) was the great resource England had at her command in the sons of her colonies, and in my subsequent travels these views have been confirmed.

The Colonial's life tends in every way to make better fighting men of the untrained soldier, than is the case at home. There is a vast country, and the life is, generally speaking, that of a yeoman. Horses are cheap, and every man rides. Game abounds. not as in England, but in the rough, and lends itself rather to the sport of the rifle than of the shot-gun ; in fact, although every man possesses the former. the latter is not so frequently owned. Here you have every practical accessory which is essential to make a fighting man, whom we may call a mounted infantryman. The rest depends upon the man himself when he sees his enemy in front of him ;

for pluck must be born in a man. With the average colonial this is the case, but I do not for an instant believe that you could bring him down to the red-tape rule of fighting which exists only too strongly in our army of to-day. He is a natural fighter or nothing, possessed of a commonsense and power of experience of his own, the only difficulty being to get him to retreat or to understand the full value of the meaning of that word, when defeat is imminent.

No sooner did the Kreli campaign subside than the Basuto War fermented and hostilities broke out. My duties never drew me into any particular episode in this campaign, and I need not dwell upon it.

The Basuto War finished, and several hundred pounds being due to me from the Government, I thought I would return home, and making up my mind to do so, I received an order on the Standard Bank, signed by the Commander, payable at Williams Town, for nearly £400, and drawing the amount in gold I took a passage to England, only to be wrecked off Robben Island, and with the exception of £70 odd which I had in my trousers when I reached shore, I possessed nothing in the world. We had struck a reef, the sea rushed into the engine-room, and the boilers exploding, she foundered and sank in twenty minutes. What added to the quick sinking of the Dunrobin Castle was the fact that her cargo was one of steel rails. There I stood on the shores of Robben Island with £70 in gold, a pair of trousers, and a helmet with a brass spike in it.

With the dawn we represented a very unhappy family, with the relief of a comic spectacle, some men scarcely even clothed to the extent that Adam is reported to have been, while some of the ladies vied with Eve. Of all the men I was the only one with a head covering, and that a white military helmet surmounted by a brass spike, making me look more grotesque than ever. A single spur would have completed my outfit as a buffoon.

A tug coming to our assistance, we reached Cape Town

safely. I paid a visit to my old haunt, the billiard room, but the marker had gone to the front. Billiard balls in peace, cannon balls in warfare must have been his motto.

Embarking on the next boat to England I retraced my homeward course after some two-and-a-half years' stay in South Africa, being now just about nineteen years of age, and as the vessel ploughed onwards, naturally, although my mood was never sentimental, I looked forward to reaching home ; a term all travellers use with hope and satisfaction in lieu of naming their country. It was not the household comforts I looked forward to. There was no sweetheart attracting my return. I had been reported in the " Times " and other newspapers as having been shot through the jaw. There was no cable between Madeira and South Africa in those years, and I knew what anxiety my mother would be suffering. My view in coming to England—what hastened my desire—was quite possibly that one word " mother."

## CHAPTER V.

## MY DEBUT ON THE STAGE.

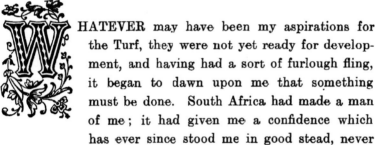 HATEVER may have been my aspirations for the Turf, they were not yet ready for development, and having had a sort of furlough fling, it began to dawn upon me that something must be done. South Africa had made a man of me; it had given me a confidence which has ever since stood me in good stead, never once forsaking me, at times perhaps when others might have sunk never to rise again. My experiences had taught me that fearlessness was a great conqueror of danger, while bravery tempered by sagacity and linked with determination, was the happy medium between foolhardiness and cowardice. All half-hearted tactics had been swept away by my exploits in Cape Colony. The open life and country, the continual up and doing something, no matter what, had imbued me with enthusiasm, had made me a Jack of all trades, a master of none, but not a failure in any.

You have now some idea of what I was at nineteen years of age. The world was before me revolving on its axis every twenty-four hours, while I revolved in and evolved from my mind what step I should take to lead me to that golden future, the feeding chamber of ambition. Ambitious? Of course I was. Conceited? Most certainly; but as a man, not as a fop. 1 was conversant with French, African Dutch, and

Kaffir, but whatever commercial value these accomplishments might have carried with them, I betrayed no symptoms of a desire for a City life. In fact, at this time I scorned a City man, a very narrow-minded position to take up, and one I quickly disabused myself of. Yet how prone are we to be prejudiced against men we do not know and things we do not understand. My case exactly. During this period of deliberation on the future I cannot express how keenly I felt not having a father. I had to decide for myself. I decided upon going on the stage.

I had represented Hamlet most successfully at the 'Varsity fancy-dress ball at Cremorne! Why not again? Some day perhaps at Drury Lane? Who knows? After all, Hamlet was hardly a maker of friends, and yet there is a touch of the character about me. He hated sycophancy, he loathed eaves-dropping — the fate of Polonius was an example of this! Hamlet acted up to his convictions, but he was a wretched lover, as any man must be who would send a woman to a nunnery. Imagine a man of ordinary enlightenment and intelligence sending a beautiful and graceful girl, as Ophelia is always depicted, to a nunnery. However much I may resemble Hamlet in some respects, I should incline to the very opposite in relation to Ophelia.

Getting on the stage twenty-five years ago was not the same thing as going on to-day. Hard grinding work was in front of the young aspirant in those days, whereas now a man is acclaimed an actor as if by magic. Is it on account of there being more acting than sincerity in real life to-day? Be this as it may, it is indisputable that the majority of modern artists are by far better actors in everyday life than they are behind the footlights. I remember one who essayed my pet part of Hamlet. He " grew " more like Hamlet every day and less like him every night, while there was another who, believing he possessed a new reading of the part, played Romeo with not even the ordinary private life matinée success, for, his winsome wife being asked one day how she thought her

husband succeeded as Romeo, replied, " He is simply awful ;
he can't play Romeo on—or off ! "

I had played in several amateur performances, had been
a guest of the Savages, who in those days foregathered at
the Caledonian Hotel, and felt thoroughly fit and ready to
make my début on the professional stage. Messrs. English
and Blackmore were *the* theatrical agents in those days, and
had offices in Garrick Street. I entered my name upon their
books, leaving my photograph behind. The first line of stage
business comes under the definition of " utility," and all
aspirants, of either sex, who have something in them beyond
mere hope, should begin their stage career at this, the first
rung of the Thespian ladder. There are amateurs who begin
higher up and end lower down! They, like many others,
have had to learn that the art of acting is something more
than a pastime, or the mere matter of a retentive memory.
Endeavouring to imitate the painter's art, these vainglorious
puppets can criticise their own daubs, but in attempting to
hold the mirror up to nature they cannot see themselves as
others see them. Egad! if they could, and judged themselves
as they do their brother actors, how they would hiss!

My name was entered in the agents' books (for a utility
part) as being disengaged (never having yet been engaged,
this was correct), and the answer came along quicker than
I had hoped. Mr. Blackmore was a gentleman I had great
respect for, and in those days gentlemen and theatrical agents
were not quite synonymous terms, for the plethora of agencies
then in existence had a distinct minimum of gentlemen at
their heads. Calling at the offices in Garrick Street in
response to Mr. Blackmore's letter, he showed me as much
courtesy as he would to a leading actor, and told me, much
to my satisfaction, that he could offer me an engagement
at the Theatre Royal, Dublin, as " utility man " for the
Autumn Stock Season, salary thirty-five shillings a week.
I jumped at it as a young barrister at his first brief, or as
a solicitor might swallow his first client at a gulp! I was

not exactly stage-struck, but I believe I walked with an air of assumed importance, and reached even that reckless state when I did not care a rap whether I had my hair cut or not.

Then came the all-important item—the wardrobe. What, aye. what, is an actor without his "props"? Nature saved me one expense—I wanted no pads. It was not so much what I could dispense with that was troubling me; it was the necessities, and how to get them. The make-up and grease-paint were small items if one did not go in for the complete box already fitted up—one might say got up—for the simple-minded beginner! Tights, like unmentionables, were indispensable. Wigs and such other "props" which the stock actor was bound to possess to complete his wardrobe, all had to be bought. Meyer and Mortimer, of Conduit Street, though excellent tailors, did not supply this kind of garments, and Truefitt's wigs were too expensive, even though they might have been obtained on credit; but I fell a victim to a pair of Hessians and of patent buckled shoes, which I ordered at Gardner's, in Oxford Street, for which I paid *after I had left the stage.*

Arriving at Dublin. I presented myself to Mr. Egerton, the stage-manager of the Theatre Royal, who in due course introduced me to the lessee, Mr. Michael Gunn, one of the best-natured and most straightforward men it has been my good fortune to meet throughout the world. What has not happened since then? Michael Gunn, afterwards partner with D'Oyly Carte in building the Savoy Theatre and Hotel, has gone the way we all must follow. The Theatre Royal has long since been burnt down, and poor Egerton, a good fellow truly, perished in the flames. A sad record.

The opening play was to be "Hamlet." Shades of Cremorne! That hansom in Piccadilly at eleven in the morning! Barry Sullivan was announced. His company consisted of his son and a few other principals, the "stock" making up the padding. In culinary language, the real turtle was coming along, the "stock" was the mock. I wondered for what part I should be cast, but had not to wonder long, that assigned to me being Barnardo. If this had been all I should have felt I was being overpaid, for 35s. a week seemed an outrageous salary for merely speaking a few words in the dark, with the footlights, wings and flies not once full on, but in other names I was cast for two more parts, both full of cues, but without a line to speak. My histrionic abilities were not exhausted here, but were further requisitioned. There was to be a first piece, and, what was more important, I was to play in it. It was one of the old-fashioned farces, and I was cast for the servant. I attended rehearsal, and inquired for my part. This rather annoyed the prompter. Let me here mention that the old-fashioned prompter was, as a rule, an irascible, dusty person, always wearing a stale shave and a frayed collar (with a broken button-hole), which ticklingly irritated his generally well-worn-out patience. His trousers always appeared too long, and wrinkled at the ankle, while his unpolished boots matched his sombre tall hat, which gave one the idea it had had the moth in it at least a couple of seasons back. His shirt? Well, I have described enough. Standing by his little table, the rehearsal progressed. At last my entrance was called, and again I asked for my part.

The little prompter answered with a venomous sting in his tones: "Your part, sir—your part is this—when this gentleman says, 'I will ring for the servant,' you enter, and, placing the things on the tray, exit with them as you came. I assume you can do that?" I remember my answer, and it has often since been repeated to me. I replied: "Your assumption does me honour. I trust I can aspire to it, but I cannot answer your question off-hand. Permit me to rehearse it." That dirty little prompter and I were friends from that moment.

To show how the uninitiated may fall into a trap by betting, I will here explain how I was nearly caught. When I knew I was cast for the servant, I made a bet of five shillings with an actor called Edward Major, who was our leading juvenile,

and was cast to play in the first piece, that I would play two
speaking parts on the opening night.  He *knew* I had not a
speaking part in the farce ; I *thought* I must have.  Of course,
I had lost, but I can assure those who are behind the scenes
that there is as glorious an uncertainty on the stage as on the
Turf.

The night came.  Teddy Major gave me the cue, and on I went.
Distracting the audience with some "business," he sidled
towards me with a sotto voce, " Eh, laddie—you can leave the
dollar on the table, if you like."  This was a cue I had not
heard at rehearsal, and before Teddy Major knew where he
was I looked him straight in the face, demanding, "Did you
say, sir, I was to give the cat the left milk, and the piece of
sugar to the canary ? "  The audience yelled.  He was bursting
with laughter himself at my consummate audacity, but he
replied. "Take away the tray and attend to your business."
"Business, sir, certainly," I replied, adding in similar sotto
voce, " *I've* won, and you can put the dollar on the table if
you like," and spilling the milk all down my clothes, 1
ejaculated, as I wiped it up with the napkin, "Poor puss,
poor puss," and again the audience roared.  I had fairly
beaten Major, and handing me two half-crowns—one was a
"property " one, in other words, there was no property in
it—he said, as I reached the door with the tray, "James, you
have missed your profession ; you should have been an actor.
You can go now."  "Thank you, sir ; but I might say if you
joined the constabulary it would give you the only chance
of taking me up," and I made my exit amidst roars of
laughter.  That Irish audience knew the farce from A to Z,
and followed our gag more keenly than the play itself.

My début was an all-round success, except to Teddy
Major, who lost his bet.  The part of Barnardo, making one
of the courtiers in the play scene, and helping to " fill up " the
last act, ended my first night's labours.  On Wednesday and
Thursday we played "Macbeth," finishing the week with
" Richard III."—a truly industrious programme !  I played one

of the witches and another small part in "Macbeth." I was cast for the Sergeant and another part in "Richard III." Fame, glorious fame, had set her seal upon my powers in the utility line, and in the theatre I believe I was looked upon by my brother actors as possessing a chance of some day becoming an actor like themselves. If my readers are acquainted with the profession, they will appreciate this great compliment tacitly paid to the utility beginner in the first week of his career. Strange to say, my opportunity was to come the last day of this very first week. On Saturday night, Catesby, a most important part in the play of "Richard III.," was taken suddenly ill, and could not put in an appearance. Catesby is not what would be professionally termed a fat part; on the contrary, it is mostly entrances and exits—in other words, he puts in a lot of time at the wings. To illustrate the despair the management was plunged into, Egerton came to me asking if I would play Catesby. "Won't I!" was my reply, with an eagerness which would have accepted the part of Richard III. thrown in. "You will have to wing it," Egerton remarked gravely; "dress as soon as you can and go to Mr. Sullivan." All stars were Mr. in the profession. To "wing" a part meant that, not having studied it, or perhaps never having rehearsed it, as was my case, one hung about the wings studying as best one could between exits and entrances. Well, I felt on the wing—I was soaring in my profession. I soon presented myself at Barry Sullivan's dressing-room, and at an improvised rehearsal he put me through my business with pedantic precision. He was quite of the old school, and effervescent at that. Breezy, with a rolling voice, gathering as it rolled, until it resembled a tempest at sea, but never followed by a perfect calm, is the briefest description I can give of Barry Sullivan on the stage. "Off" he was spic and span, but never dissociated from the traits of his calling. He patronised me at our quick rehearsal in the dressing-room; in fact, I believe when he looked in the mirror he patronised his reflection! He spoke with the automatic precision of the subsequently invented gramaphone—indeed, I can think of no living actor whose elocutionary powers would be better suited to this instrument, for reproduction.    He rounded his words and, metaphorically, threw them off his chest like hot cakes, and how the audience—the Dublin audience especially—ate them!

The curtain rang up. I had two things in my favour—I was not nervous, and had plenty of confidence in myself. Catesby that night was letter-perfect, thanks to the part which he stuck in his cap, nor did he take a wrong cue or give one, and his exits and entrances were measured with such ease that even the "guying" which Teddy Major attempted at the wings in no way shook his equilibrium.    Even Barry Sullivan complimented me, but advised me to speak more naturally.   This was diverting, as there never was a more pedantic or less natural speaker than Sullivan himself. He never spoke, he intoned, with a touch of a long drawn out soliloquy pervading his speech.

On the departure of the star, the stock company started in regular work; yes, and it was work. Mrs. Michael Gunn played Ariel in the production of "The Tempest." Robert Brough,* now in Australia, played Caliban. Kyrle Bellew was at the Gaiety, and he had not been on the stage long. We all foregathered, and times were not so bad. Since those days Bob Brough has been lessee of a theatre, both in Melbourne and Sydney, while "Kurley" appears to have become Americanised, and I believe, and hope, has piled up a fortune. I have been the rolling stone, gathering and dropping moss as I went.

When the veneer of "shop" does not cling to a professional in his private life, he is, as a rule, a real good man, one of the best; but when he is a better actor off than on, then, indeed, he is a—well, I cannot find the word in the dictionary. Neither Michael Gunn nor Egerton had a taint of this about them.

---

* Since these lines were penned, Robert Brough has died in Sydney.

I esteemed them both highly, and retained that esteem to the end, Michael Gunn surviving Egerton many years. The latter took a great interest in me. He asked me to study Claudio in "Measure for Measure." I did. In due course Adelaide Neilson came along, "Measure for Measure" was put up, and I played Claudio. Miss Neilson congratulated me. It was a condescending tribute, for she was as charming in manner as she was beautiful, and her beauty was only comparable to her most perfect acting.

I had a pleasant time, and was frequently the recipient of that charming, open-hearted hospitality which both Mr. and Mrs. Gunn dispensed at their house, and equally as I remember her playing Ariel, so I can call to mind her genial and "Ariel" good nature. Those days were happy ones, and I recall them with pleasure.

It was only a few years ago that Bob Brough reminded me of the billiard handicap I promoted in the theatre. It created no little excitement, and in the end Brough and I were left in. We played it off on treasury day, and I have ever since looked upon Robert Brough as a business man. He won.

## CHAPTER VI.

## IN THE WITNESS-BOX AT PLYMOUTH.

UST before my nineteenth birthday, I returned from Dublin, and after playing a short engagement at the Theatre Royal, Nottingham, I joined the stock company at Plymouth. The proprietor was a Mr. Newcome, whose chief ambition appeared to be to look younger as he grew older. I was introduced to an old gentleman well over seventy years, his cranium adorned with a jasey, his Napoleon III. moustache and billy-goat dyed a hue to match. He hunted regularly, and he went straight and stuck on; in fact, he showed such physical vitality, that it seemed hard that Father Time had interfered with his hair and general appearance as much as he had. This may be a general complaint when three score years and ten are reached.

I found the weekly programme of the Theatre Royal, Plymouth, worthy of the stories which are now often told of the old stock days, for here I played in as many as six different pieces in one week. Shakespeare was "stock." and all standard plays came under the same category. The old actor had little or no trouble—in other words, he was "stock," too—but for the uninitiated it was, to put it mildly, and without the semblance of exaggeration, somewhat of a busy time. For instance, I will give you an old-fashioned theatrical weekly menu, consisting of: Monday, "Hamlet"; Tuesday, "The School for Scandal"; Wednesday, "Othello"; Thurs-

day,  "The  Ticket  o'  Leave  Man";  Friday,  "The  Two
Orphans";  Saturday,  "Black  Eyed  Susan";  Sunday—thank
heaven!  I  played  every  kind  and  description  of  part  during
this  season,  from  a  wicked  Boer  to  Captain  Crosstree,  the
latter  always  getting  a  fat  round  of  applause  at  Plymouth.  Our
leading  actor  was  one  of  the  good  old  ringletted,  thunderstorm
school,  and  judging  from  the  effects  of  the  recent  American
introduction  of  the  dope  for  racehorses,  I  am  inclined  to  believe
there  must  have  existed,  in  the  days  I  refer  to,  a  theatrical
dope,  which  the  provincial  leading  actor  swallowed  nightly.
Nor  do  I  consider  the  effect  completely  worked  itself  off,
until  he  blew  out  his  candle  and  turned  over  to  his  rest.

The  exercises  and  gesticulations  of  the  histrionic  heroes,
increasing  from  breakfast  to  their  last  drink  at  night,  must
have  been  the  means  of  keeping  them  in  that  good  state  of
health  they  nearly  all  enjoyed,  while  their  own  breeziness
must  have  been  to  them  as  a  change  of  air.  There  was  nothing
enervating  about  them  in  this  respect;  it  rather  resembled  a
good,  old-fashioned  blow  on  the  East  Coast,  and  they  mani-
festly  appreciated  its  exhilarating  effect  both  on  themselves
and  upon  the  uninitiated.

Beneath  all  this  tinsel  ostentation  of  the  provincial  professional  of  my  youth,  there  was  generally  to  be  found  a
sympathetic  heart  and  a  generous  nature,  rising  above  the
pedantic  mannerisms  which  enveloped  him.  There  existed  an
unwritten  Bohemian  law  of  hospitality  in  those  days,  which,
perchance,  would  not  be  so  appreciated  to-day,  nor  commend
itself  to  those  superior  geniuses  who  have  leapt  on  the  stage
only  to  disappear  down  the  trapdoor.

There  is  a  great  majority  who  imagine  they  are  possessed
of  histrionic  ability,  but  the  principal  part  they  play  on  the
world's  stage  is  the  fool.  We  have  yet  to  learn  that  talent
is  hereditary,  though  a  fool  usually  begets  his  like.  I  was  not
sorry  when  the  stock  season  was  growing  to  a  close,  the  work
of  daily  rehearsals  and  evening  performances  leaving  little
time  for  leisure.  It  was  about  this  period  that  an  incident

happened which I must relate.  Plymouth in those days upheld
the gaiety of the times, then waning in London, and it was
the wont of some of us to "take a stroll" after the hotels
had closed their doors.  The police on one occasion were
perhaps a little over zealous in their peremptory orders to
"move on," and the prompter, by name Fitzroy, for once
forgetting his cue, was ruthlessly collared and run in.  It was
a most unjustifiable act on the part of the men in blue.  After
the formal preliminaries, he was allowed out on bail, and the
next day, when his "turn" came, made his début in the dock.
We had engaged a solicitor to defend him, but it was agreed,
owing perhaps to my tendency to practical joking, not to put
me in the witness-box.  The case appeared to turn on the
question of using bad language, the evidence of the police
being strong against the prisoner, while the company to a
man swore they heard none.  The solicitor felt he had lost
the case, and in desperation put me in the box.  I corroborated
the evidence given on behalf of the prompter, when the chairman of the bench turned to me and asked:

"Did you hear any bad language used?"

"Yes," I replied, upon which poor Fitzroy collapsed in the
dock, the solicitor shuffled his papers together, and all our
witnesses looked at me open-mouthed.  The police appeared
most satisfied.

"What did you hear?" asked his worship.

"I heard that policeman over there call us a lot of ——
actors."

It was true.  They asked me no more.  The case was
dismissed.  The witnesses for the defence were Mr. Charles
Cartwright, Mr. T. G. Warren, the author of "Nita's First,"
and others I cannot call to mind.  The one witness who was
originally not to be called saved the situation.  So much for
the law.  I may add that I think this was the most successful
part I played at Plymouth.

## CHAPTER VII.

## INDIA.

ONDON has a fascinating attraction for most people who are disengaged, and for actors in particular, and it is sometimes disappointingly astonishing how long some remain " resting." Why the profession has given to this period of inertia the term " resting " I have never been able to understand, for, as a matter of fact, it is not always disassociated from the most critical time of the professional's life, more especially in regard to what I may term the middle-class actor, there being always a large stock of this species on hand. A short season at the Haymarket Theatre, a few race meetings, and I was offered an engagement to make one of the company chosen to open the Gaiety Theatre at Bombay. This, indeed, had the aspect of combining business with pleasure, and on the first Sunday in November, 1879, we sailed in one of the Hall Line steamers. The passengers differed in many respects from my fellow-travellers on the African route, the distinction being much in favour of those Eastward bound. The majority belonged to the Civil Service, or were the wives of those worthy officials returning to join their long-suffering husbands, with a sprinkling of a few military men and garrison hacks. However great the pride of caste may be among the Hindus, it is infinitesimal compared with that of the white official, and according to their official rank they insisted on

5

taking precedence in a manner worthy of the traditions of the Court of St. James's. On board the boat, as in India itself, the civil servants looked down upon the soldier as though he were placed at least a step lower on the social staircase, while we strolling players were at first patronised with an excessive politeness, bordering on vulgarity. This patronage, however, gradually wore off as we became better acquainted. It was astounding to learn how many of the dear ladies returning to their sunburnt husbands hated the journey, though resigned to the respectable inevitable. The voyage progressed, we all became a very happy family, and the austere demeanour of the first few days melted as we drew nearer to the Southern sun. The old saying that familiarity breeds contempt belied itself, and the more travelled of the fair sex led the way, entering heartily into the amusements and conviviality which soon reigned supreme. They tacitly appreciated that as soon as the good vessel reached her destination each would go his or her different way, and that none of us might meet again, unless, peradventure—but then there was an unwritten code against any such contingency. These worldly wrinkles imparted a freedom on board ship non-existent ashore, and leaning over the bulwarks as the vessel ploughed along on her journey a man could watch the opaque blue of the ocean and, turning, look into a pair of blue eyes. As I look back and remember that I was but nineteen summers, I cannot refrain from recalling that they were fairly hot ones!

Malta, that fortress of the sea, was reached after a fair-weather run, and Blue Eyes came ashore. The opera house, the cathedral, the Palace, and the Catacombs were shown to us by a descriptive guide, voluble in his praise of Americans. as he thought we were, but when we mentioned London he snorted "Christopher Columbus!" and started to eulogise the English, beyond the measure of praise he had meted out to the country of Stars and Stripes. Meeting some of our fellow-passengers we lunched together, and going aboard soon after, were once more going East before the shades of night had cast their pall upon a pleasant day. Between us and the setting sun, Malta, pushing itself through the celestial blue of the Mediterranean, rose from the water's edge, its steps of ramparts rising to an eminence, dotted with the brilliant red of the uniforms of our soldiers. The light grew dimmer and dimmer, the distance between us increased, and, half in awe of, half in wonder at that great Artist, we gazed into the twilight and marvelled.

In those days travelling through the Canal at night with the aid of a searchlight was unheard of, and we were moored to the bank at sundown.

Ismailia and the Bitter Lakes were passed during the second day, and no one was sorry when we left Suez behind. Aden cannot be better described than by disjointing the first vowel and making two words of it. The days were now nearing, when as in all else on this earth, the end must come. We had arrived at the last night we were to spend on board, and merry-making continued, with half an hour's extension graciously granted to us by the skipper. To think that sober party of travellers which I first saw on board, should let themselves go as they did on this particular evening, afforded me no little amusement—dancing, games, everything went merrily along without dissent—I even believe one and all would have cheerfully entered into a general game of Kiss in the Ring had it been proposed, and those dear little wives who the next day were to rejoin their patient husbands, would have been the first to grasp hands in forming the circle. "Auld Lang Syne" brought things to a close. At ten o'clock the following morning we were anchored off Bombay, I bade adieu to Blue Eyes—I fancied I detected just the sign of moisture—I may have swallowed a lump myself—and the launch to take us ashore was alongside. Instanter, as if electrical, that austere dignity which was so marked on the first day or so of our voyage depicted itself in every woman ; the rollicking fun of the night before vanished into obscurity, caste and precedence rode the high horse, and each of them stepped on to the Apollo Bunder at Bombay with an attitude and expression befitting a saint. I landed and went my way. What of Blue Eyes? If you expect an answer you are asking the wrong man.

India, with its wealth, its semi-barbaric pomp and Oriental grandeur, its Eastern colouring, its picturesque natives of many castes and multifarious religions, ranging from the most ancient form of idolatry to Christianity, its innate conservatism in traditions and old customs in face of the white intruder, is to the visitor summed up in one word—novelty. Its scenic side is fascinating, and what it may lack in beauty, from an English point of view, is made up for by endless variety, and this distinction absorbs the traveller's interest. To the European eye all is new, and the general surroundings carry with them a freshness arousing ever-growing curiosity and interest. The enthusiastic impressionist would describe it as the land of enchantment, the country of the necromancer.

The first lesson one learns is that the unadulterated native makes the best servant, while those who have been fostered in missionary settlements, make the best thieves. The Hindu who speaks English advances with the times, as his cunning is sharpened by civilisation.

The next lesson presents itself in the shape of an interrogatory. Why should the good, honest servant, as an unalloyed Mohammedan or Hindu generally is, be inveigled from the religious path of his native contentment? There is no form of worship which does not in its finality point to God, and, in my humble opinion, paramount of all feelings should be respect for, or at least non-interference with, the freedom of another man's belief. If it is sought to make converts, why not first attempt to convert the thousands of heathens, devoid of any belief whatever, who haunt the purlieus of London and our big cities, rather than try to make a bad Christian out of a good Mohammedan or Hindu?

In every country where I have been, where the aborigine

is black or coloured, my experience is that the schoolroom is the native's first stepping-stone to ruin, and that all loose native women sing hymns.

Having lost several articles of underwear, unnecessary minutely to schedule, I discharged the Portuguese missionary boy I had taken on, and engaged an untainted idolator, to look after the remnants left behind, which he did honestly and well. I have since made it a rule, and it has panned out well, never to engage a foreign servant who is unfaithful to his nationality or his religion. A foreign valet who professes to like England better than his Fatherland generally has his eye on the jewel-case, and not infrequently where the eye rests the hand wanders.

The hotels of India may be described as veritable open houses. There are no doors anywhere, except to bedrooms and bathrooms. A piece of paper, called a chit, is initialled for anything that may be desired, and a more pleasant state of luxurious affluence could not well be imagined, while it lasts. The end of the month is the day of reckoning, when the guest is presented with his chits, both from inside and outside his hotel. A man can then count up the number of cocktails he has killed, how many gin-slings he has slung, and the pegs he has nailed down in a moon's life, and some of these totals would make a unique record of how much liquid a body can absorb in a given time. This fascinating system of chits lends itself to hospitality, and as a cheque settles it one way, it is not infrequent that a check has to settle it another.

An enervating climate is the cradle of indolence. Indolence in luxury is an accepted occupation; it is only indigent indolence that merits censure. Everything that tends to ease the fatigue of the white man is brought into use. He is perambulated hither and thither in a rickshaw pulled by the black man; he is fanned by the punkah-wallah from without; he is surrounded by body servants, each having his own special duty to perform—in short, after a certain time, a white man's existence in India renders him unsuitable for life in any other country. Novelty takes an enchanting grip of us all, but as familiarity lessens its fascination, the traveller should bid au revoir to India, and tear himself away from that monotonous life which has spell-bound the Anglo-Indian. He will then always retain a great inclination to see this Brobdingnagian fairyland once more.

"The Gaiety" at Bombay was to open its doors with the production of "Pink Dominoes," a piece which was rather of a scarlet hue than that of modest pink. I was cast to play Harry Greenlanes, not a bad part, and one which the late Sir Augustus Harris originally played at the Criterion Theatre. Our company consisted of that sterling actor, Charles Cartwright; A. B. Tapping, a safe old man, and good at that; Hewitt, a low comedian, upon whom the green curtain has finally descended—the last play I saw him in he was battling with the waves in "The Tempest," only to hear later in life that he was shipwrecked and drowned at sea; Teesdale, of Lyceum fame (who also has since joined the great majority), and others, including my unworthy self. The ladies were Miss Edith Wilson, Miss Agnes Birchenough, a sound actress, who, together with Miss Amy Crawford, has gone yonder, and those others of more or less pretensions who go to make up a dramatic company. A few primitive rehearsals had been got through on board the boat, and the Gaiety was due to open about five days after our landing. It was a good theatre, supported by a syndicate principally made up of Parsees, of whom the head was Sir Rabjeedodgy, as I called him, for in Anglo-Saxon pronunciation his name had no rhythm, except to those with a broken jaw. The eventful night arrived, and the house was packed. We scored a success. In the Cremorne scene I was quite up to the form that the part afforded, and perhaps my acquaintance with the real place infused in me a zest for the scene. Those good old days! Yet not so very old, nevertheless. Though but forty-five years of age, I can distinguish between the men of that period and those of this. We may return to those days when les nouveaux riches have a gilded ancestry. Do not think me a pessimist. We have the right men, but in most instances the wrong ones—it might be said wrong 'uns—have the money.

To enumerate all the plays we produced would be of little interest, but perhaps the best part I ever played was that of Krux, in " School," and to typify the versatility which an actor was expected to possess in those days, I next essayed to play Catherine Howard in the burlesque of " Henry VIII." I can now quite understand why this matrimonial monarch beheaded her! Then came the Usher in " Trial by Jury," followed by parts covering every line of business to which the stage lends itself. Being what is classified as a quick study, I seldom studied at all. India had greater attractions than the dry words of a part, and I am ashamed to confess that I was often not so perfect in my words as I might have been. Not that I was ever at a loss for a word, or, for that matter, a sentence, but this did not always give my brother in art his proper cue, and *he* would " dry up "—in other words, get stuck. This hit doubly hard, for the audience very naturally were of opinion that it was the other, and not I, who was the delinquent and kept the stage waiting; but I was ever ready with a gag or some stage business, which, if it did not at once advance matters, provoked a laugh, until the prompter came to the rescue and set us right.

I can call to mind two unrehearsed scenes with our low comedian Hewitt. It was his turn not to be perfect, and he failed in the middle of my best scene. It was a complete dry-up on his part, and half dazed, as it were, he stammered, " I must leave you now," and walked off. Looking after him as he disappeared through the door, I ironically mused, " If there is a go-as-you-please match at the gymkhana to-morrow I shall back you." The play was " Still Waters Run Deep," but among the audience laughter at once ran high. I then settled down and played the two parts in monologue, and got the best Press notices I ever had while on the stage. On my exit Hewitt made not the faintest effort of an apology; on the contrary, he patronisingly referred to the good turn he had done me!

Shortly afterwards I was cast for a part full of long speeches. The whole company who had to meet me during the play dreaded me. Each, according to his part, approached me with an apologetic plea for mercy. " I had such a fine part, was sure to make a hit in it," and so forth! Among them was Hewitt, who had a scene in which he scored off me throughout. I was a villainous earl, not the stereotyped wicked captain. The house was crowded. I had gone so far fairly perfect, and had been, I believe, reasonably successful. Hewitt's scene was reached in due course. I made my speech, gave him his cue, and as he was about to speak his first line —he had not yet spoken—I held up my hand, saying, " Stay, I have more to say," and, continuing, spoke all the points the plot of the play needed, finishing peremptorily, " Now leave me. I am weary. Leave me." Poor Hewitt! His expression to me was the acme of low comedy. To anyone else it would have appeared blank amazement. A silence followed. I broke it by repeating, " Leave me," and sank into a chair as if in deep meditation. Hewitt mustered his shattered forces, and pleaded, " My Lord, I cannot leave you thus. I have matters of moment to impart to you." I rose, and with a patrician frown, said : " I will not be disturbed. Your news will keep until to-morrow, when I will give you a fair hearing ; but since you will not leave me, *I* will leave you," and off I walked, making a similar exit to that which Hewitt had made a few nights before. Next morning the Press were not so kind to him as they had been to me. This practical joking was all accepted in good part, though Hewitt appeared a little less loquacious than usual after the performance.

The fact was that life was made all too pleasant for me at nineteen years of age to seriously give myself up to study. With invitations to this bungalow, to this place, and to that, Malabar Hill became a kind of hostelry, and the theatre a secondary consideration.

In no country does temptation invite a young man through its open doors more than in India. How simple merely to initial a chit in order to satisfy the requirements of this life! How easy it is to run accounts, and thereby unthinkingly keep pace with other men whose purses are better filled, and how hard indeed it is to avoid these facilities, which are the common custom of the country, by retiring to a solitary chamber and looking out of the window vaguely to study astronomy!

The races had come and gone, and several weeks of my salary accompanied their departure. My chits were petrifying into stones, which would be hurled at me at the end of the month. John Roberts, the King of the Green Cloth, was playing nightly at the Byculla or Waverley Hotels, but necessity did not prompt me to throw down the gauntlet to him! I resorted to the old remedy, and a money-lender accommodated me. I paid my debts by a method which in truth increased them with interest. Nevertheless, they were collected into one quarter. I took counsel with myself, thought everything out, and proposed and carried excellent resolutions—with the result that I soon fell to signing chits again with renewed freedom.

Common courtesy, apart from inclination, demanded that I should make a few presents. Jewellery being the most appreciated souvenir, I felt I could not wound my pride and resort to the counterfeit.

Again another month was coming to a close, so was the season at the Gaiety Theatre—and so was I. The end of the month brought with it reflections, and it by no means appeased my discomfort when the management announced the production, on the very day of reckoning, of "The Road to Ruin." I felt if I could only play the weak hero of the piece it might prepare my creditors for the worst, but no such good fortune presented itself, and I was doomed to represent the very character who sells the hero up!

I came to the conclusion that as I had no chance of touching the sympathy of my creditors across the footlights, I had better try to create confidence, and the way I abused the poor hero when he could not meet his honourable engagements must have inspired them with a false hope.

Alas! those chits! Why should the mere fact of being a white man be a basis upon which rests abnormal credit? Such were the thoughts which passed through my mind. Not once did I ask myself why I had succumbed to the temptation of extravagance. I candidly confess I felt very much ashamed of myself, but it is extraordinary how this initial consciousness wears off with the progress of life, as the blushes from a maiden's cheek.

I was encompassed by the inevitable. This has been described as having to face the music, but the difficulty is to play the tune. I strummed over the keys, but could only produce a discordant crescendo of inharmonious sounds. The presence of the dusky money-lenders and jewellers made things blacker than ever. I interviewed Sir Rabjeedodgy, the head of the Gaiety syndicate, with the hope of his advancing me a month's salary, but that lynx-eyed Parsee, with his hands folded across his bosom, only smiled that Oriental smile, so subtle and snake-like, which puts the non possumus upon any subject in question. I then said I must conclude my engagement forthwith. This did not create a smile, but provoked a frown—that almost imperceptible Oriental frown. I was obdurate and insisted, but to no satisfactory purpose, so I had nothing left to me but to resort to the instincts of the rabbit, and bolt. I borrowed fifty pounds from Charles Cartwright, which, together with the money I had, settled all my smaller accounts and the hotel bill, and arranging to sail in the "Rydal Hall," the same vessel which had brought us out, and which had made a return journey, I paid my devoirs to my friends at Malabar Hill, and said good-bye to the company. I had stipulated in England that a part of my contract should include a return ticket, and this was a forethought which at this momentous juncture stood me in good stead. Going aboard in a suit of immaculate white, with helmet to match, I outwardly looked an emblem of purity, but the empty pocket told a different tale. The majority did not know this, so, like many before me, and many who will follow, I passed muster. As I steamed in the tug to the vessel I felt the "novelty" of this mystic land was on the wane!

No sooner had I got comfortably aboard than I espied a launch steaming all haste towards us, and as she neared I recognised Cartwright and a friend. Meeting him at the top of the companion, he clutched me by the arm, and, speaking in a mezzotone close to my ear, said, "You must hide yourself —the money-lender," and, pointing in the direction of a boat being pulled by two men, added, "There he is, sitting in the stern, with two officers to arrest you for debt." I thrust both my hands into my empty pockets. This helped me at once to grasp the situation! On the voyage out the chief engineer and I had been on friendly terms. The predicament was explained to him, and down the engine-room steps I went, in my immaculate white suit! Oil and coal-dust had no terrors for me! With little space to move, he left me in the vicinity of the shaft of the propeller; indeed, I was in the tube in which it revolves! Above me was a windsail, with rough rungs running up its interior like an improvised ladder. This connected with the deck, and down the funnel I could hear voices, as through a speaking-tube. On the other side of me coal was being shot down, and I could only distinguish broken sentences, such as. "Arrest—he owe me lot of rupees"—a shoot of coals would drown the rest—a lull—"He no pay me for lovely jewellery" —coals—a lull—"Me catch him and put him . . ."—coals —a lull—and I hear the third and last bell ring out its final warning, "All ashore." The shooting of the coals ceased. My enemies had gone ashore, but worse was to come. The shaft began to revolve. ·I had to bend in a semi-circle for fear of becoming inextricably entangled in its grip! A second's reflection, and I was mounting the bars running up the interior of the windsail. I poked my head out of the top of the funnel—a nigger! receiving the cheery salaams of the chief engineer and many others. Sqeezing myself out, I gained the deck on all fours, looking like a demon from the depths below! Oh, those chits!

Going full steam ahead, I waved my hand to Cartwright, who to this day says he recognised me because I was the only black man on deck. Leaning over the side of the vessel, watching the fast-fading distant hills and rocky coast, I bade adieu to Bombay and "au revoir" to my creditors, and watched the fading coast with "mixed feelings." Waking from my reverie, my attention turned to a more practical point, and I had a bath. Begrimed with coaldust, which the oil had encrusted on me, it was a moot point if I should not have to resort to the holystone used for cleaning the deck, but by the aid of the shower and a hard brush I succeeded in removing the "enamel."

After dinner that evening I lit my cheroot, and threw myself into my deck-chair and my thoughts. Everybody had retired. I strolled round the deck. Leaning over the end of the vessel, I watched the phosphorescent trail. I turned, and straight before me was the empty seat which not long ago I had occupied with Blue Eyes! Blue Eyes? I turned in.

We were not so lively a crew as we had been coming out, and I fully appreciated that beggars could not be choosers! Amongst the passengers was a Parsee, to all appearances full brother to Sir Rabjeedodgy. He was suffering all the evils the sea could give rise to, now and again looking at the sun in vain reproach.

At Suez I posted a letter to an uncle of mine, a clergyman, asking him if he would lend me the money which I owed in India, setting forth the facts without seeking to excuse myself.

The still waters of the Canal suited the Parsee far better than the rolling sea, and he asked me, I may say supplicated, that I would leave the boat with him at Malta and go overland to London. My affection for Malta must have touched me, and I agreed, cabling to my uncle to send an answer to my letter to the Quirinal Hotel, Rome. Disembarking at Valetta, we booked our passages to Palermo in a Rubattino steamer. This short journey again discovered the weak spot of the Parsee, and on going ashore at Palermo he vowed he would never get on a boat again, which, as I explained, meant that he would never leave Sicily, for the simple fact that we were on an island.

I here met some friends, and accepting their invitation to stay, the Parsee was left to find his own way across the Continent to London, and taking him to Reggio, the southernmost point of Italy, I waved my hand to his dusky face as it hung out of a second-class window as the train departed.

After staying a month in Naples I reached the Hotel Quirinal in Rome, and found my uncle's reply, which, instead of a cheque, contained a sermon, telling me that I had committed a great wrong in getting into financial trouble, and that I had no right to attempt to borrow money without being able to offer security for the same. I answered this briefly by stating that I thought as a clergyman he would appreciate that I could not have offered better security, for "He that giveth to the poor lendeth to the Lord."

## CHAPTER VIII.

### HATCHETT'S TWENTY-FIVE YEARS AGO.

HEN an Englishman is abroad he doubtless appreciates his own country more than at any other time, and to the traveller who finds himself thousands of miles away from home, in an indigent state, with nothing but bare hope to help him towards his passage back, the distance one's native land then appears away is incapable of estimation, for it is measured by despair.

South Africa having in my silent moments impressed me with this possibility, I had taken the precaution, as I have already stated, to secure my return ticket before I embarked on the theatrical trip to the Gaiety Theatre, Bombay. Hence whatever my adventures might be in that fascinating country, I always felt that I had a certain security behind me, which, if not an asset for my creditors, was one on which I put great reliance as security for my person!

On my arrival in London I took up my quarters at Week's Hotel, 49, Dover Street, Piccadilly, facing Hatchett's, before the old building, with its sporting traditions, was demolished —a historic hostelry to which I shall refer later on.

Having deposited my luggage I went to see my mother, and in narrating to her my experiences I am afraid I rather dwelt on the parts I had played on the stage than those off.

I then turned my attention to raising the money to

liquidate the debts which I had left behind me, the records of which were now doubtless slumbering in peaceful tranquillity among a mass of others in the safes of my creditors. I laid the bare facts, surrounded by my guilt of extravagance, before the then Vicar of Keswick, with whose family I was on friendly terms. Unlike my preaching uncle, he came to my assistance, and the money was forthwith cabled to India.

Like many others of my acquaintances, death has long since claimed the Vicar, but among my sincerest friends to-day are the members of his family.

Living in such close proximity to Hatchett's, it would have been astounding if I had not visited this most celebrated coaching house, with its merry men and jovial conviviality.

And what a real high-spirited lot they were. At this time the revival of coaching was at its zenith, and in the White Horse Cellars, underneath Hatchett's, was the booking-office for all the road coaches. Piccadilly in those days was rarely without the tootling of the guard's horn, and the departure and arrival of the many teams was an attraction to all those who loved the sound of champing bits and the rattle of the splinter-bars.

Easily first amongst the coachmen was Jim Selby, rubicund of visage and portly of person, dressed to fill the part, whose teams were always good and turned out in faultless style. Jim's coach, the Old Times, became world-known, and the journeys to Oatlands Park and Virginia Water were generally undertaken with a choice lot of spirits on board. To the last Selby played the game, and died in harness, more than respected by all who had matriculated under him.

Other coaches there were whose guards enlivened the morning with their music. The Dorking, horsed and driven and well looked after by Sheather; the Guildford, with which Walter Shoolbred, one of the best and most generous of friends, was associated until his quite recent death; the Brighton, for which Stewart Freeman was responsible; that to Burford Bridge, whose pilot and principal proprietor was that most excellent and reliable of whips, John Bolding, a man who never made an enemy in his life; the Windsor, driven more often by Captain Bailey than anyone else, but always a popular drive with the tourist section.

It was a cheery crowd who constituted " the see 'em home club," and whose headquarters were the coffee-room at Hatchett's. Sportsmen, all of them. They could give you the points of a horse as easily as those of a pretty woman, and there was no question of sport upon which you could not get a reliable opinion from them.

They looked upon the coffee-room as their own holy of holies, and woe betide the stranger who tried to force himself unasked into their select coterie. Divers ways and means were adopted to make him unpleasantly aware that his company was neither appreciated nor desired; and on one occasion a more than usually thick-skinned intruder was lifted from his chair and placed bodily on the fire before he could be convinced that he was not wanted. The presiding deity of Hatchett's in those days was Miss Wills, and she understood her customers perfectly, and ruled them discreetly. William, the head-waiter, was the guide, philosopher, and friend of them all.

The coffee-room window was a wonderful point of view, from which you could see the entire length of Piccadilly; and gathered there at all times of the day could be found some or other of Hatchett's members. Walter Blake, then in his bachelor days, lived at the place; Bill and "Juggins" Cosier; Willie and David Hope-Johnstone; Freddy Hobson, of Austerlitz renown; "Suss" Nesbitt, generally on his way to Sam Lewis's or his tailor's; "Pot" Franklin—why "The Pot" no one ever clearly understood; Eddie Stratford, who in after years was my secretary; good-looking Joe Posno, whose tragic death a year or two since removed a real good chap; "The Parrot," whose other name escapes me for a moment; George Rush, who swore he *had* to stay at Hatchett's for six weeks, as his place in Northamptonshire was snowed up; all these belonged to Hatchett's, and were of it. Another division, much addicted to pigeon-shooting, included Walter Nixey, quietest and most self-contained of men ; Poutz, who could execute a commission as cleverly as most ; Walter Maas, one of the old reliable sort of shooters ; and many others. Free of the coffee-room, too, were such horsey and coaching men as Major Dixon ; Ernest Beckett, about as good a man with the ribbons as ever sat on a box ; Macadam, whose hands were as hard as his ancestor's roads ; " Swish " Broadwood, with a wealth of language that was inexhaustible ; and Walter Dickson, with his " Cheer oh ! " ; " Squire " Goodman, whose nutbrown ale every coachman stopped to quaff when arriving at the little house on Kingston Hill ; his brother, a partner in Aldridge's, about as good a whip as you could find ; and many others. What rattling good fellows they all were ! and what times they had ! Heigho !

One curious thing about the coffee-room at Hatchett's was that it was always breakfast-time. No matter what time of day you went in, some one or other was having poached eggs— and such poached eggs !—they vied in popularity with the old brandy, than which there was no better in London. Curious things took place there, too. Wrestling matches were not un- common, a sovereign sweepstakes forming the pool ; and a little game that was peculiar to the place was the flicking of a coin from the edge of the table into a circular hole in the centre ; much money changed hands at this simple game, and much excitement reigned at times. Such was Hatchett's at the time I resided opposite, and all must wish there were now such men as those who added to the gaiety of life in those days.

Having attended a few race meetings, I caused an announce- ment to appear in that theatrical organ called " The Era " that I was " resting." This in the profession is a polite term for " out of work," but in my case it might have read " gone to the races."

Knocking about the world had shown me something of the

6

practical side of life, and that the next step to knowledge should be application.  As I went on I saw that the stream of learning was ever running, and those capable of following its course would find it never ending.  Those who could not swim with the stream were soon left behind, while those who clutched at one of the buoys invariably found themselves in a sorry plight.

In life's whirligig there are buoys and boys!  The latter extended my knowledge of the world.  The examination papers were three cards, and the place of examination was a first-class railway carriage, specially put on for Sandown Park races, while I, the Juggins, was the examinee.  There were three other players in all, one confederate to each card.  I have since thought that I must have been the fifty-third of a pack—the Joker.  To these three gentlemen I lost all I possessed, alighting at Esher in their debt to the extent of £40.  This sum I borrowed from the late Mr. R. H. Fry and paid them, for I then held, and my opinion remains unaltered to-day, that if I was fool enough to attempt to win their money, nothing would justify my not paying if I lost.

At least two of these three-card-trick men have advanced with the times, and I can to-day place my hand on one who is a member of a prominent racing club, and another who is an owner of racehorses on a small scale under National Hunt Rules.  If they read these lines they will remember the circumstance, and I take this opportunity of publicly thanking them for the object-lesson which they taught me, though I feel under no obligation.

It may appear puzzling to know how I ever got into the financial position of being able to lose this money ; but I had at this time gained the affection of someone, that family relic most of us must have possessed—a maiden aunt.  She shuddered at the idea of my being on the stage.  Having a dutiful respect for her feelings, I did not increase the shuddering by telling her that I had attended several race meetings. Had she had the sole selection of my future, she would doubt-

less have chosen the Church for my profession ; but I am afraid
the cloth would not have hung fittingly upon me, nor can I
quite distinguish in what way I might have succeeded, unless,
perhaps, as Chaplain to the Jockey Club.

The news that I had been plucked like a pigeon by the
three-card carrion travelled among "the boys" by the aid of
the tic-tac, which may be better defined as a crude form of
Marconi signalling. The unknown acquaintances who quickly
claimed me were more in numbers than in merit, but feeling
that I had gained sufficient experience among strangers for one
day, I had the whole of the explorer's ambition knocked out
of me. and preferred being left to my own devices rather than
to lean on the advice of others. I was not unlucky in my
speculations, which was perhaps equally a stroke of good
fortune for my good-natured aunt.

Derby Day was approaching, and I looked forward to my
first visit to Epsom as one of no small degree of importance.

The race of 1880 is generally referred to as Bend Or's
Derby, but I would rather describe it as Archer's, and instead
of saying that Bend Or beat Robert the Devil by a head in a
most desperate struggle, I am inclined to say the account
should read that Archer beat Rossiter.

This race made a great impression on me, for, apart from
the prestige of the Derby, it was a tremendous finish, and
from that day I thoroughly appreciated what good jockeyship
meant ; and my closer association with racing has more than
endorsed the opinion I then formed. Of the many endless
details connected with horse racing, jockeyship is almost the
paramount one, and every trainer of any capacity knows
what he has to fear in this respect.

Opposite my rooms, which were immediately over
Solomon's, the fruiterer's, was a hotel, recently demolished,
called "The Bath." This at least suggested cleanliness, which
a proverb tells us is next to godliness, which possibly induced
me to pay it a visit one Sunday just prior to my lunch.
Amongst its habitués was Mr. Fred Gretton, the owner of

Isonomy. After my morning tub I kept up my acquaintance with " The Bath " across the road, and I soon had reason to fancy that the owner of Isonomy appreciated something beyond the drinks which the young lady at the bar poured out for him. She was a good-looking girl—very. On better acquaintance I took her to the Aquarium. Perhaps there was something analogous between " Bath " and " Aquarium." However that may be, an excellent dinner, washed down with champagne, melted our acquaintance into convivial friendship.

From what had been whispered at the " Bath," I backed Isonomy for the Manchester Cup of 1880 to win nearly £3,000.

Seated in Hachett's, many of us were awaiting the result of the race, when suddenly the shout of the paper-boys penetrated the room, with the crys of " 'Ere y'are! Winner! Manchester Cup! " I rushed out and bought a " Globe," and, shouting out " Isonomy's won! " gave the boy half a crown. Disregarding the traffic, I rushed across the street and entered " The Bath " at a bound. " Isonomy's won! " I shouted. We were quite alone—well?

Some of my bets were for ready money. I had 1,000 to 30 with Milner, and the rest had gone on, at 20 to 1, in tenners, and so on. I remember the janitor of the Gaiety bar, recently one of the staff at the Carlton Hotel, put a pony on for me. This knocked acting into a cocked hat. I furnished and decorated my lady of the " Bath " as any young gentleman ought, and on the following Sunday Skindle's Lawn at Maidenhead was alive with my friends, while the lady, seated at the head of the launch, was a veritable belle de la rivière.

Undoubtedly the thick end of the wedge of racing which had penetrated my life received a very substantial knock with this win, and one which was encouraging, dissipating any prospect of that inevitable knock which nearly always visits all young plungers, unless they are closely connected with the Bank of England. The goody-goody people would describe this as the ephemeral success which tempts man to damnation.

I continued racing with extra vigour, and by the book-

makers was looked upon as a man of wealth, for, needless
to say, the £3,000 which I had won—£500 of which I had
already given away—was magnified doubly and trebly, as all
such transactions are.

Following in the footsteps of many others, I managed to
decrease my capital in my efforts to increase it, and I soon
learnt the practical lesson that to win a few thousands is not
to win much, but to lose a few thousands is to lose a lot.

It was now the autumn of 1880. Just about the period that
pheasants become rocketers, I became rocky. Yes, I candidly
admit it. I took the knock. Needless to add, R. H. Fry was
my biggest and almost only creditor. Forsaking my name-
sake, Robert the Devil, in the Cesarewitch, I returned from
Newmarket a sadder and "unwiser" man.

Again I soliloquised without words. It was not a mock
repentance. It was not what I would have done and what I
would not have done if this or that had happened. I merely
reflected what a jolly good time I had had, and how delighted
I was that I had not received my temporary quietus earlier.
The knock! Ten seconds, and one is counted out. In other
words, Monday, twenty-four hours, and it is past—until
animation is restored by payment.

Nothing brings with it better resolutions than failure.
I crossed the road, saw my lady "Bath," and told her everything. Had I permitted it, I could have settled my account
on Monday. I felt my position, and I have always felt
everything keenly in connection with racing, good, bad, or
indifferent—instinctively, possibly from my love of sport, and
this branch of it in particular.

In those days the major part of the settling took place at
Tattersall's. My chambers were a pleasant half-way house
for my creditors. The late Mr. Fry, ever urbane, would have
continued my credit, to my discredit, had I so desired—and
here let me break from the line of my story, and say that the
ring has never seen a man like him before, nor will they
ever, in my opinion, see his like again. He was a speculative

gambler. no matter whether he received his gains or not, and
had he died worth a tithe, not of what he was owed, which
in itself was a fabulous fortune, but of what he gave away
in charity, those he left behind him would not have had to
fall back upon that prop of which he himself was so great a
support.

What was I to do?

I went boldly to my aunt, and I admit that it took me
longer to screw my courage up to do this than any act I can
remember in the whole of my life. I respected the dear old
lady, and to this day I revere her memory. She listened to
me without interruption. I told her my story, ungarnished,
without reservation. Without a word of rebuke, she said how
glad she was that I had told her everything, spoke with no
little affectionate emotion, wrote out cheques for R. H. Fry,
Milner, and a few others for small amounts, which were then
and there posted.

In those days ladies grew old. Nowadays they never do.
They had that refined simplicity of manner, that true sincerity
of womanhood, which has left its influence to-day upon every
man who remembers that innate courtesy which marked the
generation to which I refer.

She has gone, and with her the customs of her age, which
had then been long on the wane ; and her maid, who is now
seventy-eight years of age, has, I am pleased to say, through
all my vicissitudes always been cared for. It is sad to record
that this old woman, in the fulness of time, has succumbed
to the temptations of the Turf, and her record is that she has
had a sovereign on Sceptre every time she ran.

Aunt Minty favoured the stage against racing, and
favoured neither against her convictions. I was then
approaching my majority, and her good nature prevailing, she
agreed that I should take out a dramatic company. Needless
to say, I did not dissent.

I played stock repertoire, with Gilbert and Sullivan's
"Trial by Jury" to finish each performance. Whether

Hatchett's had installed in me extravagant ideas, or India had lent, or I might say given to me an inclination to extravagance, I cannot say ; but one thing is certain, that, though the company was nominally a financial success, my hotel bills and expenses swamped all the profits, until we ultimately dried up at Birmingham.

Everything had pointed to a burst of success without being able to finish. Fun we had, and successful as this may be across the footlights, one does not get an audience or receipts for it inside the theatre. The salaries were paid, and after a short speech from me the company dissolved.

On returning to London I threw myself into an armchair, wondering what I should do next.

## CHAPTER IX.

## OLD HOSTELRIES.

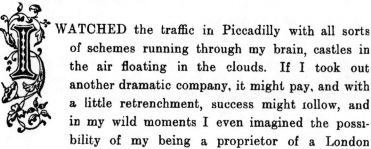 WATCHED the traffic in Piccadilly with all sorts of schemes running through my brain, castles in the air floating in the clouds. If I took out another dramatic company, it might pay, and with a little retrenchment, success might follow, and in my wild moments I even imagined the possibility of my being a proprietor of a London theatre! Then, on the other hand, my mind's eye would rest on the racecourse, which with me was a softer spot, and I pictured to myself the possibilities of some day winning the Derby. 1 had already tasted the sweets of winning, and there is no greater incentive than this to the new beginner, whether it be in racing, acting, or aught else. I took a short engagement at the Haymarket Theatre, and the approaching winter compelled me sternly to realise that racing, at least for some months to come, was a dead letter. Prospective Isonomys were hibernating.

Many of the frequenters of Hatchett's coffee-room patronised the Blue Posts, in Cork Street, celebrated for its good English fare ; it was also celebrated for the fun and practical joking which went on inside its hospitable walls, while it was no less a pleasant resort by reason of the company of the haut demi-monde, who were more in evidence in those years than now. Their names were as well known in

the West End of London as those of any leading ladies in the
land, and many of them married well. To name them perhaps
would be unfair, for they were all a good sort in their way,
surrounded by a good time.

Another hostelry less frequented was the Crown, in
Rupert Street, now the Hotel Florence. Here Dr. Harvey,
Charley Johnson, the Pot, Dr. Dougall, and a host of others
ran riot at times, and any stranger presenting himself in what
was called the " upstairs club parlour," was generally received
with volleys of flour. This kept the place secluded from
strangers! The barmaids were the most fashionable the proprietor could obtain, and amongst them were prize-takers
at the Woolwich Barmaid Show.

It is needless to say that the decorum which one might
expect in the restaurant of the Savoy Hotel was not to be
found in the " upstairs club parlour " of the Crown in Rupert
Street. Chaff, practical jokes, things that men in their more
sober years wonder they ever did, were the sum and substance
of the meetings at the Crown. The landlord found it difficult
to keep time with his guests, and one evening closed his house
punctually, which was against the rules and inclinations of
every member of the " upstairs club parlour." The next day
it was decided to mete out punishment to him as a mark of
disapproval of his overnight conduct. He was a married man,
and his wife was good-looking and full of spirits. It was proposed that a trip by sea to Aberdeen would blow the cobwebs
off everybody, and the landlord agreed with some others to
go. By the time he reached the boat, in company with the
rest who were supposed to be going with him, he had had
more to drink than he could reasonably carry, and taking to
his cabin long before the boat was due to start, he went to
sleep. Now was the time to mete out to him that punishment
to which the club had sentenced him. One of the members
took his return ticket out of his pocket together with all the
money he had on him, and left him still peacefully slumbering.
The party then wished him " Bon voyage " in ceremonious

dumb show, and soon after they watched the boat safely off with its cargo.

That evening the Crown in Rupert Street hardly closed at all. Dancing and rollicking fun was the order until the break of day. The lady who appeared to enjoy the proceedings most was the landlord's wife! But the fun had scarcely begun yet. In due course a telegram arrived from Scotland which ran somewhat as follows:—"Where are the rest of the party? Here all by myself with neither ticket nor money. Reply." The landlady, with an eye to the welfare of her business, consulted some of the revellers of the night before, who eased her of all trouble in this respect, and promised to attend to the matter; but this poor landlord was sent from one town to another by telegram saying he would meet one man in this place, or another man in the other, or, failing that, receive the money somewhere else, and he was kept out of London for five whole days and nights.

The night of the landlord's return might have been expected to be a stormy one, but such was not the case. A dinner was laid for several, with the head of the table reserved for the landlord, who in due course arrived. Garrulous explanations were made drowning anything the landlord said, and he was positively carried and put in the chair at the head of the table to sit down and eat the dinner which was arranged in honour of his return by his guests, who had, he was informed, spent a very dull time anxiously wondering where he was; but they welcomed the prodigal husband back, and so ended a huge joke, which the husband was compelled to appreciate as much as the rest of us.

Of all the frequenters of the Crown whom I can for the moment remember, only two are alive, Dr. Dougall and the Pot.

Another hostelry which at this period received much sporting patronage was Long's in Bond Street. In the eighties, and many years earlier, this was a celebrated house, and the entrée to the coffee-room was perhaps more difficult than to the majority of clubs. It may be said that the habitués of the coffee-room at Hatchett's were accepted as honorary members, and a list of the influential names of those who frequented Long's would run into hundreds. Amongst many others the Duke of Hamilton, "Jimmie" Shaw, Lord Gerard, and others of that ilk kept the ball rolling. A wet devilled sole and champagne cup, served in silver mugs, was the standing breakfast. William was the head waiter, every inch a gentleman's servant.

Limmer's, just round the corner in Conduit Street, might be styled a full sister to Long's, but these old-time hotels were part of an era which, I fear, is never to come again. Limmer's is now a pianoforte warehouse, but whatever tunes they may be able to produce there, not one of them will compare with those of the sparkling days of old, while Long's has been no less desecrated, and what were once the celebrated coffee-room and the old smoking-room are now turned into shops ; the drawing-room is a public bar, and what was in recent years a billiard-room is now used as a make-shift dining room. The old associations have disappeared, and the new landlord, Jenks, a former proprietor of a gambling club off St. James's Street, has transformed Long's Hotel beyond the recognition of the sportsmen who used to patronise the place. There is an incursion of palatial hotels where one gets little else but an ample supply of coloured glass and music, and the solidity of the good smaller hotels which had their own particular clientèle, and gave to their guests the comfort of home, is now out of the fashion and dead.

## CHAPTER X.

### TURF UPS AND DOWNS.

O N May 30, 1881, my coming of age was celebrated at Long's by a breakfast, and I determined at that moment to sever my connection with the stage. From that day forth I took to racing more actively and generally than I had heretofore, and was to be found on the racecourse at almost every important meeting in England. I was fortunate, and soon won enough to repay "Aunty Minty" the bulk of what she had advanced me. I was thus early well known to the regular followers of racing, and I had pulled more than one out of a tight betting corner.

From the day I saw Archer ride Bend Or in the Derby I always favoured his mounts if I had the shadow of an encouragement to back them, and this stood me in good stead. Having taken up my quarters for the Sussex fortnight at the Old Ship, Brighton, when Mr. "Arthur" was alive, I drove tandem daily to Goodwood, having two changes on the road. To my mind, Goodwood is never complete without lunch underneath the trees, hence I had my table there, a custom I never relinquished any one year except when I have been abroad. Entertaining my friends, I had not time to go into the ring, so sent round to have £200 each way on Dutch Oven at starting price in the Richmond Stakes with R. H. Fry. She got home at 6 to 1, Archer up, and I landed £1,500, not a bad opening bet, and good seasoning for a youngster who had just touched his majority ! She won by a head from St. Marguerite and the flying Kermesse, who ran a dead-heat for second place, and to show what a good jockey Archer was, and how much he must have had in hand, she later on at the meeting again met St. Marguerite in the Rous Memorial Stakes, over the same course, at a difference of 3lb in the latter's favour, and on this occasion Dutch Oven beat her by three lengths! Having backed several good winners, I had £500 on Dutch Oven at 3 to 1, and on Monday morning when I settled up with R. H. Fry at Brighton, before he went up to London, he handed me a cheque for over £6,000—and there were others !

Brighton and Lewes were not unsuccessful, and I finished up the Sussex fortnight as "a man ought to." Then I continued racing with those fluctuations, which are too well known to need description, more especially when my twenty-one years and the early success which I had achieved are taken into consideration. Had I led a less liberal life, or have been brought up surrounded by the drudgery of a city office, or have shut myself out from the world generally by locking myself up in the Temple, or through one way or the other have narrowed my ideas to a business degree, I might have plodded on without a reverse ; but this was not my nature. I was not greedy to win, nor did I hoard up my gains, and during my racing career I do not think I have gained the reputation of being other than reasonably liberal, in proportion to my successes. This gives a man who does not brood over his gains the right not to brood over his losses. In colloquial terms, I followed a "happy-go-lucky" line of my own. I never looked back to pat myself on the back, nor did I attempt to look into the future and wonder how long it was going to last. "Sufficient for the day is the evil thereof ! "

I would not for an instant suggest this maxim to a professional or business man ; but personally, if I am not a bold speculator I am nothing. Had I introduced commercial instincts, and treated my racing career in a purely commercial spirit, I might to-day have been a rich man, for I have at different times acquired three large fortunes on the Turf, each amounting to over £200,000. These ups and downs have afforded me great opportunities of studying human nature—the ebb and flow, and that overwhelming majority which floats with the stream.

After a bad Doncaster I determined to give myself a rest, and once more paid Plymouth a visit. I began dabbling as an amateur bookmaker, which was a little slow and did not quite satisfy the ambition of a young plunger. Whether it was that the "Plymouth Brethren" knew a bit, or that my vein of bad luck still pursued me, I cannot say, but as a result of my amateur efforts I never won on any one week, and this, as it continued, gave me a kind of professional bite.

My mother's cousin, Major-General James Freeth Williamson, having at one time commanded the 23rd Welsh Fusiliers, gave me an introduction to the officers of that regiment, who were at this time stationed at the Citadel; and, following in the footsteps of the "Plymouth Brethren," they backed Foxhall with me for the Cesarewitch to a man! The result of this considerably reduced the balance of my account at my bankers; in short, it nearly left me high and dry.

I then opened a book on the Cambridgeshire, and that the Welsh Fusiliers were conservative cannot for an instant be doubted, for they backed Foxhall again to a man, and, not content with this, introduced one or two friends, who followed their example. On the day of the race I found myself rather with a "Foxhall Book" than a Cambridgeshire one. The result is common knowledge—that is, so far as the winner of the Cambridgeshire is concerned—but the result of my settling my account on the following Monday is not ancient history. Add up my bank-book as I would, I could not find sufficient to meet my liabilities. This knocked all the amateur out of me. I became deadly professional. I interviewed three of the officers to whom I was more largely indebted, and asked for "time." At the early stages of my interview with them I believe they would have obliged me had they been magistrates! After a prolonged explanation, in which "hope" played no small part, they generously agreed to wait. I settled with everybody else, packed up my traps, and returned to my rooms in Dover Street, not a sadder, but a wiser man. Here, although the winter was approaching, I felt at least no concern as to the price of coal!

It was not until my first return from Australia in 1886 that I paid my debts to the three men of the 23rd. It came as rather a surprise to them, for they had all forgotten the matter, and had long since wiped it off as a bad debt; but there are two things I have always done—firstly, never to forget a debt I owed; and, secondly, never to allow it to trouble me. Moodily brooding only retards the prospective chance of getting out of debt.

During the close season, I paid more than one visit to Fitzroy House, Newmarket, which was then kept by old Martin, the grandfather of E. Martin, the present trainer; and here I renewed my acquaintance with Dick Budge, in his day a celebrated trainer of gamecocks. Dick had brought off a main for me at Plymouth. He was a Devonshire man, and I have an idea he looked upon me as a blossoming millionaire patron of the sport. I did not undeceive him; stern facts do quite enough for us in this respect, without any aid or assistance. Gamecocks brought him in touch with the late Tom Jennings. In this roundabout way I gathered that Poulet was expected to win the Lincoln Handicap of 1882. I backed it, amongst others, with Mr. Pottle, of the Royal Exchange, who, I regret to say, is now deceased. I got all sorts of prices, ranging from 40 to 1 down to 20 to 1; and when Mr. Pottle had to pay me on Monday his cheque did not arrive, but in answer to a telegram on Tuesday he came to Newmarket, "as he would like to have a look at the young gentleman who had won so much money from him." He left his cheque behind for a most acceptable sum, and asking me what he had better back to get his money back, I advised him to have a pony or so on Iroquois for the City and Suburban, but he went lame soon afterwards, and with this my business with Pottle also broke down.

This was opening the season well, but it was not to last, and before a fortnight had elapsed I had lost nearly all my Lincoln Handicap winnings.  I then took a trip on the Continent, stopping at Monte Carlo and many other places, ultimately reaching Naples.  Here I re-visited a few of the old spots, and thought of the Parsee I had put in the train at Reggio, and other circumstances which the surroundings brought back to my recollection.

Shortly after my arrival a large vessel came into the bay, and, looking at her, I inquired her name.  I was told she was the Liguria, one of the Orient liners.  I then inquired, " Where is she going to ? "  " Australia," was the answer.  A second's thought, and I hailed a fly ; and, driven by the aid of a nose-band and Neapolitan ejaculations, I reached my hotel.  Hey presto ! and my servant had packed the things ; I paid the bill, and we were on board the Liguria sailing for Australia.

Again I met a distinctive lot of passengers compared with either of those on the South African or Indian routes.  The South African travellers represented what Whitechapel is to London, the Australians the suburb of Brixton, and the Indians, Mayfair.

Our complement of passengers may best be described by the one word " mixed."  Old hands returning to the colonies, whither, perhaps, their initial passage had not cost them so much, and in more than one instance might have cost them nothing ; others going out in search of those fortunes which are won and lost on the goldfields ; in short, men of all classes, doubtless mostly those who had not been as successful as they thought they should have been in the mother country.  A sprinkling of youths, who in earlier years might have been the hopes of the family, were being sent out by their fathers to gain what is called colonial experience, which generally means that the unruly youth at home discovers, on landing, that he has much more scope, and is subjected to a great deal more temptation, than is the case at home.

A traveller on board ship has three courses open to him. He can keep himself to himself, he can become one of a certain circle, or he can be amiable and courteous to everybody, with a result that each circle tries to ensnare him in their meshes. The latter is by far the preferable stand to take, and affords plenty of amusement to the man who is a worldly angler.

The Orient line at this time ran straight from Suez to Adelaide, which is a long run without touching a port, and seldom is a sail to be seen on this stretch. Sweepstakes on the distance of the run of the vessel, concerts, dances, and ship's athletic sports, helped to pass the time away. Amongst our passengers were fifteen nuns, and though I hope each one may be blessed, I am compelled to confess they did not add to the conviviality of the voyage. It was no small relief when Adelaide was sighted, where I landed on May 30, 1882, my twenty-second birthday. I had ascertained that the York Hotel was the best in town, which was inducement enough for me to put up there. The Adelaide autumn races were just over, and many sportsmen from Victoria and New South Wales still remained behind. Amongst others, I met Mr. Joseph Thompson for the first time, Mr. J. Eden Savile, an Englishman who subsequently trained The Assyrian, who won the Melbourne Cup, and many others whose names would be of little interest. What I was going to do I had no idea. I had no plans in going to Australia. I saw no prospect if I was going to stop there; in short, I felt little better than a peripatetic stroller.

The life was purely colonial, everybody knew everybody else, and the hotels, which were not quite up to the class of the Savoy or Claridge's, were the general meeting places of all.

Wide streets with huge telegraph poles running along either side of them, shops with corrugated fronts projecting over the gutter to protect them from the sun, dust—which on hot-wind days vied with the desert of the Sahara—the eucalyptus stud-

7

ding the street at regular intervals but giving little or no shade with its vertical leaves ; such is a brief description of the general impression Adelaide leaves on the stranger. It has its suburbs, which are extremely pretty, and its public institutions are worthy of an architectural description. The men were one and all a good-natured lot, and they extended to me the hand of hospitality.

I am now strictly referring to those who live in Adelaide, and not to the bookmakers of Australia, to some of whom I shall have to refer in a less pleasing tone as the recital of my life in Australia progresses.

A one-day's race meeting was advertised to be shortly held at Morpethville, which is the name of the Adelaide racecourse, and before going on to Melbourne I determined to wait for this meeting. Just prior to its taking place I resolved to make a book, and assuming my mother's maiden name, that of Sutton, for racing purposes, I was proposed, seconded, and elected a member of Tattersall's Club in Adelaide, and this brought me into contact with the majority of owners in South Australia, and I made many friends. The day arrived, and I drove to the racecourse with more confidence than capital.

## CHAPTER XI.

### AUSTRALIA.

USTRALIA! In this hemisphere of topsy-turvey-dom—where the aboriginal is black, where the trees shed their bark and not their leaves; where the gean grows tasteless, with its stone outside the fruit; where the native pear ripens into a pendulous pod of wood; where the marsupial kangaroo fosters her young in her pouch; where the bandicoot doth procreate upon her nipples; where foxes fly as bats by night; where the birds have no song; where the rivers are destitute of water; where all things indigenous are inverted—a traveller may expect to encounter impediments of all kinds.

I knew that in starting to make a book on the racecourse as a new man among strangers, I should be confronted with no little opposition from men who had followed the calling of bookmaking for several years and were locally known.

The Australian system of betting was not on the more liberal lines customary in England. It was the general rule of the colonial bookmaker to bet on double events, and seldom, if ever, to have a straight out book, except on important events, such as the Melbourne, Caulfield, and Sydney Cups. Every bookmaker carried his own book, having no clerk, and would generally offer to bet on "this and the next," which meant that the punter was expected to find not only the winner of the first event, but also that of the following race; and if he backed a winner in the first race, but in the second event his horse did not start, he would lose his money. Cash betting was unknown, and if a stranger wanted to make a bet he would have to deposit his money, but, in the event of backing a winner, would not receive his gains until the regular settling day. The foregoing shows the crude state betting was in at the time of my arrival in Australia. When, therefore, I took up my position on the Adelaide Racecourse with a clerk by my side I created no little excitement, and when I gave out that I would pay over every race immediately it was decided and the winner had weighed in, and that my transactions would be confined to single and not double events, the bookmaking fraternity looked upon me in wonderment mingled with despair, while the public came up smiling, and I did a roaring trade forthwith.

It was only a one-day meeting, held on Accession Day, which was kept as a public holiday throughout the Colonies—an example which might be followed in the Mother Country; for we have no public holiday throughout the year in connection with Royalty.

The result of my new methods, or rather the introduction of those which were in vogue in England, caused me, before the end of the day, to transact certainly 75 per cent. of the betting on the course, and many of the local bookmakers put their volumes in their pockets as "this and the next" signally failed in face of the opposition which I had inaugurated.

My first venture showed a profit of more than £1,500 at the end of the day, and it was telegraphed all over the colony to the different newspapers, that a prominent bookmaker of the name of Sutton had arrived from Tattersall's in England, and that he had paralysed the betting in South Australia, while the Adelaide "Punch" had a cartoon of the Bishop betting with me, and some ten bookmakers belonging to the Chosen Race were depicted walking away up a hill, upon the top of which was a signpost pointing "To Palestine."

Having been so well advertised in the columns of every newspaper of the different Australian Colonies, I immediately packed up, determining to make my headquarters in Melbourne, which in those days was only get-at-able by boat or mailcart, there being no railway connecting the two cities.

The licensing of bookmakers had been recently introduced into Victoria. The licence to bet at Flemington cost £25 per annum, and it was not long before all the minor racecourses in Victoria levied some kind of charge on all bookmakers who betted at their meetings.

These licences represented a good round sum, and the money so obtained helped to swell the prizes. If this method were followed in England it might be made of great benefit to owners, who are the principal supporters of the Turf, for the stakes which are offered at the present moment cost more to run for than those of any other country in the world ; or the money might be divided amongst the different executives and a lesser charge demanded from the public for the entrance to Tattersall's and the smaller rings, while it would give the bookmakers a better standing, and knock welshing on the head, for the public would not do business with any man who had not been licensed by the authorities.

My resolve to visit Melbourne, and actively continue the business of a bookmaker, had been well discussed, and on my arrival my name was already well known in sporting circles.

The Melbourne bookmakers did not disguise the fact that they failed to appreciate my coming among them with the innovation of cash betting, and in many instances attempted to put obstacles in the way of my becoming a member of the leading sporting clubs—namely, the Victorian Club and Bowes's Tattersall's. Having a letter of introduction to Captain Standish, who was Chairman of the V.R.C., the equivalent to the Senior Steward of the Jockey Club in this country, this opposition was futile, as this gentleman proposed me for the clubs, and the Hon. W. Pearson, the Vice-Chairman of the V.R.C., seconded me. Had certain evidence recently given in the Law Court, before Sir William Grantham, been true, it is not possible that these two gentlemen, holding these high honorary offices, indeed the highest that can be held under the rules of racing in Australia, would have proposed and seconded me for the principal clubs in Melbourne.

I was unanimously elected, and received a licence immediately upon my application to Mr. H. Byron Moore, the Secretary of the Victorian Racing Club.

The first meeting I attended was at Caulfield, but I decided not to bet there, so went as a spectator only, in order to gain a general insight into the way racing and betting were conducted in the colony of Victoria. " This and the next " was the order of the day, and at least 90 per cent. of the bookmakers' physiognomies announced that they belonged to the Chosen Race.

The Sydney meeting was approaching, and after some consideration I made up my mind that I would start business there, and I was immediately elected a member of the Sydney Tattersall's.

The Spring Meeting at Randwick (New South Wales) opens the ball for flat racing in Australia, which continues merrily until the autumn meeting, when it is carried on to a lesser degree. There is no National Hunt, and this, judging from the parlous state of steeplechasing at home, shows the colonials' sound sense.

At this spring meeting I went on to the course with my clerk, and, after surveying the space set apart for betting purposes, I fixed on a place which I thought would be a prominent position to take up. Such a thing as shouting the odds was unknown ; indeed, bookmaking before my arrival in Australia might be better termed " lumbering," it being the common custom to run about in search of the up-country squatter and lay him a bet, nearly always a double event, much under the legitimate price. The bookmakers did not take up a stand in any one place. The numbers went up for the first race, and I launched out, shouting a price on the field, with a result that some forty or fifty of these men stood round me, forming a large ring, and booed. I continued, taking no notice of them. It was a cowardly attack, but the public broke through the cordon they had made with a cheer, and from that moment I carried on the largest business of any bookmaker in Australia.

It was not long before many followed the example I had set, and in Australia to-day double events on minor races are, very rightly, almost unknown.

I made many friends, and was christened by the public, and always referred to in the papers as "The Englishman."

The Cornstalk is a sportsman, and the generosity he extends to his visitors knows no bounds. Wherever I went I was welcomed, and considerable sympathy was extended to me for the unseemly and contemptible demonstration of some of the bookmakers on my first appearance at Randwick.

My business increased with each race, and I netted a considerable sum, and began to feel that I was on the road to becoming a Crœsus, and had struck oil.

Returning to Melbourne, I met a friend of mine, Major Bell, and with him went to a fancy bazaar which was being held in aid of some good cause; from memory I think it was in aid of a fund for building the wing of a church, and amongst other things I fell in love with one of the ladies who kept a stall; and as I do not intend to touch upon family matters, I may say shortly that we were married three weeks afterwards, I being just twenty-two years of age, and she my junior by a year.

The Sydney episode and the large business I had done there, had reached Melbourne before my return, and I became a subject to be pointed out in the streets by different people, and frequently heard myself being referred to with "There goes the Englishman."

The accommodation and comfort afforded to the public at Flemington, Randwick, and Caulfield, put in the shade the stands and the space allotted in England. Indeed, I know of no stand in any part of the world that can compare with that of Flemington, with its spacious lawn laid out in flower-beds, where, on a Melbourne Cup day, when young Australia turns out to a man—aye, and to a lady, too—there is plenty of room for everybody, and the attendance in the stands is about equal to that at Epsom on Derby Day, while the charge for entrance to the grand stand, where one can see the races in perfect comfort, is only 10s. (and this includes the paddock), compared with the £1 or more which is demanded in England, where the pleasant surroundings I have described are next to unknown.

In the grand stand certain seats are reserved for Stewards, and a portion is kept for members of the V.R.C. The spacious paddock is connected with the enclosure ; there is no barrier or gate to go through, and no pass-out checks have to be taken to get there. Of the merits of the horses we have had a sample in England, and I need go no further than to name Merman, a winner of the Cesarewitch and the Ascot Gold Cup, though I cannot omit to mention Moifaa, once the property of His Majesty the King.

The first Melbourne Cup I witnessed was in 1882, when Assyrian, an outsider, won, and after paying out some £700 I won over £5,000 in ready money on the race; indeed, I did so great a business that I was compelled to have three clerks, the business of one being solely to hold the money.

That the meeting for the Melbourne Cup is a spectacle one cannot witness on any other racecourse, is beyond contradiction. With its garden-like lawn, its enormous stands, tier following tier, with a natural hill behind it, forming, as it were, another grand stand above the roof of that built by man, it is in every respect unique. The course is circular, a little more than a mile and a half in circumference, and though it is in every respect good, it could not compare with the track at Newmarket, or the turf at Goodwood. Ascot, with all its brilliancy, is left far behind in respect to comfort and the advantages of being able to view a race.

I generally won, I may say I always did so at the large meetings; and not being afraid of living up to my income I had a house in St. Kilda, bought a yacht, and had a country place at Schnapper Point (Mornington), which is on the coast, or, rather, on the shores of the bay.

Of hunting there was not much, the Melbourne hounds being a drag pack and there were no others, but hunting the kangaroo afforded excellent sport, and coursing the strong hares which Australia produces was good fun. One could shoot rabbits, which are the pest of the country, quicker than a naughty boy could catch flies, but with the exception of wild duck and wild turkeys there was little sport for the gun.

These surroundings suited me very well, and at the end of my first year's racing I had won over £70,000, of which I sent a certain amount to England in payment of some debts I had left behind, and assisted a few friends who had been good enough to help me at a time when I myself was in difficulties.

After some happy and fairly prosperous years, I arranged, in 1886, to return to England for a trip.

One of the passengers on board the boat was Bishop Moorhouse, who was returning to England to take up the bishopric of Manchester. A better type of Englishman, a more genial companion than his lordship one could not wish to meet. It was announced that he would administer the Sacrament at one of the Sunday services, and in due course the Sabbath arrived, but no preparations had been made for carrying out the communion service, and it was suddenly remembered that no chalice was forthcoming. Mr. Harry Haines, one of the best sportsmen Australia has ever seen, immediately offered the use of a cup he had with him. This was accepted on the spur of the moment, and after the service the Bishop was admiring the cup which had done duty for the chalice when he read on it the following inscription: "The Adelaide Gold Cup, won by Euclid, the property of Mr. Harry Haines."

## CHAPTER XII.

## A TRIP HOME AND BACK.

NCE again I found myself going through the Suez Canal, once again we touched Malta—and once again I thought of Blue Eyes. Reaching Brindisi, I disembarked and went overland to England. On the train I met an officer in the King's Dragoon Guards, whose name I need not mention, but from that day we have been fast friends. I mention this, as I shall have to incidentally refer to him shortly.

On my arrival in London I took rooms over Elvery's in Conduit Street, and settled down for a few months' holiday prior to returning to Australia. My married life had not been a success, doubtless all my fault, and it had been arranged that during my absence the matrimonial link should be legally broken.

I attended the different race meetings at Newmarket and those convenient to London, and renewing my acquaintance with many old friends, I was elected a member of Boodle's, made a member of Sandown Park, being proposed by the late General Owen Williams, and became a member of the majority of racing clubs.

Once more I found myself in the midst of a merry lot of men, whose wild oats had not yet been sown, and judging of them generally, the majority required several extra acres for the successful carrying out of the old proverb. The East

Room of the Criterion had not then long been opened, and was a favourite resort for dinner, while the Continental and the Globe were the rendezvous for many a convivial supper-party.

It was after one of these evenings, towards the end of June, that a party of us repaired to my rooms in Conduit Street. It took some half-dozen cabs to get our full complement there. On our arrival a good, true, and faithful myrmidon of the law, to wit, a policeman, was standing outside. It was a hot, thirsty night, and, like a good Samaritan, I asked him if he could not "do a drink." He followed us in, and a whisky and soda quenched the parched lips of the law. He must have had his "appreciative" eye on us, for he seemed in no haste to retreat, so I offered him a cigar, and he took a seat and started puffing away—with another whisky and soda by his side.

It dawned on me that I had never had on a policeman's helmet and tunic, and, beckoning to the constable, I took him into another room. Dressing myself up as a policeman, I returned suddenly, creating no little excitement when I demanded the presence of Mr. R. S. Sievier, for whose arrest I said I held a warrant.

No one recognised me ; indeed, they rather displayed the mighty dread which the blue tunic carries with it. The chin-strap of the helmet helped to hide my features, and it was some time before I was recognised. This done, the fun increased.

Unobserved by the owner of the tunic, who, in a loose dressing-gown, was puffing away at the butt-end of his cigar in a room by himself, I, followed by two or three friends, began to parade Bond Street as an officer of the law, and, meeting an acquaintance, immediately arrested him, insisting that he was drunk and had been creating a disturbance. He protested, but the strong arm of the law collared him, and turning his nose towards Vine Street, marched him round the corner into Conduit Street. Here I hesitated, suddenly rushed him up the stairs to my chambers, and threw him into my rooms, where he found himself face to face with a good many of his personal friends!

Nothing daunted, I went out again on "the beat." Just as I was about to turn the corner, the whole company hanging out of the windows looking after me, I ran right into the arms of a real policeman. I took to my heels instanter, the policeman after me. I soon outpaced him, and, doubling round the houses, reached Long's, and, ringing the bell, the door was immediately opened by the porter and I entered.

He did not recognise me; indeed, he stood dumfounded, and walking straight into the smoking-room. although breathless, I placed everybody under arrest, including the landlord, for serving drinks after hours; but my evening-dress trousers and pumps rather gave me away, for the police force are more celebrated for the size of their boots than for the ordinary patent pumps.

I had safely dodged the policeman who was in pursuit, but I was no less in a dilemma to know how to get back to my rooms undiscovered, and to return the tunic and helmet to the officer of the law who was doing yeoman duty with the whisky and cigars. Borrowing a coat and cap, I got back to my chambers, receiving a reception of three cheers from the occupants of the windows, together with a volley of bolsters and pillows which they had gathered from the different bedrooms and hurled down at me in the street.

I came to England for a holiday. and I was having it! Among those present that night, one has blossomed into an active and successful member of the House of Commons, another commanded a corps of Imperial Yeomanry in South Africa with great distinction, and the rest of the company of that evening are one and all alive to-day, and each holds a responsible position, and holds it honourably.

Goodwood came round, and taking one of the many rectories always to let in the neighbourhood during the race week, which is as much the rector's harvest as that of his parishioners living round Goodwood, I collected quite a respectable house-party, properly to bring off the double event—the rectory and the races. A matter which at the time afforded me great amusement, and which I have never forgotten, was the ever-ready courtesy of the rector to oblige us in any possible way he could. He had removed for the time being to a little cottage, and very graciously placed everything he had left behind at our disposal, he himself proposing that the donkey might assist in taking the lunch to the racecourse, and an old broken-kneed pony and a ricketty basket phaeton might be made use of by helping to take some of the guests to the grand stand. I caused the donkey to be used as a help, as suggested, and the old pony took two or three of the valets to the course. It was a very thoughtful offer on the part of the rector, and I felt I should like to repay this in some indirect way, so on leaving I tipped his servants with extra generosity. About the middle of the following week I received a note from this man of piety and self-denial, asking if I would kindly send a cheque for twelve guineas, being two guineas a day for the pony and a guinea a day for the donkey!

I had a very bad time at Goodwood, not so far as racing was concerned, as my account on Monday showed a small balance in my favour, but I had lost a very large sum at baccarat during the week, and one extraordinary feature in connection with this after-dinner card-playing, which goes to show what can happen in gambling, was that out of the seven players I was the only loser.

I saw the Sussex fortnight out, and though losses never troubled me, I began to consider the advisability of returning to the land of the Golden Fleece, instead of remaining in the country where I was being fleeced of my gold.

I found what money I had brought with me was exhausted, and I borrowed £300 from my friend in the K.D.G.'s, to whom I referred in the beginning of this chapter, and arranged to sail forthwith on my return journey to Australia. A few friends dined with me at Boodle's the evening before I started, and this arrangement suited my finances admirably, as members only paid their bills once a year, when the house account was sent in to them. Doubtless this custom has been a convenient one to others in times gone by! After dinner we all repaired to the Alhambra, and a question arose as to whether any of our company could successfully negotiate walking or running round the top of the dress-circle balustrade. The discussion on the point became very animated, and each of the company thought he could do it, but when challenged, discretion became the better part of valour. I offered to back myself for a pony to accomplish it there and then. This was immediately taken by one who is now the senior officer of one of our crack cavalry regiments, and without a moment's hesitation I jumped on to the top of the dress-circle rail and ran "the zigzag course" from the private box at one end to the beginning of the row of boxes at the other. The astonishment of the audience, after it was realised what I had done, may be conceived. I had the biggest round of applause in the house that night!

These were the sort of mad tricks that I was always ready to perform in those days, and even now I often wonder whether I have settled down or not. Would I play them again? Yes, if I could be put back twenty years!

On reaching Melbourne I telegraphed the £300 I had borrowed, to the credit of my friend at Cox's, and then sat down to hear the story of different events which had happened during my absence.

I found I should have to get into harness again at once, for I had not more money to carry on my business than I required. My expenses had been enormous, and at spending money it has always been my lot to be an expert.

By this time I was universally known throughout Australasia, and my name was a public one throughout the whole of the five colonies, in which I include Tasmania.

After my return I attended several meetings, mostly up-country, where I generally lost money, and the vein of bad luck which I had picked up in England still pursued me.

Having plenty of spare time, I determined to take a trip to Sydney, and took my passage on one of the coasters in preference to the 500 mile train journey. These boats started from the River Yarra, which, were it not for Hobson's Bay, evaporation would transform into a creek, and whereas the geographer asserts that Melbourne stands on the River Yarra, it is in truth the River Yarra that "stands" in Melbourne.

Gliding through the gaseous waters of the "river," the coaster dipped her nose in the ripples of the bay, and, piloted between the stationary buoys marking the channel, leaving Queen's Cliff on the starboard and Sorrento on the port, steered her course between the Heads, and, gaining the aquatic freedom of the ocean, headed for Bass Straits.

Port Jackson was sighted as the morning of the second day broke. We passed Botany Bay, the original city of the New South Wales settlement, and once a name by which the whole colony was generally known, but which is now untenanted and barren, as though performing a desolate penance with a view to obliterating its early traditions, though the spot will ever be historical as the landing place of Captain Cook.

Sailing under the precipitous cliffs of Sydney Heads, the little vessel went on until these huge mountainous rocks suddenly opened like a gigantic chasm, and disclosed, as though by magic, the fairyland beauty of the finest natural harbour of the world. Studded with islets, bedecked with semi-tropical vegetation, dotted with houses varying in size and architecture, rugged with sand-hills, symphonising with olive-tinted bushes, broken with inlets leading to nooks like a lacustral chain overhung with foliage, all rhythmically radiating into one mighty glaucescent mass of water, with a couple of British men-of-war peacefully floating at anchor, surrounded by craft of all nationalities, encircled by a broken line of hillocks reaching in places almost to the height of mountains, with gardens and lawns coming down to the water's edge, interspersed with wild flowers—imagine this, and you may have a slight conception of this magnificent natural picture—Sydney Harbour.

## CHAPTER XIII.

## UNDER THE SOUTHERN CROSS.

HE hotels in Sydney were not in my time remarkable either for their perfect cuisine or good service, the best of them being Petty's.

To the Englishman, there seemed to prevail more of a homely influence about the city than was the case in Melbourne, the streets and houses more resembling the old-fashioned style of England than the broadways of the capital of Victoria, which favoured America in their general appearance more than the Mother Country. It is needless to observe that the two cities vied with each other, and considerable rivalry, not altogether devoid of jealousy, existed between the Victorian and New South Welshman as to the merits of their respective capitals. Whatever may have been the considerations on either side, Sydney Harbour is one of the most picturesque spots of the Southern hemisphere—and the Sydneyite does not forget to trumpet it.

On my first journey to Sydney from Melbourne (1882) the railway had not been completed, and we had to do a short part of the journey by mail-cart, having to pass the Customs on the border between Victoria and New South Wales, which to the traveller was a nuisance; for, after all, he was not making an incursion into a foreign country, but merely passing from one British colony to another. The whole was the territory of the Empire, and to have one's luggage diligently

8

searched at a British colonial Custom-house very much suggested the procedure of the irritating Octroi throughout France. On the Victorian side the railway runs right through the notorious Kelly country, a wild, mountainous district, where Ned Kelly, the ringleader of this family of bushrangers, held out and held up banks for years, until ultimately, after keeping the authorities at bay for an inconceivably long period, his whereabouts was discovered and his temporary hiding-place surrounded by a large force of some hundreds of police, who, *with the aid of artillery*, succeeded in capturing their prisoner, but not before he had been severely wounded.

It is extraordinary to relate. yet it is no less the fact, that the Kelly gang had created a terrible state of terror, not alone throughout the district they were known to " favour," but throughout Australia generally. Nothing can better describe this state of wholesale fright, bordering on panic, than the fact that when the Kellys were at last run to ground and known to be hiding in a small wooden shanty. called a bush hotel, the police, numbering some six hundred or thereabouts, surrounded the isolated place, little better than a hut, and, in place of arresting these outlaws, set fire to the wooden cabin, with the result that the owner, an innocent woman, was burned to death, and a priest also perished in the flames.

Though the head of a gang of desperadoes, Ned Kelly proved himself a man on this occasion, and, emerging from the burning timbers, faced and fired on his enemy. They retaliated—we know their numbers. Ned Kelly had improvised some armour out of a ploughshare, and had covered his head with an iron pot, in which he had pierced two holes to see through. This resisted many bullets, some of the police afterwards stating that they thought they were firing at the devil himself ; but being finally wounded in the knee, he sank to the ground and was captured. He was tried and hanged in Melbourne.

Nothing remarkable happened at the race meeting at Randwick worth recounting in these columns, and I retraced my way to my colonial headquarters in Melbourne. Amongst other

country meetings, I regularly attended that of Warnambool ;
indeed, I shall always look upon this fixture and the surrounding country, as the most sporting in the land of the Southern
Cross. How far the railway now goes I cannot say, but a good
part of the journey—considering the time it took rather than
the mileage—had to be negotiated by the aid of the mail-
coach. Some hours in what is in Australia called a coach,
but what here would be called a caravan painted red, drawn
by four or six horses over a track of intermittent ruts and
stumps of trees, is not one of the most pleasant journeys on
a tropical afternoon. Yet it has its fascinations. The bush
of Australia is, generally speaking, weird  In parts, for hundreds of miles together, the sameness of the country is such
that the traveller on his journey might apparently be travers-
ing the same road or path again and again. The immaculate
precision of the virgin country, with its towering eucalyptus,
its vertical leaves offering but scant shade, one spot exactly
similar to the other, gives no guide to any direction. Once
off the track, and it may never be regained.

The coaching stage from the railway to Warnambool, however. had none of these drawbacks. The road was a fairly good
one ; on either side of it large paddocks were fenced in for
stretches running into miles, and the land was rich in grass and
herbs. A considerable portion of the journey lay between lines
of bracken alive with rabbits, and the creaking, swaying coach
ran over more than one as we sped on our journey. This
district is the garden of Victoria, much resembling Tasmania,
which insular colony is a nearer likeness to the Mother
Country than any of her sister colonies.

The Warnambool meeting was of little importance. except
that several good horses have come from the district ; but I
especially refer to it as being one of the most sporting of any
in Australasia. The steeplechase course was made up of solid
log fences. and both horse and rider required their nerves in
the right place successfully to negotiate the country, which also
included stone walls, post and rail, and was as formidable as—

if not more so than—any course of its kind that I can remember ; indeed, the jumps were obstacles which did not belie their name. I remember a horse called Dizzy winning four races in one day there ; and that he was a good one was subsequently proved by his landing the National Hurdle Race at Flemington shortly afterwards, the principal race over the sticks then run in the Colonies. From memory, Bob Batty, an excellent cross-country jockey, rode him.

A winner of four races in one day ! And this achieved without having to run the gauntlet of a single objection ! I do not refer to this as a comparison, but as an example. No objection ! Such an exploit would be next to impossible in England at such meetings as Ascot, Newmarket, etcetera, even granted one owned the horse capable of accomplishing this extraordinary feat ; for, owing to the extremely complex and tangled wording of the many different conditions and penalties, it would be almost a miracle to be able to discover what should be the correct weight to carry in the next race, in time to weigh out for it !

The betting at Warnambool was insignificant and not worth mentioning, but I always attended the race meetings there, owing to the thorough sporting surroundings and spirit which prevailed. This part of the colony of Victoria was the best for breeding horses, and the turf equally so with regard to racing them, of any I saw in Australasia. I am afraid with me it is adieu to the sportsmen of Warnambool. Would that it were au revoir only !

These so-called up-country meetings varied to a great degree, both with respect to the quality of the sport and the spirit of it. Not infrequently both were bad. At times, and in certain places, the pleasant picnic picture of a day's local racing was transformed into an oleograph depicting the most crude and barefaced malpractices. I took it all as it came, for wherever there was racing it had magnetic attractions for me, as a loadstone for iron ; in fact, if there was nothing more important going on, I am afraid I should be tempted to bet on a match between two tame white mice. As another contrast, if a match were made between the Bishop of Hereford and Lord Davey to sprint fifty yards, I should inevitably have a bet on it, even if the wager provoked the abandonment of the match! Thus it is not to be wondered at, that my following of racing took me here, there, and everywhere; and this brought me into contact with thousands who, when they were gathered together on that universal holiday, the Melbourne Cup day—I might say the GREAT MELBOURNE CUP—all betted with me to a man.

I remember at one of these small meetings, at a place called Mount Ararat, I did not take an active part in the betting, but had an equal share with Sam Allen in his book, which, according to his custom, was one of double and treble events. Things went very badly with him, and with the hope of getting our money back he extended his operations on the last three races and the final double. A local squatter had taken his full book on both the treble and final double event, and had landed the first two winners, and only had to pull off the last event to secure a very good stake. It was an open race, there being at least four horses on the spot with equal pretensions and prospective claims to victory. Unfortunately—but fortunately for Sam Allen and myself—the squatter strayed from sporting instincts, and treated the play of betting rather like a game of cards called grab. He succeeded in arranging with the three different owners of those horses who had good chances of winning the race that they should not run, though the jockeys were to attend in the weighing-room with their racing colours on, apparently ready to weigh out, but with no honest intention of doing so. Having satisfied myself that this was so, I remembered I had been taught that justice was meted out by " an eye for an eye, a tooth for a tooth." I at once approached the owner of the horse against which Allen had laid this man, who, disregarding all sporting feeling and the common code of honour, which racing demands, had resorted to such contemptible scheming. My conversation with the owner was

brief; in a few words I told him the facts, making no comment, but nevertheless making a business offer. The parties
concerned met in the weighing-room—I had become one of
the parties concerned. Three horses were weighed out for,
leaving the four jockeys who had any chance of winning
hanging around the scales.

"You had better weigh now," said the squatter to the
jockey of the horse he had backed in the doubles and trebles
with my partner for the day.

"Not until the other three have weighed out, Mr. ——," I
observed.

"What business is it of yours, Mr. Sutton?"

"I am the owner of the horse; I have just bought him;
here is the receipt," and I laid it on the table in the weighing-
room.

There was a momentary silence. When those present had
recovered the shock, some made their way hurriedly out, going
towards the betting-ring. Turning to the clerk of the scales I
said, "When the other three have weighed out—I presume they
are here at scale for that purpose—then my recent purchase
shall weigh out, or I scratch him." A few hurried words
followed this observation, and slowly each jockey weighed out,
and as the third left the scale I tore up the receipt for the
horse and presented him to his late owner. After a desperate
race he was beaten a short head!

Among the landowners in Australia, Tyson was the largest,
the whole extent of his property being estimated equal in
square miles to something like the size of England, while his
wealth was reputed to be enormous. He was a man of extraordinary habits, which, owing to his inordinate riches, polite
mothers referred to as eccentric, for he was still a bachelor,
and, evading maternal snares and lassies' beauty, died one.
His sole aim—he must have been devoid of all other ambition
—appeared to be the continued accumulation of money, not
the enjoyment of it. He would carry his meals with him, and
sleep in his waggon or cart, to save the charges for the

comforts, such as they were, a bush hotel could afford; nor would the clothes he wore be calculated to advertise or increase the business of a tailoring establishment. How rich might not many men become if they lived in poverty!

These characteristics by no means depict the general run of Australian squatters, who, as a body, are sportsmen and men of liberal natures. Their visits to Sydney or Melbourne rather incline to what is colloquially called a spree, and in town, or at home on their stations, they are the very essence of generosity. There is no class of men on the face of the globe who extend the hand of hospitality to the traveller more readily and more willingly than the Australian squatter, and these are the kind of men who go to make up the majority of owners of horses on the Turf of Australasia.

Of the horses in Australia, some of the best would, in my opinion, compare not unfavourably with their English brothers. Such as Ormonde and St. Simon belong to the phenomenal; how often do we see their equals? Again, unless horses meet to fight it out, it is impossible definitely to pronounce a verdict, except as bare estimate of the superiority of one over another. Is this not the case to-day even with our own horses, Ormonde and St. Simon? I am inclined, therefore, to base my deductions on the general average run of the best horses of the two countries rather than on the invidious pitting of one against another. Were I compelled to name the two best horses which came under my observation in Australia, I should unhesitatingly name Carbine and Malua. The former was a great horse, as the majority of racehorse followers are aware, and by winning the Melbourne Cup, a handicap of two miles, with £10,000 *added* (a prize which should make some of our racecourse company officials hide themselves), carrying the welter weight of 10st 5lb, must be credited with a very grand performance. This race is equal in every respect to our Cesarewitch, if not surpassing that, or any other handicap in the world, and when it is remembered that Carbine won the Cup from a very large field in a canter, with Highborn, carrying only 6st 12lb, second—the latter subsequently winning, among many good races, the Viceroy's Cup in India—his victory stands out an international record. I shall always look upon seeing this race as one of the greatest sporting pleasures I have experienced; it was a scene and an achievement not to be forgotten.

Carbine was bred in New Zealand, and for 1,500 guineas was purchased by Mr. Donald Wallace, who, adopting Lord Falmouth's colours (black, white sleeves, red cap), was a worthy upholder of the popular magpie jacket in the Antipodes. A thorough sportsman. and one of the most charming gentlemen it has been my good fortune to meet, it nigh broke Donald Wallace's heart when Carbine was compulsorily sold. I have been told he died some few years ago in poverty, an ill reward for one whose better days were marked with so much generosity.

To give some comparative idea of Carbine's quality (this is merely an opinion), if requested to handicap him with Merman, who won the Cesarewitch and Ascot Gold Cup in this country, I should have asked Carbine to concede him anything between 21lb and 2st, and should have backed the heavy-weight. Merman's best champions could not have expected him to give more than a stone to a horse like Highborn.

Malua belonged to a different man, a Mr. J. O. Inglis, and the combination by no means favoured the horse. J. O. Inglis was an amateur jockey, and a real good one, too, but I am afraid he preferred the commercial side of racing to the sporting side, for Malua was more than once inexplicably beaten.

Amongst other successes, Malua, with top-weight, won both the Newmarket Handicap (six furlongs) and the Australian Cup (2¼ miles) at Flemington, beating large fields and the best horses of his day, and when the extremely different distances of these races are taken into account, this was a good all-round performance—one that some of our more modern trainers might look upon as a miracle! He also won the Melbourne Cup, carrying 9st 9lb, beating Commotion, a real good horse, and Plausible, who were second and third respectively. Malua was never a popular horse, but this was no fault of his own. At the stud he got many winners, amongst others Malvolio, who, following in the footsteps of his sire, won the Melbourne Cup.

As an instance of the irregular management of Malua, he was engaged in the Adelaide Cup with a heavy impost; the exact weight I forget, but it was a welter one.

For some reason, best known to the stable, I was requested by Mr. R. A. Inglis, brother to J. O. of that ilk, to back Malua for the stable. I executed the commission, and then started to back him for myself for a good round sum—over £10,000. One feature of this business I could not explain away to myself. It was that the regular stable commissioner was ever ready to lay against the horse, even beyond his own limit. I am not a suspicious man, but I am a great believer in first impressions. In respect to Malua and the Adelaide Cup there was that something floating in the air which emitted an unpleasant odour. The regular agent for the stable was backing another in the race, named Conjecture, and laying against Malua!

Everything pointed to a very fine game of hankey-pankey, and the betting market reflected this, Malua going from bad to worse, in face of my continued personal support of him. I summed up the situation and came to the conclusion that I had been made a scapegoat of to assist in successfully carrying out the stable designs. I did not attend the Adelaide races on this occasion, but remained in Melbourne. On the morning of the race, my opinions by then being more than verified, I sent a brief but concise telegram to a friend of mine who was at the meeting. There was no law against jockeys betting then, nor were the more severe restrictions since introduced into the rules of racing in force. My telegram ran :

" Lay Ivemy 2,000 to nothing for me against Malua to-day."
Ivemy rode Malua.

It was a terribly wet day. The going at Morphetville, the racecourse of the South Australian Jockey Club, was of the heaviest, all against a top-weight. The result tissue came into the Victorian Club, and when hung up on the board read:

### ADELAIDE CUP.

Malua ................................................. 1
Conjecture .......................................... 2
King of the Vale ................................. 3

Betting: 100 to 7 agst Malua, 3 to 1 agst Conjecture, and 4 to 1 agst King of the Vale. Won in a common canter by three-quarters of a length.

Ivemy, though successful on Malua, never rode for Mr. J. O. Inglis again

## CHAPTER XIV.

### ITEMS.

WENTY years ago and earlier, gambling in Australia might have been styled the custom of the country —as, indeed, it is the custom of any body of free men, especially those who have lost their hymn-books. At Tattersall's in Sydney, the hazard "school" in the seventies and eighties would have vied with old Crockford's, upon the site of which, in St. James's Street, the Devonshire Club now stands. I have seen men of all classes sitting round the table, with thousands of pounds at stake on the turn of a die. "How awful!" 1 hear Mrs. Grundy remark. But what does Mrs. Grundy know of the world, men, and their ways? One thing is certain—the money did not melt, and the world was no worse off at the end of a night's play. Poor men could not be much worse off than poor, and rich men could afford to lose. Philosophy? Certainly. A man would indeed be a poor thing without it. Many more men by far have, in my experience, made a successful start in business through a "flutter" than have been ruined by gambling. I could name several successful business men in Sydney who now support happy homes through a start thus obtained.

The chances are that a man who is such a weak fool as to lose his fortune at cards, or by the aid of some other instrument of the devil, would, even if he had been an abstainer from all games, find some other means of gratifying his weaknesses. It is the weak man who is the author of whatever may be deemed wrong in gambling ; and what is more pitiable than a weak man—except a drunken woman?

This play continued throughout the year, increased on the occasion of the race weeks, and during the whole of my stay there, extending over eight years, I cannot call to mind a single case of a player having been ruined, or of a scandal in connection with the play, except that it came under the censorious ban of the anti-gamblers. Money was in freer circulation in Australia then than it is now ; or, as it is called in the City, " money was easy."

I may say that I have lost thousands at cards and hazard, and add that I do not regret a penny of it. I can call to mind one evening—it was on the day that Le Grand won the Champion Stakes at Flemington—I lost within a fraction of £5,000 at hazard in the little back parlour of Solomon's shop at Swanston Street in the space of a couple of hours or less. Joe Thompson and his brother Barney were present. The players were Harry Haines, George Alderson, Humphrey Oxenham, W. T. Jones (later on destined to be the owner of Airs and Graces, winner of the Epsom Oaks), and myself. Why I particularly remember this incident is that I lost to everyone present (after parting with about £4,000 in cash), except to Jones, who owed me somewhere about £300 at the end of the play, and this was paid to me with more " airs than graces," and only after a bit of a wrangle. From memory, I was the only loser.

Misb Solomons always kept a good cigar, not a common commodity in the Antipodes, and in the same little back parlour of his cigar shop I lost a larger sum at solo whist one evening than I care to name ; indeed, with the exception of five good wins, three of which have never been honoured, I have never won at cards or hazard any stake worth mentioning, though I have given the Casino at Monte Carlo a good shock more than once.

A member of the two principal sporting clubs in London and Melbourne, I think my fellow-members never, or very seldom, saw me leave the card-table a winner of anything worth mentioning. There is a good reason for this. I used to be too reckless—not in my play, but in my stakes—much the same thing, perhaps.

Harking back to sport, outside the area of the principal meetings, I remember seeing a race at Cranborne, Victoria, which would have made some of our gentleman jockeys, not sit up, but fall off. It was a bare-backed Hurdle Race, distance one mile and a half, over six hurdles, amateur riders only. Mr. Watson, son of the starter at Flemington, rode the winner, and all competitors completed the course. Do any of our clerks of courses think a similar race would fill in England?

An annual meeting used to be held at Frankston, a small seaside resort just beyond Mordialloc, and about ten miles from Schnapper Point, my country residence. I can remember riding at these races over a course which, what with fallen trees and the absence of flags or posts to mark out the track, placed the dangers of the Grand National at Aintree in the category of mother's milk. In the first event I was beaten off, but in the second, on a horse called Charles II., *I rode a course of my own*, and won, amidst hilarious, not to say ironical, cheers, by a distance! Be it said for the sportsman on the second, a good fellow named Sinclair, there was no objection. Had there been, it would have taken the ingenuity of the whole of the National Hunt Committee, with all their vast experience, to have decided what was the course, or even what was not.

Having mentioned a horse called Le Grand, and his winning the Champion Stakes, I may here chronicle an episode in connection with this race which I think unique with regard to another race—that of the Chosen People. Some time previous to the day of running (1886), the Hon. James White's Norden-feldt was favourite at odds ranging from 2 to 1 to 5 to 2 laid

on him.   By an extraordinary coincidence I had good reason
to believe there was a screw loose somewhere.  It happened in
this way.  About a week before the race I entered the telegraph
office at Melbourne for the purpose of sending a message to
James White, a bookmaker who resided in Sydney.   I handed
in my telegram, and it was apparently despatched.   I then
remembered I had another to send elsewhere, and I began to
fill up the form at the writing-desk set apart for this purpose.
A telegraph clerk returned to the counter, and, looking across
at me, inquired :

"Did you hand in a wire to White ? "

"Yes," I replied.

"Is this the correct address ? " he asked, handing me the
form.

I read the message with no little interest and astonishment.   It ran as follows : "The Hon. James White, Sydney.
—Afraid to go on with Nordenfeldt ; leg slightly filled."  I
told the clerk the address was quite sufficient, but that it was
not my telegram, finished the one I was writing, and sent
it off.

If all is fair in love and war, this adage applies with
equal force to backer and bookmaker.  I entered the Victoria
Club.  The first man I confronted was Maurice Jacobs, at the
time the commissioner to the stable.

"I'll bet on the Champion Race," he challenged.

"The cat's out of the bag," I thought.

"What do you want to do ?" I inquired.

"Nordenfeldt—what odds do you want ?"

"I'll take 500 to 200."

"I'll lay you 9 to 4," he replied, interrogatively, his little,
restless, dark eyes quizzing me.

"How much ? " I asked.

"900 to 400 ? "

"Book it."

"I'll lay you two monkeys more," said Jacobs.

"Done."  A pause.

"What price will you lay me Matchlock?" I asked. It was a horse in the same ownership, second-string to Nordenfeldt.

"1,000 to 100," replied Jacobs.

"Book that also. Again?" I demanded.

"Twice," he replied.

"Right," I said.

The bets were hardly booked before I was besieged by many of his brethren desirous of laying the liberally short odds of 2 to 1 on, and I booked many bets, and at the end of the business I had thirteen names in my book, all Jews.

I told them that night that thirteen was an unlucky number, though I did not refer to the origin of the proverb. A few days before the race Nordenfeldt was scratched. Matchlock, about whom I had taken 2,000 to 200 from Maurice Jacobs, won.

I owned a few horses in Australia, but not many, and none of any note. With Spero I won the Sale Handicap, beating Arsenal, a subsequent winner of the Melbourne Cup. In paying the stakes, £2 was deducted "for champagne," in which the clerk of the course, stakeholder, &c.—offices pretty well all rolled into one individual, on the system of which Pooh Bah was a past master—were presumed to have drunk the winner's health.

I trained the little horse myself in Albert Park, on a track called after our Rotten Row, and the Rottenest Row it has been my lot to come across. About four feet in width, mostly tan and sand, with a scarcity of the former and the latter the natural soil, the attempted innovation turned out a dire frost, except that I utilised it occasionally as a pastime, and for training an old nag or so. Partner won a race or two for me, and in a selling race at Flemington equalled the record for five furlongs. If the time test is accurate, then the Australian plater is by it proved to be as good as his superior "class." Class smothers, and always will, the horse tried by the watch to do wonders.

It was my pleasure to sail my own boat, the " Zivola," a little four-ton centreboard, winner of some thirty races. With her I had a nearer chance of losing my life than I at the time appreciably realised. Sailing from St. Kilda, which may be styled a suburb of Melbourne, two of us set out one Sunday morning for Schnapper Point. The weather was not fair, and it was blowing hard when we started. I had continually to tack. The wind and sea increased. Storms in Hobson's Bay are treacherous, rising with little warning, resembling the mistral of the Mediterranean. The sea continued to rise, and I frequently had to ease off. A boat called the "Iolanthe" started about an hour before me, and I sighted her ahead as she rose on the waves. We shipped water almost quicker than we could bail out. The wind was blowing a gale in our teeth, and at last I turned her head towards Brighton, due west of Frankston. I was unacquainted with this place, never having gone ashore there. We had been out about six hours. The spot offered no shelter, the wind blowing straight on to the land. Nearly water-logged, I determined to run ashore. We landed without accident, except to the tight little "Zivola." At about this moment the "Iolanthe" turned turtle, and all on board were drowned. Some days later a shark was caught off Frankston pier. It contained in its stomach the waistcoat and watch of Iolanthe's owner, and the boot of a friend who accompanied him. The shark and "his meal" were exhibited in Melbourne.

## CHAPTER XV.

## AN EPISODE.

T is with some regret and great reluctance, that I am compelled to refer to an incident which happened in Australia in connection with Viscount Deerhurst. I might have dealt with this matter in a few words, or even passed it by, had it not been for the fact that this incident was referred to, and most unfairly and unjustifiably commented upon, in the case in which I was engaged before the Law Courts in May, 1904.

A cowardly attempt was made, in the case to which I refer, to prove that I had assaulted Viscount Deerhurst in Australia, and, as a result, had suffered fourteen days' imprisonment.

I will avoid further comment, and go straight to the point.

We were both young men. We happened to meet on the pigeon-shooting ground at Hurlingham, in Melbourne. A good deal of betting took place on the shooting ; indeed, speculation in this respect in Australia used to far exceed that at the Tir aux Pigeons at Monte Carlo, at Hurlingham, or at the Gun Club in England. This gentleman lost during the day a sum of £281, which he did not happen to have with him, and as the settling on pigeon-shooting takes place at the end of each day, it placed his lordship in a somewhat embarrassing predicament. I relieved him of his difficulty by settling his account myself, which, including an amount which had been lost to me, amounted, as I have stated, to £281. Not receiving

9

this from Lord Deerhurst, after waiting some considerable time I wrote him a letter, in which I said that I should feel much obliged by the receipt of a cheque. I received no answer. Several weeks passed, and I found I was being avoided by him, which I resented. One evening I attended the performance at the Opera House, Melbourne, and during the first act Lord Deerhurst took a seat next but one to me. On the falling of the curtain after this act he left his seat, and after the lapse of a few minutes I followed.

His lordship did not return. After the performance I made my way to the Melbourne Club, and met him going up the steps. I expressed my surprise at his non-return to the theatre, insisted on a settlement between us, and then left him. The next morning I received a letter, of which I subjoin a copy:

"Melbourne Club. Sir,—I shall be in a position to pay you before Friday 12 noon. In the meantime post me, and be damned.—DEERHURST."

My reply to the above was as follows:—

"Sir,—I am in receipt of your letter. I shall be pleased to receive the amount you are in my debt for settling your account at Hurlingham, and will answer the latter portion of your letter when I meet you in person.—Yours, &c."

I did not receive the amount at the time stated, and shortly afterwards lodged a complaint with Mr. Thomas Haydon, the secretary of the Victoria Club, and was requested by him not to press the matter. I concurred in this, and later on the money was paid. Some time after I entered a private bar of Gallaher's Hotel, in Burke Street, and Viscount Deerhurst was there in the company of a Mr. Agnew. Waiting an opportune moment, I spoke to his lordship in a subdued tone so that no one should hear our conversation (all of this has been substantiated on oath in evidence), and the first words I addressed to him were, "I should like to speak to you privately on the subject of a letter you wrote to me." He then sat on the counter of the bar, and in a loud, almost truculent tone, said, "Whatever you have to say to me you can say in public." I replied, "As you wish," and then adverted to the latter portion of his letter, where he consigned me to a place to which I was not at all inclined to go. He merely laughed. I then firmly asked him to apologise or leave the bar. I did so a second time, and jumping from the counter he laid hold of my coat, saying at the same time, "As an officer of Her Majesty's police force I arrest you."

Brushing his hold away, I drew my hand across his face, rather than struck him. I repeat we were both very young men, and I have regretted losing my temper after he had laid hands on me, as I trust he has for being the aggressor. He did not then retaliate. He left the bar, which was a parlour where only those known to the hotel were admitted. Unfortunately, perhaps, for both of us, he brought the matter before the Committee of the Victorian Betting Club, and, by the aid of his influence, caused my name to be struck off the list of members. With respect to this I reprint a cutting from the Melbourne "Sportsman" as follows:—

"The decision of the Committee of the Club was naturally received with astonishment by all the members on Friday evening, and the sentence was so hugely out of proportion to the paltry nature of the offence, if any, that the members of the Club, both backers and book-makers, are, we hear, about to petition the Committee to reinstate 'The Englishman,' or, failing this, call a general meeting of the members of the Club. We are informed on good authority that the Victoria Racing Club will, under the circumstances, not move in the matter."

The Victoria Racing Club is the equivalent of our Jockey Club, and they took no notice whatever of the matter. To

clear myself in the eyes of the public, and that the facts should
be ventilated, I caused a summons for assault to be issued
against Viscount Deerhurst. He then took out a cross
summons against me. The evidence given on both sides
exactly tallied with the facts as I have already given them,
and did not vary in any way whatever. The Bench was
packed, more magistrates sitting than had been the case for
over twenty years. My counsel, Mr. Duffey, who has since
been raised to the Bench in Victoria, told me at the luncheon
adjournment that I should be sure to get imprisonment, that
he had been informed of this on good authority, and that it
was iniquitous. At this time no evidence had been called for
the defence! By the casting vote of the chairman I was
sentenced to fourteen days imprisonment without the option
of a fine. The judgment was received with an outcry in the
Press throughout the whole of Australasia, and every paper
was unanimous in its condemnation of the grossly unjust
decision of the so-called justices. Letters filled columns in
all the papers in the various colonies, and excitement ran high.
The " Sportsman " stated : —

"Seldom has a magisterial decision evoked more
adverse comment than that of the District Court Bench,
which adjudicated on the Sutton-Deerhurst case. The
matter carries with it so much interest to racing men
that we publish in another column a review of the facts
of the case as illustrated by the evidence adduced last
Thursday. We have already commented on the extraordinary action of the Victorian Club in the matter, and
it is satisfactory to note that our comment—the first, by
the way, published—has been endorsed by all the principal metropolitan journals, sporting and otherwise. Mr.
Panton's sentence of fourteen days fell like a thunderbolt
on all present, and from the moment the decree was
recorded, public, Press, and Bar have for once been
unanimous, and the whole of the proceedings have

evoked universal condemnation. Temple Court, to use a legal luminary's own expression, is ' up in arms,' and so largely have the public interested themselves in the matter that, hazarding a prediction, we are inclined to think that on the rehearing of the case next month, the magisterial verdict is bound to be upset. From whichever standpoint the two verdicts—the Victorian Club and District Court—are regarded, whether looked at in a legal or rational light, there can be no two opinions as to the manifest partiality evinced towards the lord, and the gross intolerance shown to the commoner."

The "Age," a leading Melbourne daily paper, published a request that the Mayor should call a public meeting in the Town Hall to consider the action of the magistrates. The "Argus," indeed every leading journal, followed on the same lines.

Against the decision of the magistrates I immediately appealed. Directly after the case, several gentlemen came forward who had dined with Lord Deerhurst at the Melbourne Club on the night of the incident at Gallaher's Hotel. These testified to the fact that Lord Deerhurst had after dinner invited them to accompany him and see the thrashing he was going to give to Sutton.

The following is taken from the "Melbourne Herald":—

" Mr. Duffy, who appeared in support of the appeal, commented strongly upon the non-appearance of Lord Deerhurst. He first stated that his client intended to fight out the case, and had subpœnaed all the witnesses whose evidence would relate to the occurrence in the hotel. He referred to the cowardice, meanness, and malignity of the spirit which prompted Lord Deerhurst, through his counsel, to press for a sentence of imprisonment on Mr. Sutton, and then to decline to come forward when the case would be reopened and heard in its

entirety. The magistrates, without a tittle of evidence
to justify the conclusion, had sentenced his client to
fourteen days' imprisonment. The listeners in the Court
were all agog with astonishment when Mr. Duffy told
His Honour that Lord Deerhurst, according to evidence
which had since been obtained, had invited his friends
to see the fun he would have with Mr. Sutton. It was
of importance that the matter should be ventilated,
because the full disclosure of the facts would doubtless
lead to Mr. Sutton's reinstatement in the Victorian Club,
from which he was expelled by a small coterie. Mr.
Duffy hinted that Lord Deerhurst had taken fright at
the expected disclosures, and thought he was safe out
of Court. He probably had heard of the very ancient
and apposite motto, 'He who fights and runs away may
live to fight another day.' The Judge allowed the appeal
with costs. The quashing of the conviction was cheered
by those in Court and continued in the streets—the vast
majority of people will re-echo that feeling in view of
the unjust sentence of the magistrates and the toadying
sympathy practically expressed by them for the lordling."


The Judge decided that all costs would go with the quashing of the conviction, and that I was to recover these from
Viscount Deerhurst. These costs not having been paid, an
application was made to remove the issue from the Sessions
to the Supreme Court to enable me to effect service in
England, when they were subsequently liquidated.

I deeply regret having been compelled to refer to this
matter at all, and more especially in extenso; but having
regard to the fact that the case has been so misrepresented
so recently, I have had no recourse left but to give the full
details in my autobiography, which, under the circumstances,
would be incomplete without them. The facts of the case
were so twisted in the Courts of Justice, and in Mr. Justice
Grantham's summing up, that I have no alternative but to

set out the actual facts in order to remove the false impression his observations may have made.

My readers have now before them the plain, unvarnished truth, and I can only conclude by an expression of regret to Lord Deerhurst that unfair events should have compelled me to refer to this matter again.

## CHAPTER XVI.

### LONDON, 1887.

RIOR to the case to which I have reluctantly been compelled to refer in the last chapter, I had booked my passage to England by the P. and O. This, in the ordinary course of events, would have been partially forfeited, but, owing to the extraordinary verdict, the hearing of my appeal against which I was then awaiting, the P. and O. Company addressed me a courteous letter, saying a cabin was at my disposal on any of their steamers, and they would, under the circumstances, not claim a penny of the money I had paid for my passage on the steamer for which I had originally booked it. This marked courtesy to me in no small degree re-echoed the general feeling the case had provoked. It was only the appeal which had detained me in Australia, and as soon as it was over, foregoing many invitations, some of a public nature, I left Melbourne for home by the first mail steamer available. I take this opportunity of publicly acknowledging the courtesy which the officers of the P. and O. Company in Melbourne extended to me on this occasion.

Our passengers consisted of a lively lot, and they were a source of amusement from many points of view. Many appeared anxious to make my acquaintance, though I already knew the majority; others, from a mere feeling of inquisitiveness, got into conversation with me, and, of course, there were the different " sets " on board. These " wingy " coteries have often been a great relief to me, and helped to pass the general monotony of a long voyage. Treat them as they *believe*, in their narrow conceit, they should be treated, and they are sackfuls of fun. On the lines of "humour a lunatic," one should never argue with a fool. On this basis, never contradict the wingy, starchy fraternity, and always answer in the affirmative all sentences ending with "don't you think so?" Among the passengers were Mr. and Mrs. Armstrong and their little baby boy. He is a man now, and good luck to him, wherever he may be. I have always had a weakness for youngsters, and many a toddle he and I have had on the deck, and many a romp. Mrs. Armstrong was the daughter of Mr. Mitchell, a large contractor, who built the Melbourne Exhibition. She was a very charming lady, with darkish hair and fascinating eyes, while her two sisters who accompanied her were quite a contrast, being fair. Mrs. Armstrong was not liked by the lady passengers, her great fault being that she was the best looking of her sex on board. Someone must always suffer in this respect. She had another fault. She possessed a charming voice, which was, if possible, more fascinating than her charming personality. So high does jealousy run on board ship—what a narrow little world a floating craft is!—that few, if any, availed themselves of the great pleasure of hearing her sing when she condescended to do so. I never once missed the opportunity, and often I have sat alone with her in the saloon, turning over the leaves of the music, while she sang. Tosti's "Good-bye" was then in its young days, and how well she sang it! How the other married ladies hated it!! As sung by her!!! That lady is now known over the whole world as Madame Melba.

There was generally something going on, and I have always looked upon this voyage as one of the most pleasant of my experiences in connection with sea travelling. We had a full complement of passengers, among them all sorts and conditions of men, not to say characters. One I remember well. He was quite a sport in his own little way. It was astonishing how accurately he could guess the length or height of anything on board, while he was equally expert at estimating the weight of different things, such as deck chairs, buckets, &c. Strolling about, he would turn the conversation in this direction, and then make a bet as to the height of the smoking room at a certain part, or the length of a rope, or what not. He always won. This did not arouse my suspicion so much as the absolute accuracy of his guesses. It happened that I slept on deck one night, and in the morning, just before the break of day, I sat half-hidden behind the wheel, when I espied this sport carefully examining different parts of the vessel. At times, after taking a look round, he would hold up a chair for a second or so on what appeared to be a hook, and then replace it on the deck in the exact position he took it from. Finally I saw him distinctly measure two pieces of hanging rope which dangled loosely from their fastenings. I now had a shrewd idea how this gentleman's extraordinary accuracy, through which he had won several bets in money and many champagne cups at lunch, was accounted for. I always like to make war, if war I have to make, in the enemy's country. That day, just before the mid-day eight bells, I found myself in conversation with this gentleman in the vicinity of the dangling ropes. One or two joined us. It was apparent that these two ropes had a great fascination for him, for he never took his eyes off them. At last I inquired what it was that interested him so much. He replied that he was mentally measuring the length of the two ropes, the end of which did not reach the deck by some two and a half feet. I fell into the trap at once, offering him to bet he could not guess the length, and after some haggling he backed himself for a fiver to do so within three inches. He made a few more stray wagers of half a sovereign and a pound. I suggested that whatever the result of the bet I would go him double or quits that he could not guess the length of the second rope within the same allowance, three inches. "Done," he cried. And done he was.

I had hauled them up a good six inches that morning while he was at breakfast. After he had paid the money, which came to just about as much as he had previously won from others, a couple of bottles of champagne were drunk at the bar, and the balance left found its way into the collecting box of the Seaman's Orphanage Fund, which stood by the saloon companion. Later on I told him if he played any more such tricks I should give him away. He never did, and I kept my own counsel.

Arrived in London, I took up my quarters at 1, Burlington Gardens, just off Bond Street, and next to Sam Lewis's ; hence I should not have far to go in the event of the proverbial rainy day. Sam was in his time an "umbrella" to many. I had been, as I have said, elected a member of Boodle's the previous year, and used the club fairly frequently. It was the year of the first Jubilee of our lamented and revered Queen Victoria, and I witnessed the procession from here ; and having been fortunate enough to draw two ladies' tickets, with a couple of other members, we made up a pleasant party for the day. Boodle's was most convenient, as, possessing an entrance in Bury Street, we had no crowd to break through in making our way to the club-house. Seeing the illuminations that evening was a matter of duty, and our brave little ladies footed the streets round London with us, and leaving them at their homes well after midnight, we men waded our way through the crowds to the Continental (Regent Street). This hostelry is not now what it then was, and its supper-tables were nightly crowded by the most fascinating and high-class cocottes. These have gradually disappeared, and have been supplanted by the alien lady who, from appearances, one would judge to be a derelict from the Continent. Those days were the fag end of a fast-fading era, and times and customs have now completely changed. The "class" is missing. Narrow-minded legislation, skulking along hand in hand with faddists, has closed the doors on that open-hearted, good-natured fun that used to exist, with the result that what they were pleased to decry as bad is now worse. The grievance of many appears to be—and there are females in their ranks—that money and everything else should be kept in the family. With what result? Many of the sprees which would have been over, forgotten and unchronicled in twenty-four hours, nowadays more often reach the precincts of the Divorce Court.

The crowds and cheering in the streets continued throughout the night, and everybody was happy, jolly, and cheeringly cheery. There was no getting up or down the winding stair-case of the Continental, and a couple of us, to get to the lower room, descended by a rope from the balcony. Even the police in this particular neighbourhood, where they are not infre-quently too aggressive, were, on this particular evening, reasonable, if not jovial. To get back to the first floor was next to impossible, except by the aid of the rope, and by this novel way we went, hand over hand, to the upstairs supper-room. Cheers from the crowd. Scrambling of silver and coppers among them in the streets. All went on merrily.

About this time there were two institutions being run, for the purpose of providing amusement for those who objected to being sent to bed by Act of Parliament. They were called respectively the Gardenia and the Corinthian Clubs, the former being at the south-eastern corner of Leicester Square and the latter at the back of the present Sports Club in St. James's. In fact, the present smoking-room of the last-named was the ballroom of the Corinthian.

Very much in vogue just then were two buck niggers, who were known as the Brothers Bohee, and who had acquired considerable popularity from their singing, dancing, and banjo playing. The creation of the Gardenia was due to them, but I think they called their venture by their own name—the Bohee. Their tenure came speedily to an end, and Dudley Ward took over the premises and gave the club its horticultural name. Blessed with a circle of friends as large as any man, Ward was not long in gathering together as his members all the best of the men about town, and a remarkably lively lot they were. In speaking of the one club it may at once be assumed I am speaking equally of the other. Their frequenters were mostly composed of the same crowd; and, as poor Hughie Drummond once explained to a fellow-member—he is commanding a distinguished regiment of dragoon guards now— "the · difference between the two clubs is that between a cabbage and a cauliflower." Either of them was a rendezvous for fun in the early hours, and as everyone knew everyone else there was a delightful absence of ceremony with respect to both sexes. There was an orchestra, but not much dancing, except when the spirit moved one of the men, who would execute a pas seul that for weirdness and eccentricity was unique. It was a high crime and misdemeanour to call a man by the patronymic his progenitors had bestowed upon him. There were nicknames for all. Two of the best were "the Finches of the Wood," Dan and Clem, brothers of cheery Joe Aylesford. A trio of brothers, a singular contrast to each other, were the Drummonds, Hughie, Archie, and the Salt— the last-named now one of the soberest of H.M. Consuls. There was no devilment of which Hughie was incapable, but the flame burnt too fiercely for his constitution. Willie and Charlie Barron, Tom Baring, Jackie O'Donnell, Capt. Pirie, Walter Blake (always one of the first to go home), Stiffy Smith (then in the zenith of his comet-like career), Bogie Horn (always swaggering and staggering), The Criminal (who would sit up as long as anyone), Long Dummy (who is still with us), Frank Jessel, Marmaduke Wood, Joe Posno, Jack Hotham, Arthur de Vere Smith (Captain Evergreen, best of good fellows), Harry, Robbie, and Lindsay Garrard, Harding, Arthur and Fairie Cox, Edmund Routledge the hospitable, Shirley Brooks (Blobbs), Willie Goldberg (Shifter), Carlton Blyth (Hullo There!), Swish Broadwood (with a command of Anglo-Saxon many envied), Dicky the Driver, Ernest Beckett, good old Partner, Mark Cazenove, Skipper Holmes (now of the Reformed Raleigh), Leycester Barwell, Hugo Chadwick, Arthur Chetwynd, Long Giles (the guide, philosopher, and friend of Randolph Churchill on his visit to South Africa), The Treasure, Billy Fitzwilliam (who little dreamed of the mayoral honours that awaited him), Swears, with his reminiscences of real life. How the names come crowding to the mind as the pen runs on! The recollections of the good times are tinged with regret for those whose names are now only shadows of the past; but the times were good, and the fun, if fast and furious, was genuine, and hurt no one. It was the hey-day of their youth, their hot blood was cooled under the eyes of their fellows, and Society was saved from much of the scandal that breaks out nowadays in spite of—probably because of—the hypocritical restrictions by which London is bound.

Dudley Ward soon tired of the Gardenia, which, after all, was only a hobby. Perhaps the suggestion of one of the members to change the name to Malmaison may have affected his determination; be that as it may, he sold his interest to a Hebrew, Ike something or other, and a police raid closed it.

The history of the Corinthian was much the same, and it came to an end from a similar shock. It was affected more by the youth of Aldershot than the Gardenia, and there was generally an exodus about three in the morning of those who had to catch that most gruesome of all services, "the dead-meat train," in order to be on parade.

The years that have passed since those days are not so many; but what a change! *Autres temps, autres mœurs*, with a vengeance. Is the balance of advantage with the present day? Are the morals of the class from which the men I have spoken of were taken, more decent for the restrictions our narrow-minded Bumbles have placed upon their liberty? Have those restrictions made the present generation a more wholesome one, a more moral one, or a more MANLY one than the last? I take leave to doubt it very much.

## CHAPTER XVII.

## MY PRESENTATION.

R. STEPHEN TUCKER, then the Somerset Herald, had during the previous year proposed that I should be presented at Court. It would seem superfluous to suggest that, of all men, one of the Heralds of the Heralds' College should be better acquainted than any other official with the legitimate social eligibility of any man to this distinction. The pedigrees of all families of any standing are to be found in the archives of the College, and the patents for arms are granted by it. Both my grandfathers bore arms, as did their forefathers. The Somerset Herald died, and I was subsequently presented by his successor at the levée held in June, 1887. Lord Dudley attended the levée. Later, I believe, he informed the Lord Chamberlain my name was not Sievier, but Sutton. He should have known better, for he had been accommodated with a seat on the Bench when the first Deerhurst case was heard, and I swore to my name when he was present. But this is not the first mistake by many that Lord Dudley has committed. There was an undercurrent at work. One or two of the minor papers wrote inspired articles, and in due course they reached the Australian Press, which doubtless was originally meant to be their destination. What I may describe as my hereditary claims to Society were not once questioned. I was not personally attacked, but the fact that I had made a book in Australia was criticised. These statements in the Press were then brought officially before the Lord Chamberlain, my enemies' aims were gained, and my presentation was cancelled some eight months afterwards. I here reproduce extracts from the official letter I received from the Somerset Herald, addressed from the Heralds' College on February 24, 1888:

> "The causes which have led to the cancelling of your presentation are, shortly, these: Immediately after levée some people came forward and testified to the fact that you were engaged on the Turf in Australia as a bookmaker, and that in such transactions you bore the name of Sutton. Shortly afterwards the affair was noticed, I think, in an English paper, and a little later it went through all the Australian Press, and, of course, was much spoken of in London. The best that can now be done is to help me in getting clear evidence that you were not engaged on the Turf, as I mentioned in the first part of my letter, *and then, I am sure, the announcement cancelling your presentation would be removed.*"

Nothing could have been clearer or more straightforward than this letter to me. I had professionally embarked in betting in the colonies, and, rightly or wrongly, this was deemed a technical breach of the customs of Society. There was nothing else assumed against me. There was not a tittle of suggestion that I was in any other respect ineligible. Looking at the situation from the strict sense which must be upheld at Court with unbending rigidity, I readily admit the Lord Chamberlain had no other course open to him when his hand was forced—as it had been. If I entertained a regret, it was that I ever made a book—none other. Except for this, I was eligible.

I say the Lord Chamberlain was right—just as right as Sir William Grantham was wrong and unjust in his biassed harangue to the jury in May, 1904, at the Royal Courts of Justice! He more than misrepresented this incident, misled the jury, never once touched upon the facts, and finished off the finest bit of modern clap-trap by audaciously asserting that "Her Majesty would sooner have vacated her throne" than that I should have been presented. But later on I shall deal with the case in the course of which these observations were made, and I shall then have the opportunity of summing up Sir William Grantham's summing-up.

I remained a member of Boodle's.

In London, as I have previously stated, I had my rooms at 1, Burlington Gardens, immediately over Holbrook and Walker's. They faced the Old Burlington Hotel, where Monsieur Jules reigned in all his glory before the whole staff migrated to the Berkeley, and many a good dinner he has served me with. He was subsequently at the Savoy, and is now successfully running a restaurant of his own in Jermyn Street.

At an angle which almost caused one to wink I could look down the Burlington Arcade (who hasn't done a wink in this Arcadia?), while all travellers from Piccadilly to the Blue Posts had to pass my door, and it was not long before my chambers were treated with little more respect than that bestowed on a half-way house, and in time were a standing rendezvous for many noted patrons of the Turf.

I was passing along the switchback ups and downs of racing, and more than once had been very pressed for money, but by some means or other, perhaps by the aid of the little cherub who sits up aloft, I somehow managed to fall on my feet when things looked at their worst. True, the land of the Golden Fleece was always open to me, and I knew I could return at any moment, and by renewing my racing avocation

10

in Australia, probably acquire sufficient means to put things right again if they took too serious a turn. I need hardly say that in face of the mean—I might reasonably add, cowardly—action of the committee of the Victorian Club, I was not inclined to pay the Antipodes another visit, though I had the whole of Australia, this small coterie excepted, on my side.

Hard up, "financially bent," or what you will, I managed to keep two or three hunters always going, and in 1888 won the South Notts Point-to-Point with North Kilworth, a horse I afterwards sold at Tattersall's. He was bought by Sir James Miller, then quartered at Brighton with the 14th Hussars, lately one of the Stewards of the Jockey Club, but now, I regret to say, deceased. North Kilworth won many races subsequently, owned and ridden by that fearless rider, Mr. Charles Thompson. And I also always had a bit of shooting, more or less rough, mostly rough.

I had experienced in 1887 what those uninitiated in racing and its attendant pitfalls would possibly call the coup de grâce, but such a state of things is only temporary with men who have any spirit. I had, in racing parlance, taken "the knock." It was over the Cesarewitch won by Humewood. I was an intimate friend of the late Captain Shaw (Jimmy), who was on most friendly terms with the Duke of Hamilton, with whom I also was on terms of acquaintanceship, and he had a horse called Jacob running in the race. He had a month previously cantered in for a welter race of two miles at the Derby Meeting, and unfortunately, for the time being anyhow, I had over-estimated him and this performance. Woodburn rode him, and I backed Jacob to win me about £50,000, and saved on Bendigo, an old favourite of mine, standing to win about £10,000 over him. Bendigo ran second, beaten a length, but Jacob failed to climb the ladder as of yore—and I fell with him between the rungs. Losing a large sum at cards that week and running amuck generally, I failed to settle on the Monday. If we could temper ourselves with that regularity which brings Monday round to us each week—but what is the use of attempt-

ing to moralise? Like many men before me, and not a few
that will follow, I could not settle. The Ring knew me, and I
believe I was more exercised over my failure in this respect
than were those who should, under ordinary circumstances,
have been the receivers. It was too late to think of Australia,
so I hunted. For wealth? No, the wily fox. I was, as they
say in the theatrical profession, resting. Nor was I any better
off the following spring, and the little racing I did was n\
successful; not, at least, to the extent of my being able to
liquidate my affairs. I must here say, and I thank my friends
in the Ring with all sincerity, that not one of them really
bothered me; they were satisfied that it would come along
some day, and that as soon as that day dawned they would
feel the warmth of the golden sun.

I went to the Epsom Spring Meeting of 1888 with the late
"Bob" Howett. I may here observe that I kept my hunters
at his hospitable home, Woodborough Manor, in Nottingham-
shire. On the first day I had won £110, my transactions being
in ready money owing to the "suspension" of credit. The
second day I took 500 to 100 about Mr. Arthur Cooper's
Cardinal Wolsey, which won with F. Barrett in the saddle.
I followed this up with 1,600 to 200 Good Night, and I remember as he passed the post I turned to Bob Howett and
said, "Another winner, and it will soon be good morning."
Having collected my money, this brought us to the City and
Suburban, and I went solely for Fullerton, the property of
Sir George Chetwynd. The first bet I got was 7 to 1 to £300
with Ben Cooper. I then took 800 to 100 from Ben Hyams,
and Bob Howett put £300 on for me at an average of about
8 to 1. Afterwards I went on to the course and saw them
canter past, and returning to the Ring took 800 to 100 more
from the Brothers Dreysey, then at their zenith, and had
£200 more on in broken sums, making a thousand altogether.
From Tattenham Corner to the winning post the result of the
race was never in doubt, and Fullerton won easily by two
lengths. Then came the collecting. I had won nearly £8,000

on the race, and was stuffed with notes, so much so that I left a large balance owing to me standing. The news spread like magic hrough the Ring, and not a few accosted me with the enquiry, "Shall I claim mine on Monday?"

And there were also some, to whom I owed not even the shadow of an obligation, who had a pony handed to them for the asking. My betting did not end here. This was the mere greasing of the wheel which had set things in motion, and it was exhilarating to feel oneself going along once more after standing still for some six months. Woodburn, who had ridden Fullerton, had the mount on Chilwood in the next race, and following my luck, not without a few necessary inquiries, I had 3,000 to 1,000 Chilwood, and, following Fullerton's example, he won by two lengths also. On the next race I lost £1,000, but soon recouped myself from this temporary break, by backing P. and O., perhaps on account of the many thousands of miles the P. and O. had carried me, but more than likely because I knew something, and taking all sorts of odds between 7 to 4 and 9 to 4, I won nearly £4,000 on the race. I had not another bet that day. To show what can be done, and more, what has been done, I started at the Epsom Spring Meeting, one of two days' duration, with a "pony," and won by playing up my winnings over £16,000. Needless to add, Bob Howett settled my old account on Monday, and once more Mr. W. Clowes began to settle for me every subsequent Monday until —but I must not get in advance of my story. Before I finally quit this episode, I feel I must once more refer to the generosity which the bookmakers as a rule extend to their clients when a bad time overtakes them. I could, of course, name one or two who are not too leniently inclined, and have in their grasping endeavours been known to chop off their noses to spite their faces; but as a body of men if they beat you, they do not kick you when you are down.

Had I not bucked up, faced the situation, and determined to extricate myself how could I possibly have succeeded? Ought I to have retired to a garret and meted out a small annual pittance to my creditors, insufficient to liquidate my debts unless I lived to the age of Methuselah, when my creditors' remote descendants would have been drawing the instalments? What a weak resolve!

## CHAPTER XVIII.

## MORNING WORK.

SPEAKING of ups and downs, I ought perhaps to refer to one of the downs which befell me in Australia. Always of an energetic nature, there was not enough horseracing to keep me occupied, hence I found myself engaged in every kind of sporting pursuit. One at which I never did any good was coursing. In Australia the Waterloo Cup, which out of compliment to the Old Country bears the same name as its Liverpool prototype, a 64-dog stake, is an enclosed affair, better known as " Plumpton." These enclosed meetings minimise those chances of a surprise which the open sporting plains at Altcar provide so plentifully. The result was that favourite after favourite won, and being a gambler I lost very large sums of money, and more than once lost a " pad " at the game. It was after one of the Waterloo Cups that I found my ready money was much diminished, and I went on to the racecourse at Flemington with a smaller sum than I usually took to the meeting. It was one of those " freezing " days when everyone is of a mind to back one horse, and that one wins. I continued betting, and losing, and quite unconsciously found myself at the end of the fourth race with not enough money to pay out to everybody who had won. Suddenly realising this, I intimated to my clerk that he had better go and have a drink

and take the book with him. This gave me breathing time,
and I borrowed what little money I could, for, like myself,
the fraternity were pretty well cleared out. On the return of
my clerk I playfully abused him for not attending to business,
and then started to pay out with a little less alacrity than
usual. The numbers went up for the next race, and I fielded
with foolhardy bravery. As is usual with most men who
gamble, luck always runs in " trots," and up came the
favourite again. This was a blow, not that I cared a snap
for my losses, but the whole ring was cleared bang out by
this last performance, and we were all running from one to
the other trying to borrow. For once the ring was unanimous !
The dodge of sending the clerk for a drink was of no avail,
for he would have had to remain at the bar—or elsewhere—
the whole day, so there was nothing left but to pay as much
as I could. This I did, and when I came to the silver, all
that was left, I took the satchel from my clerk's neck and
scrambled the coins among the punters generally, finally
throwing the satchel itself among them. I was well known,
and the next day, as soon as the banks opened, I redeemed
my credit. I have often laughed over this incident, and have
as frequently been reminded of it.

To the man who devotes his time to racing, the sport
becomes real hard work. I say the sport advisedly, and by
it I do not mean merely running down to a meeting by train,
strolling round the paddock, making a few bets, and getting
back to town in time to rush into dress clothes and dine with
one's best girl—or somebody else's. That's not treating racing
as a sport, but merely as an amusement. A man who enjoys
it as a sport, and I may fairly claim to have done so to the
full, must know a racehorse when he sees one, must possess
a knowledge of his make and shape, and, more important than
aught else, of his action. Winners are of all shapes, but if
the action is not there, well—neither is the horse. Apart from
all other fatigue connected with a week's racing, no end of
labour, both physical and mental, is entailed by the advisa-

bility, almost the necessity, of knowing a horse in his work
as well as in his races. Only the wonderfully healthy, open-
air conditions, under which the all-important watching and
observation are done, enable a man to accomplish this task.
The life of a racing man, who is a sportsman as well, is harder
than that of almost any other class. The true sportsman must
be capable of forming his own opinion, and must base it on
his own observation and his own judgment. How many men
who go racing can do this? Not one in a hundred! To the
uninitiated the element of chance is so great that they allow
superstition to take the place of sound judgment. And the
man who once gives way to weakness of this kind is indeed
undone, for indecision will hamper the workings of his mind,
and prevent the formation of a definite opinion. A man who
wishes to acquire the indispensable practical knowledge and
the strength of character necessary to the forming of a sound
personal opinion must be one of the early birds, and must
watch the work of the different horses daily during a meeting.
He must make it both his business and his pleasure to be on
the course each morning, and to see the work done. Now,
to do this a man must be either a sportsman or a man of
commerce, or he may be a little of each, or even half-and-half;
if winning he will perhaps pose as the former, but if losing
he is strongly imbued with the business instinct to set himself
right again! We are most of us keen business men when it
is a question of getting our own back.

I maintain that a man must be able to form his own opinion
on racing, or he will not succeed as a regular racegoer. And
to do this after the manner of a true sportsman requires
tireless activity. It entails rising at the break of day, and
greeting the sun as he rises above the horizon. Yet surely
the crisp freshness of the morning air, the dewdrops sparkling
on the grass, the singing of the birds, form more than an
equivalent for an hour or two of slothful slumber. Suitably
equipped with thick boots and the indispensable glasses, our
early riser makes his way to the course, where, if he is a man

of practical experience, he should know nearly all the horses by sight. Many eke out their superficial knowledge in this respect by the aid of the clothing the horses carry, and the initials of the owner or trainer on the cloths. This conceit is common enough, and reminds one of the man who cannot read, and yet holds a paper in front of him, even if it is upside down, rather than admit the fact of his ignorance. The man who has his heart in the sport, and I grant you that he may be a gambler as well, knows his animal at once by its walk, its carriage, its canter, and its characteristics generally, its colour being merely a confirmation of the whole.

In the early morning our sportsman observes the different strings as they walk round, watches them canter with a critical eye, and then judges their gallops as they negotiate their day's work with their companions. And if he is a man of keen discernment, he may see improvement in a horse more readily than the trainer himself. For a man who has not seen the animal for a fortnight or so is much more likely to observe a difference than one who has watched him every day. Many a good bet have I won through keeping my eyes open for points of this kind.

Again, on the book a horse may appear a certainty for a race, but in his early morning work he may show considerable falling off both in condition and in action. If the latter is at fault, and he goes short and scratchy, it is any odds against his being within pounds, or even stones, of his previous form ; always provided that one has seen him galloping, and reasonably extended, for nothing, in the case of some horses, is more misleading than to form an opinion of their merits solely from seeing them in their slow paces.

Then there are the hundred-and-one things that always crop up in connection with the early morning work, and should occupy the sportsman's keenest attention. He will find it ten o'clock or later before he has had his tub, and can comfortably sit down to breakfast. He then has an opportunity to run over in his mind all that he has seen, and to do what is most essential, yet very rare among racegoers generally, viz., *make up his mind and act on it.*

Many a good man and true do I remember who seldom, if ever, missed the morning work. First I may mention that keen sportsman, Lord Cholmondeley, good horseman and huntsman too; Lord Lurgan, who unfortunately has of late years taken less interest in the game; Lord Marcus Beresford, who has been manager of the studs of a crowned and an un crowned King; Lord Buchan, in those days Lord Cardross, spick and span even in those early hours. Then there were Captain Milligan, ever on the *qui vive;* Walter Blake, who has gradually grown tired of exercise since the days of Exmoor; W. Allison, the "Special Commissioner," always ready to insure any horse, or, for that matter, anybody's whole string; and "Bob" Pryor,* chary of taking off his hat so early in the day. At Ascot and Goodwood one often met Prince Christian, consistently inquiring the name of everything that galloped past, and occasionally Lord Farquhar, who has more than once been known to ask the name of one of his own horses. I must not omit to mention Charles Hibbert, who is his own judge, and has on that account much to be thankful for; the late Arthur Cooper and his partner. Johnnie O'Neill; or Bill Riley, who is said never to have missed a day; and of course the usual crowd of touts and tipsters, and host of others, not forgetting Old Mary, the card seller.

Earlier in the eighties, amongst those who regularly watched their horses at work on race mornings were the Duke of Beaufort, the Duke of Hamilton, the Hon. James Lowther, Prince Soltykoff, and many another pillar of the Turf. The sport of kings has sadly missed their whole-hearted support, and it will be long before we shall see their like again.

Well, the horses have finished their work, and we must

---

* Mr. Pryor has died since this was written.

get back to breakfast. And what an appetite the keen morning breeze has blessed us with! When the inner man has been satisfactorily attended to there are the papers to be read, and the day's programme to be studied in further detail. Then comes the racing, with all its attendant bustle and excitement, its frequent visits to the paddock, and its close study of each race in its turn. The keen betting man watches every move of the market, and now is the time to turn to good account the knowledge gathered in the early morning. After racing, the book should be made up and checked, to prevent any possible error, for mistakes occur easily when the balancing is left until the end of the week. When this is done one has just time for a snatch of rest and a rub-down, and then comes the most comfortable part of the day, the change into evening clothes. If this is not a solid day's work I should like to know what is. Yet a more healthy mode of life it would be difficult to find ; for one practically lives in the open air. Think of it, you whose lives are spent in stuffy offices and in scarcely less stuffy suburbs ; think of the hours every day passed out of doors, with the fresh breezes blowing the cobwebs from the brain, and the blue sky for a canopy. Of course, the sky is not always blue, or if it is one cannot see it for grey and stormy clouds, and sometimes the wind is too keen to be altogether pleasant. But bad weather seldom hurts those who are properly equipped to face it, and, at any rate, one lives !

Many are the practical jokes that have been played upon unsuspecting victims. I could fill pages with anecdotes that I know to be true, and in many of these performances I have taken no small part. I remember a certain bookmaker—who shall be nameless, for I do not wish him to become again the butt of his brother pencillers—who one day boasted that he had secured the finest piece of silverside of beef that had ever been seen. In the fulness of his heart he invited two comrades of the Ring to help him do justice to the feast, and so much was said of this marvellous silverside that everybody knew of it. It was a real bad day for the bookies, and favourites rolled home in unbroken succession, so it was with somewhat glum faces and surly tempers that our hero and his friends repaired to the scene of festivity. However, a wash and brush-up refreshed them, and they entered the dining-room with every intention of atoning to some extent for the disasters of the day. In came the landlady, a nervous old soul with ancient ringlets, bearing the precious joint, which was hidden from view by the only electro-plate cover of which the house could boast. The host was all smiles, and sharpened his knife as he said, "Now, boys, I've got a bit of boiled and carrots for you ; the best you ever saw." Then the landlady raised the cover, and what he beheld on the dish drove every vestige of a smile from the bookie's face. He looked as if he had himself been welshed. He glared fiercely at the joint, and more fiercely at the poor old land-lady, whose ringlets were by this time dancing with fright. "Madam!" he hissed, "this was a prime silverside of beef, and I told you to boil it; but, by all the gods, you have roasted it! *Roast* salt beef and carrots!" Then words failed him, and the old lady, shaking all over, fumbled in the depths of her pocket, and at last produced a crumpled telegram, handed in at the racecourse by an anonymous practical joker, which ran : "Kindly roast silverside to-night, carrots as usual."

When racing is so far away from town as to make it impossible to return home for the night, many of our middle-class sportsmen form themselves into small parties, take lodgings, and mess together. As most of these gentlemen fancy themselves not a little as judges of good living, there is frequently keen competition for the office of caterer-in-chief, and a good deal of chipping goes on. A certain prominent backer, who to this day poses as an epicure, always insists on being the chief of commissariat for his particular party, who, it may be mentioned, have suffered many a time from his peculiar predilection for boiled mutton. For even the rudest and healthiest of appetites cannot be expected to appreciate boiled mutton and turnips as a standing dish. One day he came in radiant, saying he had just been buying some blue trout. " Blue trout, boys! " Then he hesitated a moment and took stock of the company. "And I saw such an extra special leg o' mutton—such a boiler—so I got that, and we'll top that up with a plum tart and cream, and a corona-corona, what ho! for the merry punter!" None of the party said a word, but suffered in silence. When they got back at night, the lady of the house announced that the fishmonger's boy said as 'ow they was sorry they couldn't send no blue trout, so they sent some *blue turbot.* There was no one in the crowd bold enough to say that no such fish existed, and in due course the blue turbot was put on the table. Blue!—it was as blue as the Mediterranean! They all looked dubiously at one another, and then stared silently at the fish. There was a long pause ; nobody wanted to be the first to brave the dangers of the unknown ; but at last, half in shame and half in desperation, the unhappy caterer ventured on a mouthful, which speedily found its way into the folds of his napkin!

"It is blue, ain't it, Charlie? " asked one. " Are blue trout anything like that? " inquired another. "I didn't order it," snarled the sufferer ; "go and take it out of the fishmonger— it ain't my fault." On came the boiled mutton—the inevitable boiled mutton, caper sauce, and mashed turnips. The cover was lifted, and behold! the mutton was blue, as blue as the turbot! "That turbot has been swimming about in the wrong pot, for certain," remarked one candid friend. "Yes," said another ; "blue's catching—just look at our blue mountain mutton! " "Well," chimed in a third, "I thought we were going to have a good old English dinner, but give me the à la business in future." Hastily the provider of the feast rose and left the room, consigning the party, all and sundry, to regions unmentionable. The truth was that one of the "mess" had been to the fishmonger's and substituted turbot for the trout, and had concocted the supposed message from the shop.

Then he placed a ball of washing blue in each of the pots—and a blue dinner it was!   One satisfactory result was that boiled mutton has not since made its appearance on the menu.

Another dinner that went wrong was that of a bookmaker famous, in plain language, for his gluttony.   He asked two kindred spirits to dine with him, and for their delectation provided two geese.   Two geese between three is not starvation allowance, but he quite reckoned on attending to one himself. This got about, and the usual kind friend sent a note round to his house saying the geese were to be boiled!   Boiled goose sounds as bad as, I should think, it would eat, and "the three pigs," as they were called, had to adjourn to a neighbouring hostelry, where they are stated to have devoured three fowls and a whole ham between them!

## CHAPTER XIX.

## AUSTRALIA AGAIN.

IME passed on with the usual ebb and flow attendant
on racing affairs, the only exception to which is
that of the bookmakers, whose fortunes seem
always at the flood. Ascot, the Newmarket July,
and that queen of all meetings, Goodwood, came
on with their wonted regularity. But I cannot
dismiss Goodwood so briefly, for its course,
besides being in other respects one of the very best in the
world, carries that natural down turf of which few can
boast. Indeed, the July Course at headquarters and the
courses at Salisbury and Bath are the only others which I
can call to mind as approaching it. "Glorious Goodwood"
stands out alone in the beauty of its surroundings and the
silent charm of its scenery. The approach to the course is
perfect. Entering at the lodge-gates, the drive leads past
the mansion itself, and then through avenues of beeches and
woods gay with their summer foliage. After ascending the
hill the famous Birdless Grove is reached, and passing through
this the racecourse presents itself to view. From the summit
stretches away as far as the eye can reach the undulating
Sussex scenery, studded with coppices and plantations, whilst,
on a clear day, a glimpse of the blue Solent can be obtained
in the distance. What finer holiday can be imagined than a
real summer day at Goodwood, with its luncheon under the
trees, and its racing for racing's sake? On no other course

can one obtain such complete relaxation and relief from the ordinary cares of life.

Yes, all went on in just the same way—the St. Leger, the Cesarewitch, the Cambridgeshire, and finally Manchester, which so often decides whether the punter's winter is to be cheerful or the reverse. To the uninitiated the continued round of racing may sound monotonous and uninteresting, and this may in truth be said of almost any other avocation but a sporting one. The chief attraction of racing is its glorious uncertainty, which carries with it an unfailing and indescribable fascination.

My restless spirit, however, could not settle down quietly, and had not yet reached that calm and composed state which prompts a man to say, *"J'y suis, j'y reste."* So in 1890 I determined upon another voyage to Australia, not with any idea of business, but as a pleasure trip pure and simple. The old associations of the place drew me, and I wanted to see again a few old faces of those whom I looked on as my friends. I went out on the " Austral," a steamer which had once, when coaling, made an expedition to the bottom of Sydney Harbour. She was an excellent boat, and carried a very good lot of passengers of the usual mixed description. It was one of the voyages which I shall never forget, and its memory will always be a pleasant one.

There is not very much to note in this, my last trip to Australia, but I may remark, in passing, that I was received with, if possible, more enthusiasm than usual, solely on account of the scurvy treatment I had experienced at the hands of the committee of the Victorian Club. I renewed old associations, and lived old times over again. The length of time which had elapsed since my last visit made the revival of old acquaintance all the more pleasant.

The city of Melbourne had made great progress. Many of the old-fashioned houses in Collins Street had been knocked down, owing to the falling-in of the leases, and had been rebuilt. An underground system of drainage had been substituted for the surface method which had obtained on my previous visits. In the earlier days I have seen Elizabeth Street, a road on a decline, which crosses Collins Street, in such a state of flood that foot-passengers had to hire a four-wheeled cab, which in Australia was a wagonette covered with American cloth or oil-skin, in order to be able to cross with safety. It is even on record that people have been carried away by the rush of water during heavy rains, and have been drowned through getting caught under the bridges which crossed the gutters. All these traces of primitive methods had vanished, and the city had been much modernised. No doubt the improvement has continued 'in accordance with the motto of the colony, " Advance Australia ! "

It was on this visit that I saw the never-to-be-forgotten race in which Carbine won the Melbourne Cup, carrying the enormous weight of 10st 5lb. I have already referred to this wonderful performance, but I must be allowed some brief further allusion. Merman, The Grafter, and many other horses bred in the land of the Southern Cross have given us in England a taste of their quality, but Carbine was the greatest of them all.

Any horse that can give a subsequent winner of a Viceroy's Cup 49lb must be a phenomenal one. A bay, with black points, Carbine, by Musket, resembled Best Man more nearly than any other English horse with which I can compare him, but there is no comparison as to which was the better horse on the racecourse. It is common knowledge that the Duke of Portland gave 15,000 guineas for him, and that he now stands at Welbeck. So far as my opinion is of value, I have no doubt whatever that the cross will make itself felt, especially in years to come.

I cannot dismiss my visits to Australia without referring to Tasmania. The climate being cooler than that of Australia, it is a charming summer resort, whilst Hobart is one of the prettiest towns to be found on the other side of the equator. It has an excellent racecourse, and is, generally speaking, a charming place to live in. Instead of the monotonous post and rail fences which abound throughout Victoria and New South Wales, the eye rests on hedges such as we have in the home country. Originally called Van Diemen's Land, after the name of the explorer who discovered the island, it was one of the early penal settlements, and I paid a most interesting visit to some of those individuals who had survived their sentences, some of whom are perhaps living at the present day. These men, bent with age, live in a settlement set apart for them, which I cannot better describe than by comparing it with the almshouses to be seen in some of our small provincial towns. Here they have their gardens and different plots of land, and the few who remain are fairly comfortably off. They are allowed to visit the town at certain periods, and walk about perfectly free and unguarded, for "the devil" which once possessed them is now dead.

A more villainous lot of faces it would be hard to imagine, than those which confronted me on my visit to the place set aside for these men, while some of their stories were blood-curdling. It is usual for visitors to take with them tobacco, or some similar present, and it was extraordinary to notice how each vied with the other, to get an extra amount of the weed, by recounting their criminal experiences almost to exaggeration, and boasting about what they had done to receive the sentences which had sent them to transportation for the "term of their natural life." I remember one old man with a jaundiced eye, who sat on a rough wooden form and told the story of how he had shot a policeman by "accident," and had heard his own death bell tolling, when the reprieve arrived just in time to save his neck. In those days telegraphy and railways were not, and it was only by the aid of post-horses that his life was saved by some quarter of an hour. The authorities had taken what is called in legal terms a "merciful view of his case," and had, in spite of his conviction, apparently accepted the theory set up by the defence that the shooting of the policeman "might" have been an accident. Or perhaps the authorities in those days did not place so great a value on the life of the " bobby " as they do now. No sooner had he finished his narrative than up jumped a comrade, and addressed me somewhat as follows : —

" 'Im, he ain't done nothing. Shot a policeman and then tried to get out of it by cracking it was an accident. Why, he ought to have been proud of it!

" I was sent out 'ere after doing a sentence of ten stretch, went home again, and then got back at the old game. Why, bless yer, guv'nor, when once you've had the taste of doing the trick it's impossible to keep away from it. I got into a mess over a little shop-lifting, the nearest tick in the world, guv'nor, that we didn't get all the swag ; but just as we were going, up wakes a bloke from under the counter—they called 'im the night watchman. There he was a-snorin' till just the finish. Well, I downs 'im with a chisel, and blest if he doesn't fall against a china vase, and the smash brought down a couple of chaps from upstairs. I downs one of 'em, and my mates have a struggle with the other, when in come the coppers, and there was a rare set-to. Talk about shooting one by accident! Well, you should have seen 'em after me and my mates had finished with 'em. Well, they gave me a lifer, and I'm proud of it, for if they didn't send me here I should never have been as comfortable as I am now. Perfect independence, and what more does a man want? Good luck to you, sir." With a victorious glance, almost of scorn, at his brother in crime, who still sat on the form, he held his hand out for a stick of tobacco.

But no sooner had he finished than another began his story, endeavouring to outdo his predecessors in depth of guilt and picturesqueness of gory detail. But the most extra-ordinary of them all, was a man by the name of Charlie Dennis, a gentleman born, who had been condemned to death no less than three times. He still bore traces of having been a handsome man, and though bent with age, he must in his earlier days have stood at least 6ft 4in. The sentence of hanging in those days was not reserved for murder alone, as people were strung up for forgery, sheep stealing, and similar offences, but this man in his time had murdered two warders and had attempted to kill one of the junior governors of the prison, these being the three offences for which he was at different times sentenced to death. The story, which is almost to-day a Tasmanian legend, was that a certain governor's wife fell in love with him, and that a liaison had existed between them, and it was through her intervention that he was reprieved for each of these crimes, once when actually on the scaffold. And so I listened to the different stories, nearly all of them interesting, but the whole merry party of convicts burst out into guffaws when one man said that the only offence he had committed for his sentence of transportation for life, was stealing a pocket-handkerchief. They all jeered at him as though he were an amateur among a lot of professionals, and such remarks as, "Why don't you own up like a man?" "What have you got to be ashamed of?" "What's the good of kidding you're innocent now?" and so forth, were hurled at him. He bore the nickname of the "Curate," which was doubtless given to him because of his continual protestations of innocence. They were all dressed in ordinary clothes, nor was the sign of the broad arrow to be seen. They were not allowed to go beyond certain landmarks in the place assigned to them, nor were they ever permitted to be out after dark, unless they had written permission. In earlier days many used to attempt to escape, and some even starved in the Bush rather than return to complete that dreaded sentence, "the term of his natural life." They have in the past at different times broken out and raided small townships, and the history of the penal settlements of Tasmania and Australia would fill many an interesting and thrilling volume. With the exception of these few men there is no trace of the convict to-day in Australia, and if a native has any doubt in his own mind of his ancestry it is the custom to assume that his father had been governor of one of the gaols! This, to some extent, is true, inasmuch as his father had probably been an inmate of one of the many prisons which in those days abounded in South Australia, Botany Bay, and Tasmania.

I cannot dismiss Australia without once more referring to some early experiences there, and relating one or two stories, for the truth of which I can vouch. Of all the men I met in the Colonies, perhaps the most extraordinary and certainly the most interesting was Joe Thompson, now established in England as a leading bookmaker.

When attending up-country meetings, there was little or nothing to do in the evenings. Hence much time was given up to smoking and yarns, washed down by libations according to one's taste or the temperature. The worst of these meetings which I remember was Wagga Wagga. Here until sunset one has to wear a fly net over one's hat for protection from this insect, which in this particular district is most pertinacious, and declines to be brushed off in the ordinary way. Then goggles have to be worn, for the glare is most oppressive ; so that the racing man at Wagga Wagga resembled a motorist of to-day, with the addition of a net covering all over his head and face. In Australia, and, for that matter, in England also, Joe Thompson and I have had many friendly battles in the betting arena, and it was at these up-country meetings, when the racing was over, that I found him one of the most interesting of raconteurs. The bushrangers of Australia have been many, and they were in their time all known to Joe, except one whose name was Morgan, and as this individual had already a record of having shot twenty-seven men, perhaps on this account Joe Thompson forswore his acquaintance. "Joe," through the whole of his career, has shown considerable tact and discretion! Morgan was the worst of all the outlaws, and was hated by his brethren in the "profession." He was a blackguard of the worst type, and indulged in crimes which his fellow bushrangers despised, for he numbered women among his victims. There was an unwritten code among these bandits that women should always be spared under all circumstances. The notorious Kellys, Frank Gardner, and all the rest of the gangs always adhered to this, and there was never a charge made against them on this account. On the contrary, it is on record that they have assisted women in many instances, at times going out of their way to do so, even at the risk of their liberty. It was owing to their respect for women that the Kellys and others of their like received so much protection from the public and those living in the Bush districts, where they sought refuge, but Morgan was hated by them, and Frank Gardner, the bushranger of New South Wales, when in gaol, stated that he hoped to live to finish his sentence that he might have the pleasure of shooting Morgan for the dastardly deeds he had committed in shooting down anybody and everybody at sight. Gardner, as he pleaded to his sympathisers, "*only* killed policemen." It may seem strange in England that these outlaws remained uncaptured for such a number of years, but it was, as I have stated, owing to the fact that they never once laid hands on a female, and they therefore frequently found sanctuary where, under ordinary circumstances, they would have been lost.

A short time ago I had the pleasure of meeting Joe Thompson again, and our conversation turned upon old times, and he reminded me of some things I had forgotten ; amongst them the incidents I am now dealing with. It was the habit of these outlaws, when an up-country race meeting was in progress, to send in a messenger to Joe Thompson or his brother Jack, whose death every sportsman in Australia lamented, saying that they would like to meet them at a given trysting place at a certain hour. The late Jack Thompson was one of those big, good-natured men—all heart. Though straight as a die, yet he had no little sympathy with these outlaws. I do not say he was right or wrong in his views, but every outlaw has his sympathisers ; therefore, the Kellys and Frank Gardner, who were sought after by the police, and who could have been shot by any man at sight (and that man would have received a reward), sent messages to Jack Thompson making some appointment whenever he attended the race meetings in the Benella, or "Kelly gang" districts. The last time Joe Thompson, accompanied by his brother Jack, saw Frank Gardner they both endeavoured to persuade him to desist, and his reply was, "The day I shoot Morgan I will never fire another shot as long as I live." Morgan, it should be observed, belonged to Victoria, and perhaps the petty jealousies which have ever existed between the two colonies may in no small way have affected the respective bushrangers; but I am strongly inclined to think that what was uppermost in Frank Gardner's mind was the dastardly treatment to which, as I have just said, Morgan had subjected many women. There must have been some good in Frank Gardner after all. Some influence was brought to bear; and after having served, at different periods, thirty-two years in gaol, he received a pardon at the hands of Sir Hercules Robinson, the Governor of New South Wales, on the condition that he left the country, and in due course he migrated to California. His two mates, Gilbert and Hall, had long since been shot on sight as outlaws.

Morgan's end was different. The races were being held at Beechworth, in Victoria, and it became known that Morgan was about the district. Joe Thompson found himself in rather an awkward predicament, for he had loudly proclaimed, as had every man in the Colonies, his hatred for Morgan, while it was understood he had some kind of admiration for Frank Gardner. Not "taking any chances," Joe saddled his horse just before midnight, and set off to Wangaratta. The same night Morgan came out of his lair ready to hold up anybody; but, being fore-warned, the town was forearmed, and he went outside to the station of a gentleman named MacPherson. On his arrival there he calmly entered the house, revolver in hand, ordered all doors to be locked, and, throwing himself into an armchair, demanded a cup of tea, and, placing his pistol in front of him on the table, he added, "If I sleep, I do so with only one eye shut." Had MacPherson taken up the revolver at that moment he would have found that it was empty! Long immunity had made Morgan recklessly foolhardy. Being aware that Miss MacPherson played the piano with more than ordinary skill, he called for a tune. He was obeyed in everything; but, despite his precautions of having the doors locked, he had made one mistake—he had not previously searched the out-buildings. One of the female servants had been away. On returning to the house, and finding the doors locked, she grew apprehensive, and peering through the window saw Morgan seated in the armchair, the revolver in front of him, and Miss MacPherson playing the piano! She recognised him at once, for his likeness had been freely distributed about the country. With some forethought, she threw off her skirts, and started to run in her petticoats to Wangaratta, a distance of six miles. Reaching the township, she informed the police of Morgan's whereabouts.

Police and volunteers arrived at MacPherson's station in the dead of night, and lay in ambush until daylight. In due course Morgan appeared on the scene, impudently walking about the place arm-in-arm with Mr. MacPherson, as if he had been an old friend and an honoured guest!

They were making their way to the stables, as Morgan had demanded the best blood horse that could be provided. As they walked up the path Morgan must have observed something, for turning to MacPherson he said suddenly, "What's the matter? What are you shifting away for?" As a matter of fact, they were close upon the inspector lying in ambush; MacPherson had caught his eye, and had been waved aside by him. As he took a quick step from Morgan, the latter turned and must have realised the situation. Immediately the report of a rifle rang through the air, and the bullet went through Morgan's back. He reeled and fell, and hardly had he touched the ground when the whole of the forces, civil and military, rushed upon him, and he was literally cut to pieces. So eager were his assailants to get at him that he was unrecognisable when he was lifted from the ground and carried to the outbuildings. His head, which had been severed from the body, was sent post haste to Melbourne. Within twenty-four hours a plaster cast had been taken of it, and it was exhibited the same day at Kreitmayer's waxwork show.

The peculiar part of these stories is that both Joe and Jack Thompson were on most intimate terms with the late Captain Standish, who was chairman of the Victorian Racing Club and head of the Victorian police. Hence it might be said that with one hand Joe Thompson could touch the shoulder of the chief of the police and with the other that of the outlaws. Perhaps the best friend the Kellys ever had was Jack Thompson, who sympathised with them to an extraordinary degree. They most certainly chose the more romantic side of highway robbery, for they never held up anything but a bank, or stole cattle from any stations except those belonging to the richer classes. Had one of their gang attempted to lay hands on a woman he would doubtless have been shot on the spot by one or other of his mates. They were once officially interviewed by Jack Thompson, who acted as a kind of intermediary, and begged them to throw up the game. He offered them an unofficial truce, which could have been arranged had the Kellys agreed ; but no, the life they lived had become second nature.

The fascination of the bush, the mock romance of their surroundings, held them, as it were, in a spell, and in spite of all Jack Thompson's entreaties the only answer he came back with was, " They say it is too late, and they could never exist without killing another policeman or two." The Kellys' greatest delight was to waylay and entrap a policeman, and to hang him on a tree by the wayside, where he could be seen by all passers by. It is recorded that once they hanged as many as three at one time.

No one in Australia has had the same varied experiences of the country and the men in it as Joe Thompson. In the

early days Ballarat was the scene of a great rush, for gold
was discovered there, and he was one of the first to arrive
on the scene.  The claims were called " jewellers' shops," they
were so rich, and were pegged out only twenty-four feet square
for eight men.  The mines proved extremely wealthy ; in fact,
it is said that the diggers sometimes got up more gold in a
bucket than dirt!  These were the reckless early days of
Victoria, and if a miner was not working he was singing or
drinking.  All classes of all countries rushed to Ballarat.
Chinamen worked at the mines, and at Mount Ararat they
themselves discovered a lead of gold which they called the
Canton Lead.  From this spot, unknown to the European,
the "Heathen Chinee" brought parcels of gold into the
market for sale.  When it was discovered whence they got
the precious metal, the Englishmen rushed the ground, ousted
the Chinamen, and gained the spoils.  It turned out to be
extremely rich in ore, and gold to the tune of hundreds of
thousands of pounds was extracted.  The Chinamen's tents
and all their belongings had been burned before the police
had time to get on the ground, and Johnny Chinaman had fled.

There is no doubt that Joe Thompson is the biggest bookmaker Australia has ever seen, for I never remember him
having a volume of less extent than £20,000 on any of the
principal ante-post betting races.  That is all over now, owing
perhaps to the fact that they race almost every day in one
part or other of Australia.  That the colonies have produced
some excellent horses, Carbine, already referred to, exem-
plifies, nor can I close my notes on Australia without mentioning Abercorn, Grand Flaneur, Commotion, Malua, Trenton,
Darabin, Tim Whiffler—indeed. I could go on enumerating
scores of good ones.  Joe Thompson was the owner of many,
amongst them Don Juan, for whom he gave £50, and won
with him the Melbourne Cup.

It is remarkable to relate that as racing has changed in
England so it appears to have changed in the Colonies, and
is daily concentrating itself round the cities of Melbourne

and Sydney, to the disadvantage of the sporting country meetings. The heavy betting which used to take place has also much diminished, and with the exception of the Derby and the Melbourne Cup there is little done. Some years ago the Colonies were almost in a state of bankruptcy over the delusive land boom. So great was the excitement that land was once sold at public auction in the city of Melbourne at a greater price than similar plots have fetched in the city of London. Needless to observe, that when things settled down and reached their normal state the speculators and nearly all the public who had their savings, and more, invested in land, were left bankrupt. It has taken her some years to recover, but I am glad to be able to state that the prosperity of Australasia and racing is well on the go again.

## CHAPTER XX.

## MONTE CARLO.

EAVING Australia in December, I spent my first Christmas aboard ship. It was far from an auspicious time of year to choose to return from the Antipodes, and England in the depth of the winter of 1890-1 was by no means a genial change of climate. It was freezing hard, and as my wardrobe consisted for the most part of summer garments, the East wind of my native country made me keenly alive to the fact that I had " come home."

From the Southern Sun to the Northern Snow is a far and cold cry. Equatorial climates thin the blood. I suffered considerably, and could not stand the climate, for, do what I would, I could never get warm. Hunting was stopped, and no fire appeared big enough to heat me through. With numbed fingers and cold feet I started for Monte Carlo—to thaw. My anticipations were more than realised. It not alone melted me, but also my cash. The irresponsible wheel, the irresistible trente-et-quarante, had invincible attractions for me, and though I had no intention of playing—oh! those good intentions and the road which is paved with them—no sooner was I in the Casino than I searched for a seat, and got it. It was about all I did get. Though I played steadily, and did not rush after my losses as so many do, a persistent run of bad luck pursued me, and I seldom found myself with a winning coup of any description. Day after day I lost my limit with that

regularity which foretells one's doom, and there I sat, waiting
for the break which never came. It has always been the
same throughout the whole of my transactions, I have either
cleared out the lot or have been cleared out. Still, I felt
warm, and no longer frozen. The sun was welcome, and if
one did pay dearly for it, its value is surely inestimable.
Never having suffered from the blues, I was able to enjoy the
hue of the Mediterranean. I did not aggravate my losses by
brooding over them, and thereby spoil my visit to Charlie's
Mount. Besides this, there are plenty of attractions " down
South " beyond those of the Casino. A walk to Cap Martin
and back before breakfast is an excellent restorer to an " overnight," while another healthful bit of exercise is, having sent
a change to the hotel at La Turbie, to take train to Mentone
and start for a climb up the old Corniche Road to that edifice.
It is a real good bit of hard walking, all on the collar, and the
surrounding scenery is unsurpassed ; the olive trees growing,
as it were, on the top of each other out of the precipitous rocks,
intermingled with huge boulders of different crude colouring,
till they touch the edge of that vast salt lake called the Mediterranean, with its silver-crested waves. On a clear day
Corsica is to be discerned, floating far off on the azure surface.
Arrived at the summit upon which La Turbie stands, a tub
and change, and one is ready for a hearty breakfast. I found
it was only those of the impecunious brigade, the losers, who
ever attempted this walk!

Altogether, my position was an unenviable one. It was too
cold in England for me to return comfortably, and too expensive to stop. In this impecunious state, between two stools,
as it were, I found myself one sunny morning watching the
waves lazily breaking on the shore. Sitting on the rocks in
the warm rays of the Riviera sun I determined I would be
regulated by King Sol, and stop where I was. It was the one
comfort which the clouds alone could take from me. But what
was I to do? I was not anxious to risk the little that was
left at the Hall of Enchantment, commonly called the Casino ;

while, on the other hand, I was not built with a temperament
that would permit of my doing nothing.  All this passed
through my mind in an instant, and I continued cogitating
more lazily than seriously.  At last I made up my mind, and
decided I would have a shot at writing a farce.  Farce?  I
had not far to look for a plot, for surely my surroundings
were sufficiently quaint in themselves.  I must have quickly
concluded that any play I was going to write would not be
of an ethereal nature, and at once settled in my mind
that something sporting would be more in my line.  I
thought out a scenario and became so engrossed that I even
muttered a few sentences as though I were rehearsing it.  But
the title, that was an all-important point.  It came to me
naturally.  I would call my little curtain-raiser " Stone Broke."
Most apropos.  I regret to say the story was not one which
would leave much of a moral behind it, but that was not my
aim.  The play is the thing, and as long as I could complete a
one-act farce which would create laughter throughout, what
did I care?  It would, at any rate, afford occupation for a time.
I will briefly give the rough outlines of the plot, with the
gratuitous advice to my readers to avoid ever becoming one of
the characters in real life.  The curtain rose on the scene of a
modern sitting-room in one of those houses which display in
their windows, "Apartments to let."  Breakfast was over, and
two young "sports," Dick Swift and Jack Sharp, were discuss-
ing the ways and means how to pay their bill, when the
landlady entered, intimating her resolve not to wait any longer,
or to listen to any more promises.  She, like most London
landladies similarly placed, was obdurate.  With threats of
seizing their belongings, locking doors. and so on, she departed.
There was the lodging-house "slavey," who conventionally
came on at the wrong moment and complicated matters all
round.  At last a wicked idea struck Jack Sharp.  Looking at
the breakfast table, he noticed that Miss Hicks, the landlady,
for some unaccountable reason, had sent up the one and only
silver coffee-pot, "which had been in her family for years."

Eyeing "temptation," Jack Sharp remarked that he knew a certainty for the big race that day, but—how could they raise the wind to back it? How? Swift, without any further intimation from his friend, grasped the situation, and spinning his only coin—copper—said as it fell in his hand,

"Toss you who pops the pot!"

"Done!"

Sharp won. After much theatrical business Swift left with the pot and Sharp barricaded the door. The former was to pawn the silver, back the certainty, and as soon as the result came up on the tape redeem the landlady's family treasure and pay their bill with the winnings.

The confidence of those in extreme straits when a chance of escape offers itself amply verifies the proverb that a drowning man will clutch at a straw. During his absence, the landlady and the servant gave plenty of scope for fun and comical complications. At last he did return—but without the sacred coffee-pot.

"Second!" he cried. The situation can be imagined. The landlady went off into hysterics, the "slavey" followed her mistress's example, when the voice of the newsboy was heard in the street calling,

"Winner! Winner! Winner of the big handicap."

With a hasty word of advice to Swift to try to keep them quiet, Sharp rushed from the room. The landlady and the maid-of-all-work-and-everybody's-business came to. The three then started to search for the coffee-pot. In vain did Swift plead that he was sure they had had tea for breakfast, and in vain did he try to pacify the head of the house. The situation grew bluer and bluer, and was reaching a climax when lo! Sharp returns unseen, and replacing the coffee-pot on the tray, flings himself into the armchair and lights a cigar. Suddenly he calls to the landlady, and with the *sang froid* of a Crœsus offers a Bank of England note in liquidation of the bill, &c. Being asked by Swift how he had accomplished this, he explained that the winner had been successfully objected to for bumping, and concluded by adding, " Didn't I tell you it was a certainty? "

That is the rough story which I sat down to mould into a farce. Many a millionaire to-day may have gone nearer to singeing his wings than did the hero of " Stone Broke." The same evening that I conceived this very irregular story I started on my work, and before morning I had completed it. On my return to London I sold it for £50, and it was first produced at the Grand Theatre, Islington, Mr. Charles Cartwright playing Jack Sharp and Mr. D'Orsay, now a leading actor in the United States, Dick Swift. It was subsequently played in nearly every theatre in the provinces.

Returning to England, the first thing I bought was a betting book. True, I was not overburdened with capital, but one has to keep a record of one's transactions, no matter how small. I have been blessed with a good memory, and strange as it may appear to many an old racegoer, I never carried a book of form in my life. If a race had not left an impression upon me I never sought a " guide " to make one for me. In this respect I think I have been the gainer. It was in May of 1891, that a race at Kempton Park—a maiden plate, run over a distance of a mile—left me with one of these " impressions." It was won by a filly called Comedy. She scored easily by ten lengths, and belonged to a Mr. W. W. Fulton, an Irishman. He had a very jovial idea of the Rules of Racing! I gathered this from Comedy's next performance, and for reasons which are obvious I must refrain from expressing my " impressions " of this race. The season progressed, and in due course the weights for the Cambridgeshire appeared, and Comedy, then a three-year-old, was allotted 7st 3lb. To obtain correct information regarding Mr. Fulton's horses was not the easiest task; it was, in fact, as near as possible an impossibility. There are some stables which are run to-day on quite the same lines— indeed, I have known some of these people who have told so many different tales about their horses that they have ulti-

mately got into a tangle themselves as to what to do or say.
Mr. Fulton was much addicted to schemes of this kind, and
ruined that brilliant mare Laodamia by running her unfit and
out of her course. In prosecuting inquiries, I satisfied myself
that Comedy was being trained for a distance over which the
Cambridgeshire was then run, and started to back her quietly
whenever an opportunity arose. I was experiencing reasonably mild luck at the time, and as I won put more on her.
Commencing by backing her for various sums at the rate of
100 to 3, I never ceased supporting her up to the day of the
race, the 28th of October. I stood to win a very acceptable
sum of money over her—some £16,000—while if she lost the
small amount I should have left to call my own would be
not worth mentioning. As was usual in connection with all
Mr. Fulton's horses, she was the victim of all kinds of
rumours, which caused her to jump about in the market like
the proverbial parched pea. Before the race there was a
considerable hubbub going on as to who would ride her, but
Ibbett, who had been up on the filly in the two races she had
lost, claimed the mount, and Mr. Fulton, wisely, if
reluctantly, did not take him off. Making nearly all the
running, Comedy won by half a length from Breach, the
property of Lord Hastings, with His Majesty's (then the
Prince of Wales's) Derelict third. The Stewards held an
inquiry after the race—the exact grounds I never could
correctly understand—and the air was full of all sorts of
scandal, and there was even a wild report that all bets would
be declared off. In the result the race remained as it stood,
nothing being done. I won my stake over the Cambridgeshire solely from the "impression" Comedy had made on
me by the style she won "A Maiden Plate" at Kempton early
in the season. I was again on my legs—not that I have ever
felt off them—and if they have perhaps once or twice suffered
from a slight after-dinner "dubiosity," they have never let
me down!

Yes, the winner of the Cambridgeshire in 1901 was quite a

12

Comedy to me.  True racing has its varieties, its chops and changes, and in turns may be a comedy, a tragedy, and not infrequently, with many, a farce.  The latter is the dangerous side of the game, and the sport of kings has suffered through the wanton conceit of many who have assumed a knowledge of horses which they did not possess.  But presuming a man to be a judge of a racehorse, he has many other obstacles to combat before he can approach, let alone reach, success on the Turf.  He must be a keen judge of the market, and this particular is, perhaps, the most important of all  No matter what may be the real or apparent merits of a horse for a certain race, the betting market must endorse the estimate of his chances, or one had better lay against him rather than back him, even if he has pleased the critical eye.  In City phraseology, on such occasions it is better to be a "bear" than a "bull."  Then, on the other hand, the market is often false.  That is to say, a favourite is frequently backed at a ridiculously short price, which does not represent his chance.  His actual chance is less than the market odds.  On such occasions the race should be severely left alone so far as betting goes, for the backer who takes a false price will soon find himself in the shallows and quicksands.  And at racing they take a lot of getting out of.  There are no lighthouses or danger signals to guide the unwary.

Again, assuming the horse is fit and backed, there is yet another matter for grave consideration—the jockey.  This is an all-important "component part."  Some jockeys ride better on one course than on another, and not a few discredit their calling altogether.  Again, some "fit" a horse, and there are instances when a particular animal will go for one rider better than it will for another.  Then there is the trusted jockey and the suspected one.  In the case of jockeys, as in all other walks of life, rumour is frequently rife, and blows hot and cold according to results.  It never makes allowances for bad horsemanship and jockeyship.  This latter combination is sadly wanting in many who are riding to-day.

One without the other is like an omelette without eggs ; on the other hand, a bad imitation is even worse, and savours of an omelette made of rotten eggs !

Those hands which were the admiration of Tom Cannon's followers ; those strong, vigorous finishes of Archer, George Barrett, Charlie Wood, and a host of others ; the rushes of poor George Fordham ; the "head" riding of these artists in the eighties and earlier, where do we find their characteristics in our jockeys of the present generation? Monkeyship has supplanted jockeyship, and the question whom to put up is, at the present moment, more crucial than it was a decade or so ago.

All these details have to be studied by the racegoer, and he must not permit a screw to be loose anywhere. The least hesitation on the part of a jockey and the situation is lost ; the same applies to a backer with all its force. If racing has been blamed in this respect, it is in itself not responsible. The sport cannot hold itself sponsor for the weak who venture where strong men refuse to go.

Then there is the owner to take into account, and he is no small item to sum up. Since I first joined the "glorious uncertainty" he has greatly changed. He comes in many shapes. He generally knows how to take care of himself and his own, and often enough a bit of someone else's, much more so than did his predecessor. The present stamp of man, in by far the majority of cases, is a different person altogether from that of past generations. We live in a claptrap era. Some call it going ahead, but I am inclined to call it going to ——.

Twenty years ago there were no Jewburg owners running horses on our English racecourses. Since then dealers in stolen diamonds, fugitives from justice, the scum of swindling speculators who, like leeches, have sucked the life-blood of many a noble family, have taken the place of their victims, lamentably so for the Turf. With this gang the spirit of the sport doesn't enter into the game ; indeed, racing is rather utilised as a key with which to open the door to Society. Such is the evolution for the worse to which I can testify.

Yet another consideration crops up, and this no small one —that of the trainer. There is no harder worked man than this too often abused individual, if he conscientiously sticks to his business. I am inclined to believe the work is treated a little more lightly than it used to be, for I have noticed an increasing inclination among not a few of the more modern trainers to leave a great deal more to the travelling lad than was customary in the "good old times." Apart from such meetings as Ascot, Goodwood, and the like, one has only to be out observing the work done in the early morning on the race days at many of the suburban meetings, to discover that the number of trainers present, compared with a decade or so back, is most palpably on the decrease. This makes the question of trainers an even more serious consideration with the racing man than it used to be. Small races frequently take more winning than classics, for in the latter case the trainer knows his horse and his capabilities, whereas in the former the animals engaged are generally so bad that they are almost unknown quantities. It is far easier to gauge the merits of a good horse than of a middle-class one. There is no reliability in the latter. They beat each other. Therefore, do not the second division require even more care and study of detail to be bestowed upon them by their respective trainers? Do they get it?

Hence the things which a legitimate racing man has to weigh and settle before he ventures to support his opinion are illimitable and innumerable. How many of the thousands who had a bet on this year's Derby have given any one of these points a moment's thought? Yet, let them lose their money, and there is a body of hypocrites, sanctified in their own sight, ever ready to hold up their hands in horror, and, turning their eyes skywards, to abuse the Turf as being part of the Devil's machinery. I venture to think that if Providence decreed that as a punishment for the bookmakers every favourite should win for, say, one week in a year, there would not be one of the shocked division who would not be a sport, if only for the brief space of those seven days.

True, the beginner or the uninitiated has much greater facilities at his command than were available to our fathers. Nor is the young man of to-day given to act on his own judgment to that degree which marked the era of that great plunger, Lord Hastings  The result is that whereas I can remember the time when bookmaking was a most profitable certainty, it is now a near thing whether the game is worth the candle. There is no fresh blood joining the ranks of layers. Betting has been on the decrease for years, and the introduction of that nail in the backer's coffin, that artificial instrument, the starting-gate, has made the cautious speculator doubly careful. I say without fear of contradiction that where thousands were betted years ago hundreds are not invested to-day. The ring is not nearly so rich as it was by a very large amount, and the fortunes that were made in the past are but traditional history, and are not realised in the present. No sport, no institution, has been sucked so dry as racing. All this has helped to compel the owner to look at his horses through commercial spectacles, and to live up to the sporting spirit which once existed has been made pretty nearly impossible. The gigantic profits of gate-money meetings, the major portion going out of racing into unknown hands, never to be returned ; the enormous entry fees compared with those in any other part of the world ; the increased and iniquitous charges which are imposed on all who attend race meetings—all these impediments have blocked the way, and I have lived to see the betting market fade into a state little better than bankruptcy. And why ? Everything is going out and nothing coming in. Owners, trainers, and every man who helps to support racing, are bled by aliens to the sport. I have been asked two pounds a night for a bedroom at Doncaster, a room I would hardly have assigned to my valet under ordinary circumstances. At Ascot many of the residents expect to pay their annual rent by letting their place for the race week, a period of four days! At Goodwood, so close to Chichester, with its cathedral, the whole of the local clergy look forward to the harvest which the letting of the rectory or the vicarage brings in. Indeed, it may be said that their harvest thanksgiving should rather refer to the rent they annually pocket than to the carted corn of the farmers. The charges for the stabling of racehorses in this neighbourhood, and, for that matter, at Ascot, and also many other meetings, is a scandal, not to say a robbery. I have been charged as much as two guineas a night for a loose box, and compelled to take it for the whole meeting at that! It is quite time these "highwayman" tricks were put down. At Goodwood I must exempt Mr. Waters, who has a farm on the Duke's estate, and who lets his excellent boxes at a rate which would be considered moderate at any time. It is to these persecutions, to which the owners and trainers have been subjected, that I attribute much of the decline of the true sporting owner, who finds to his cost that he cannot continue the pursuit of the Sport of Kings after the manner of a gentleman, and is thereby compelled to retire. These are my experiences, and I believe I am a reasonably observant man. In mediæval times it was the survival of the fittest; the custom is now slightly altered to the survival of the most tricky.

Comedy, and the merriment its success brought with it, in due course played itself out, and was followed by the usual varied luck attendant on racing. But my experience was beginning to make itself felt to some degree, and though I was still reckless beyond discretion, yet I was not as foolhardy as I used to be.

## CHAPTER XXI.

### 1891.

BOUT this period I frequently came into contact with the late Marquis of Ailesbury. I had known him some years previously, and in September, 1892, I married his sister, Lady Mabel Brudenell-Bruce.

About the end of the following year a cousin of mine started a Turf-commission agency in Bennet Street, St. James's, under an assumed name. It seems to have been at once presumed that the office in question was mine, and by many I appear to have been looked upon as the proprietor. As a matter of fact, I had no financial interest in the business whatever. Certainly I was often there, and assisted him in many ways, and during that time the place was a success and thrived. For reasons which I need not mention, as 1 was in no way, directly or indirectly, connected with the cause, the balance at the bank became greatly diminished, and the foundation which had been built upon began to give way. In due course the office failed. Its affairs were brought before the Committee of Tattersall's, who decided I was liable for the firm, and I paid the whole of such outstanding accounts as the Committee declared were legally owing according to their rules. My mistake was that I did not explain I was not a partner in the firm; at least, it was so contended, and I submitted, and paid. Had I been inclined to dispute their ruling, I had no opportunity of doing so, for there is but one tribunal to settle betting disputes, and from its decision there is no appeal. The Stewards of the Jockey Club affect to take no cognisance of betting unless a man is declared a defaulter, when they use their prerogative by warning him off Newmarket Heath, which carries with it a bar to all other meetings under their rules. The names of such offenders used to be published in the "Racing Calendar," but this custom, doubtless by reason of a high legal opinion, has long since ceased. It is now the practice to furnish all clerks of courses with a list of the black sheep, the publication of names in the official organ unquestionably constituting a libel. When the default is made good, after the preliminary red-tape arrangements have been gone through, the clerks of courses are informed of the rescission of the order of the Stewards. A good many names have been on this list, and their publication would astonish Society.

My wife owned and raced horses, and was fairly successful. They were originally trained by Sherwood at Epsom, but eventually they were sent to Sanders at Lambourn. I managed them, and superintended most of the work. Allsopp, the jockey, was then at the zenith of his fame, and won many races on them. Then I got into one of my periodical financial troubles, and I sought that asylum known to the temporarily embarrassed as "abroad." 1 was.

At Paris my son was born. My daughter had seen the light about a year earlier at 28, Lowndes Square. Time heals most things, but the only salve which heals the creditor is cash. It was rather a prolonged period before I could apply the healing salve.

On my return to England I found my cousin's brother had taken an office in the Haymarket. I assisted him in this, and it was not long before he had a flourishing business—a Turf one, of course—and, strange as it may appear, again I fell a victim to what I suppose I must call my laxity. It was just before the Ascot meeting that the late Captain Arthur de Vere Smith called upon me and asked if I would help Mr. Walter Shakeshaft by advancing him a sum of money to assist him carrying on his business as a bookmaker at this meeting. I can say that I have seldom, if ever, refused a friend, or even an acquaintance, when it has been in my power to help him over a stile. Captain de Vere Smith was the former, and Shakeshaft the latter. I advanced him a hundred pounds, and on the settling day I increased this by four hundred to get him through with his account. He had won on the week, and when I asked for a settlement he advanced excuses, which I accepted without any hesitation at the time. A few weeks passed, and on a Monday Shakeshaft failed to settle his liabilities. I then ascertained the fate of my five hundred pounds. He had been paying his old debts with it. As a matter of fact, he had won, but the usual "pressing matters at home" and elsewhere formed the basis of his excuse for treating my loan in the manner he did. All this is of little interest, nor should I remark on it, except for the sequel. Again I was called before the committee at Newmarket, this time to show cause why I should not pay Shakeshaft's betting debts. I explained my position, which the committee held constituted a guarantee, and I was ordered by them to pay the whole of this man's bets that were then outstanding, as from Ascot. That they arrived at their judgment reluctantly was demonstrated by the rider they added to their decision, which was to the effect that they felt I had been treated very unjustly, and that the creditors should express their sympathy with my position in the matter by not claiming more than 10s. in the £ from me. They unanimously consented, not one claiming more than half. I much appreciated their spirit. Nevertheless, though I uphold and admire the Committee of the Newmarket Subscription Rooms, with every respect I take this opportunity of dissenting from their judgment in this particular case. Had Shakeshaft won any monies, large or small, could I have called upon him to pay me a share of them? No. Furthermore, all partnerships in betting have to be registered before they are recognised. No such contract was entered in between Shakeshaft and myself. I merely advanced him in two sums an aggregate of £500, and a very bad turn I did myself, for apart from losing it, I had to pay a large amount for the privilege!

Things had taken a turn for the better with me. I had written, and Downey and Co. had published, a book called "A Generation," which ran into 480 pages. Rather a tall order for a maiden effort, but over 7.000 copies were sold, including a Colonial edition, a large number finding their way to Australia. It was fairly well reviewed, but the story was a complex one, and it is a marvel to me, in these days of sing-song, sketchy plays, how so voluminous and heavy a work ever found its way into public favour in any degree at all. I often wonder how, in the midst of racing, I ever possessed the patience to complete it; but, as a rule, when I take a thing in hand I do so resolutely, and am not the kind of man to leave anything in a half-finished state. I remember I put the first cheque I received on account from the publisher on Odour, who won at Kempton at 10 to 1, and by estimating the result on these lines writing should be a profitable pastime! But there are Odours and odours!

So time passed on. My two children were growing up, and being naturally fond of youngsters, it is only reasonable that I became devoted to my own. They have been a great source of consolation to me, more so than any words of mine can express, and no matter what I may have lost or gone through, I believe my affection for them has helped me to succeed, at a time when perhaps many men might have sunk.

## CHAPTER XXII.

### THE IMPERIAL YEOMANRY.

 ROM the day I returned from abroad, I on several occasions made headway only to fall back again, like the climber of a greasy pole at a regatta. Bad jockeyship, so often put down to bad luck, an unequal start—something always happened, and 1 could not bring off that final coup to completely clear away everything in front of me. True, I jogged merrily along, and managed to enjoy life. The man who does not embrace the latter opportunity in this world will surely some day have to answer to Providence. Yes; and no matter how greasy the pole of life may be.

It was not until November, 1899, that things once again took a decisively favourable turn. and got me out of the " ups and downs." I had owned and run a few jumpers, and Merry Mood and Shaker had won a race or so. In a quiet way this was very wholesome, and did not attract that notice which subsequent events were fated to do. It was the last week of racing under Jockey Club Rules, and there were the usual three days each at Warwick and Manchester, whilst Folkestone had been granted two, namely, the Tuesday and Wednesday. Whenever the chance has arisen of uniting pleasant surroundings with racing I have always tried to avail myself of the combination ; hence I chose a sojourn to Folkestone in preference to Warwick. I wish to make no invidious distinction between the two

places, but the Southern town is on the coast—in itself always
an attraction.

I started the week well, and though the bookmakers were
not present in full strength at Folkestone, I succeeded in what
in racing parlance is termed "packing up a parcel." I had
backed the first two winners; and, planking down the greater
portion of my winnings on Sun Bonnet (then a two-year-old), I
landed a nice stake. Indeed, I can say that during the whole
week I never looked back. At Manchester, on the first day of
the meeting, I found myself launching out, and bought that
good little horse Crarae for 560 guineas, after he had won his
maiden race there. Charles Morton, who then trained for me,
was not particularly taken with the colt, chiefly owing to his
size. But Morton never was an optimist; there is no better
nor more patient trainer in England than the little man at
Letcombe Regis (Wantage); but he is the worst of the whole
of his brother equine magicians in extending encouragement
to his patrons on the day of the race, and the earlier confidence
of winning, which he very rightly may have expressed, appears
slowly to evaporate as the day of battle approaches. This
may be the outcome of over-anxiety, or what not; one thing
I quickly discovered—that Morton's early opinions were to be
respected and his final ones rejected.

I completed my successes by backing Proclamation for the
big handicap of the meeting, and how the winner was ever
allowed to start at the very long odds of 25 to 1 with that
genius Sloan on his back, I have never been able to comprehend. Proclamation had recently succeeded in landing the
Derby Cup, with any kind of lad on his back; the same boy
who had, a week or so before, thrown away the Liverpool Cup
on him. Now with Sloan up, granted with several more pounds
also, he started comparatively unbacked. The two results—
the Derby Cup and the Manchester November Handicap—
cannot better demonstrate the enormous importance that there
is to be attached to jockeyship. In the former race Proclamation, ridden by Wetherell, beat Invincible II. (1½ miles) by a

neck, with 16lb in the former's favour ; eight days later Proclamation, with Sloan up, again beat Invincible II. (1¾ miles) by a neck, but was this time conceding 2lb, *a difference of 1st 4lb!*

On each occasion Madden rode the neck loser. Here is an instance where jockeyship has to account for a difference of 18lb.

Just that last week of the season sent me into winter quarters at Toddington Park, where I there lived with my children, with an assurance that I could face the most strenuous of winters. Yes, I had "packed up a parcel." It was common knowledge. I soon learnt this by the number of letters I received asking me to throw some of my cargo overboard. I did, and I am in a position to-day to say that a great deal of it sank!

Christmas came, and faded into the New Year of 1900. It was at this epoch that the Boer war assumed a most serious, not to say alarming, aspect. Volunteers were called for. The cablegrams from the front, published in the daily papers, caused consternation throughout the land, and it was felt that someone had blundered. That loyalty to Queen and country which has ever been dominant in all British breasts spontaneously answered to the call of duty. Among the earliest volunteers was myself. As my readers are aware, I had already seen active service in South Africa, and understood Afrikander, Dutch, and Kaffir. Sending my name in to the headquarters of the Yeomanry, I was one of the very first passed by the War Office. My previous service was doubtless the reason for this. I then had an interview with Lord Valentia at the temporary offices of the Yeomanry in Suffolk Street, Pall Mall, and it was arranged that I should see Lord Chesham, the officer commanding the district of South Bedfordshire, and obtain his consent to raise a corps of Imperial Yeomanry. This I did at the barracks at Buckingham, and my interview with Lord Chesham closed by his giving me a letter to Lord Cowper, the Lord Lieutenant of Bedfordshire, whose consent I had to obtain in the first instance. In this letter Lord Chesham recommended my proposal to Lord Cowper—indeed, he suggested my taking over the barracks at Buckingham as soon as they were vacated by the Yeomanry then ready for embarkation, under his command. If ever a man had his country's interests at heart, that man was Lord Chesham. The main object alone—victory—was uppermost in him. Losing no time, I proceeded forthwith to Panshanger, Lord Cowper's seat in Hertfordshire, in company with Mr. Montagu Sweet. Mr. Sweet I knew in Australia. He is an excellent all-round man ; and when I say he was the active secretary of the Melbourne Athletic Club, one of the best institutions of its kind in the world, I have said sufficient.

His Lordship received us with that charming courtesy which marks a fast declining era, and after kindly asking us to dinner we discussed the object of our visit. Not only did he, as Lord-Lieutenant of the County, grant his permission for me to raise a corps of Imperial Yeomanry, but he supplemented this by promising a donation of £300 towards the expenses of its formation, &c. He had already given a large subscription to the Bedfordshire Yeomanry, raised by Lord Alwyne Compton, a relative. The following is a copy of the letter written by Earl Cowper to the Mayor of Luton :—

> Dear Sir,—I have seen Mr. Sievier, and cordially approve of his scheme of raising a mounted infantry corps for South Beds. I sincerely hope he will be successful.—
> Yours truly,                                  (Signed) COWPER.
> Panshanger, Hertford, January 10, 1900.

The Mayor of Luton placed the Council Chamber in the Town Hall at my disposal, and with the assistance of Mr. Montagu Sweet and Captain McGee I proceeded to form a corps. It was hard work. Volunteers poured in, but a large percentage, certainly 70 per cent., failed to pass the examination I set them. I had each man on horseback and at the butts before I sent him to pass the doctor. A week's work at

recruiting is no sinecure. I had raised about £1,000 in
subscriptions during this period, and I received support from
all classes all over the county. From time to time I had
occasionally reported progress both to Lord Chesham and at
headquarters. I had collected 170 good, sound recruits, many
of whom had served in Her Majesty's Army, some on active
service. A better lot of men I could never hope to get together
for the business in front of us.

Having completed my establishment much sooner than
had been anticipated—but I had worked day and night—I
addressed the following letter to the Headquarters of Imperial
Yeomanry, then removed to St. James's Square:—

URGENT.

To the Committee, Imperial Yeomanry,

Gentlemen.—I have the honour to report that as the
result of the public meeting held in South Bedfordshire,
when it was unanimously agreed that I should obtain
permission to raise a Company in the County, upon the
advice of Lord Valentia I attended Lord Chesham at
Buckingham, where I received his written consent. I
then saw Earl Cowper, the Lord-Lieutenant, who cordially
consented, supplementing this with a voluntary subscription of £300 towards the local Fund. I proceeded to the
Headquarter Staff, where I saw Lord Valentia, and gave
him Lord Chesham's authority, personally, after which
he told me to proceed, and that I was under Lord
Chesham's orders, Bedfordshire being attached to the
Buckingham Hussars. I then proceeded to carry out
those instructions, with the result that I have a full Company of Volunteers from the County, whom I subjected
to a riding test with the assistance of Captain McGee,
late riding master 17th Lancers, before I entered their
names upon the enrolment sheets. This meant a refusal
of 70 per cent. Based on my previous experiences of
South Africa, I venture to assume that the men selected

are of the order required. I saw Lord Chesham at Buckingham yesterday, and he expressed regret that he had
no barrack accommodation at present, nor had he any
clerical staff, and referred me to Captain Bagot, who, he
said, would give me instructions. The men have been
waiting to be attested, and I feel sure the Committee will
give this their prompt consideration.—I am, Gentlemen,
your obedient servant,                    R. S. SIEVIER.

Toddington Park, Bedfordshire, January 16, 1900.

To this I received an indefinite reply, one which did not
fall in with my views, for the only consideration I had in view
was to get to the field of operation with as little delay as
possible. I immediately presented myself at headquarters.
To avoid causing pain I refrain from mentioning any names,
but that some members of the committee had suddenly become
hostile to me at once made itself apparent. The first difficulty
raised was whether I would object to an officer being placed
above me. Notwithstanding the active service I had seen,
my knowledge of the country and the languages, I immediately
consented, my object in raising a corps being to get out there
and do something; I was not seeking mere kudos. I felt I
could accomplish what I had undertaken. I had done it all
before, and now, as an older man with more experience,
I felt I was better able to do it.

My acceptance of the suggestion of a superior officer being
put over me gave the committee occasion to deliberate, and
I returned to Bedfordshire. I still could not get any definite
reply from them. Petty obstacles continued to be put in my
way, and on my application for attestation papers, I was
informed that "they had all been used." This brought a
second letter from me couched in terms that demanded a
straightforward answer. But even this was not replied to. I
had long before this satisfied myself that "influence" had
been at work; the country was a secondary consideration.
I was a man as fit as most men to take the field. I feel I

should have done my duty until a piece of lead stopped me. My men were without barrack accommodation; they, too, were clamouring to start for the front. I had no help for it. I had done my utmost.

IN THE QUEEN'S NAME I DISBANDED THEM AT LUTON.

After this event, which caused no little excitement in the country, I received the following telegram :

> To SIEVIER, Toddington Park, Bedfordshire.
> Committee are unable to avail themselves of your personal services. Men anxious to enlist in Imperial Yeomanry must do so through Colonels of Yeomanry Regiments.—(Signed) VALENTIA.

The whole of the daily papers, without exception, reported the matter. There was not a solitary journal which cast the least blame upon me for the part I had taken ; on the contrary, their articles were headed by such lines as "Strangled by Red Tape," "Somebody's Blunder," "Yeomanry Bungling," and severely condemned the conduct to which I had been subjected. Those responsible for this did not, nor could they, make any answer or tender any explanation. The whole cause was the petty spite of one man, a man whose name is found in the pages of the peerage, and had he not appeared on the scene I should have once again been fighting for my Queen and Country—in that event I should never have owned Sceptre.

As soon as I had disbanded the South Bedfordshire corps of Imperial Yeomanry, I advised them at once to enlist in some other troop, but I regret to say that I fear they were heartily sick of the unpatriotic treatment to which I had been subjected, and they expressed their resentment by remaining at home. The subscriptions which I had raised, and which were more than sufficient to cover the expense of

13

equipping my men, horses excepted, were returned to the generous donors. To say that I felt hurt would not adequately describe my feelings, for, apart from any other service I might have succeeded in rendering, I could have turned my attention to single-handed scouting. I had not failed in this respect in a previous campaign in the same country. But whatever disappointment I suffered, Providence or fate, perhaps good luck, possibly judgment. amply rewarded me, and during the year of 1900 I won what most people would call a fortune. In fact, 1900 was my most successful year of speculation on the Turf!

Here, then, I leave the Yeomanry and those responsible for its very numerous blunders and scandals, recently unfortunately revived by the publication of the result of the long and tedious Government inquiry into things in general connected with the Boer War.

## CHAPTER XXIII.

### SOME BIG BETS.

Y mother had been ordered to the Riviera, and there, with her and my children. I spent the tail of the winter.

Prior to my departure I had been to New-market, and the way Sir Geoffrey went in his work left upon me one of those impressions to which I have referred in previous chapters. He was engaged in the Lincolnshire Handicap with 8st 6lb, and after making such inquiries as I deemed advisable, I backed him to win me a very fair stake—several thousands. I did not hurry to return from abroad, but extended my holiday, and I made it no secret that I thought Sir Geoffrey would win the first important handicap of the season, and I have reason to believe I did more than one good turn under these circumstances to several of my friends and acquaintances. In due course I left Cap Martin, where I had been staying, and arrived at Dover on the day the Lincolnshire Handicap was run, and it was indeed a very satisfactory welcome to open the telegram which announced Sir Geoffrey as the winner of the race.

I attended the Liverpool Meeting of the same week, and by the aid of Osbech, who won the Liverpool Spring Cup, and one or two minor races, I increased my Sir Geoffrey winnings to a substantial sum, about £9,000. Northampton and a few other small meetings intervened, and I won

different amounts every week. not large, but totalling up to
a pleasant figure, my biggest win being over Mr. George
Cottrill's Lackford in the Doveridge Handicap Plate at Derby.
Then came Newmarket, and taking 1,000 to 100 about Gramcrip for a selling race, I bought him after his success for
200 guineas, and he won me a nice race later on, apart from
being an excellent trial horse at home. And so my luck
continued until the Epsom Spring Meeting came round. In
the Great Metropolitan Stakes I backed King's Messenger
to win me a good stake. Wednesday was the day of the
City and Suburban, and two candidates, both of whom had
held prominent places in the betting returns from the time the
market on the race was first started, were both trained by
Brewer, who till lately had Mr. Henning's horses at Newmarket. The names of the two horses were The Grafter and
Syerla ; the former belonged to Mr. G. Clark, in partnership,
I believe, with Mr. Robinson, and the latter to Mr. Humphrey
Oxenham, the well-known New South Wales bookmaker. I
had had a tip for both horses, and one appeared to me almost
as reliable as the other, so I determined to see them gallop
myself. I therefore went to Epsom overnight, and going
on the Downs unknown to anybody, I waited till Brewer
came along with the few horses he then had in training. On
this particular day he sent them together about six furlongs,
and I was immediately convinced in my own mind that The
Grafter was the superior of the two. That day I backed him
for a few thousands. The two horses were chopped about
in the market, and changed places daily, almost hourly, Each
had his supporters, who were equally sanguine that their
choice would win. On the day of the race I scanned the two
over in the paddock. Syerla was a nice natty sort, but The
Grafter, though of huge proportions, which have been not
incorrectly described as " camel-like," was, if one picked him
to pieces, a very fine horse indeed. He had those enormous
feet characteristic of the Waler, so abnormally large that,
except with those who had had considerable experience of

the Australian thoroughbred, they would not create a favourable impression. Again, he was "as long as a ship," and his
height gave him the appearance of having considerable daylight underneath him. He had. But he was symmetrically
formed, so far as very big horses ever are to the eye. He
possessed any quantity of bone, and as an Australian bred
one, pleased me. I had already backed him for a fair sum
of money outright, and had instructed a commissioner to
support him on my behalf in London prior to my going to
Epsom. On returning to Tattersall's Ring from the paddock,
I further supported him for large sums, Mr. Goodson laying
me in one hand the odds to lose him £5,000. From my box,
which 1 had regularly taken for years, I watched the race.
The field ran reasonably together, and Morny Cannon, who
rode The Grafter, came down the hill towards Tattenham
Corner holding a very nice position in the middle. Rounding
the bend for home he came up on the outside, and the race
was over. The Grafter won comfortably, though Halsey on
Innocence gave me the impression that he came a little late
through a piece of bad luck which happened to him in the
straight. On this race I won over £33,000. I am ready to
admit that I accepted this as a good set-off against not going
out for the Imperial Yeomanry!

The next meeting I attended was the Guineas week at
Newmarket. Here I backed Diamond Jubilee to win me
about £5,000, but in the following race I lost between £3,000
and £4,000 of this, fielding against a two-year-old, Good
Morning, the property of Captain Greer, trained by Sam
Darling. He beat Handspike over the Rous Course by a
neck, but by the aid of Toddington, by Melton—Minera, and
Winifreda, the winner of the One Thousand Guineas, I
finished up that week by adding some £20,000 to my winnings.
I had one or two horses running at Chester the following
week, and attended the meeting. Here my good luck continued, and with Crarae I won the Earl of Chester's Welter
Handicap, his starting-price being returned at 5 to 2 against.

I had £4,000 on him. I had also had a good win over Rough-side, the winner of the Chester Cup, ridden by Sloan, and, finishing the week at Kempton Park, I won a selling race there with Gramcrip, who beat the favourite by a neck, starting at 3 to 1. I won £7,000 on the race, and he was afterwards sold to Mr. W. Brown for 250 guineas, and, though never winning again in England, won several races in Belgium. Charles Morton was then training for me, and that excellent jockey, Sam Loates, riding. A better judge of a race or a trial than the latter I have never met in the whole of my experience, and whereas the majority of jockeys are too frequently over-confident, Sam Loates never expressed an opinion to me with regard to any of my horses which was not actually fulfilled in the race. It is doubtless this happy faculty which has helped him to succeed in his business as a trainer.

Toddington had made such a great impression upon me by the style in which he won the May Plate at Newmarket that I immediately opened up negotiations with Mr. Musker through the agency of Mr. T. Vigors ("Ashplant" of the "Sportsman"), and I instructed him to inquire at what price Mr. Musker would sell. He came back with the answer, 10,000 guineas. "He's mine," was my reply, and drawing a cheque for that amount, we made an appointment that evening to see Mr. Musker after racing, and the deal was then and there completed.

That Toddington was the best two-year-old seen for some time, and also of his year, I had little doubt, and the opinion I formed of him he thoroughly sustained in the trial I set him before running him in the Woodcote Stakes at Epsom. Overnight Morton and I discussed the weights, and we ultimately agreed that Crarae, a recent winner at Chester, should carry 9st 3lb, and Toddington 9st. This was in the middle of May. The pair jumped off together, Sam Loates riding the two-year-old. I may mention that Crarae, as he subsequently proved to be, was a very fast horse, but the youngster stuck to him from the moment they first struck the ground. By the side of the gallop there were some chains, and Sam Loates, not being fully acquainted with the Downs, rather hung towards them, and had to pull out of their way at a critical moment, which caused Toddington to lose at least a length or so. On they came neck and neck, and though the last 200 yards of the gallop were well on the collar, Toddington looked as if he would just do it, but the older horse, lasting the longer, finished a bare neck to the good. This was a most meritorious performance, without taking into consideration the fact that Toddington did not go quite the nearest way. One thing, we were all quite satisfied that the Woodcote was as good as over.

En passant, I cannot refrain from mentioning that at the following Newmarket Meeting I bid for a filly by the name of Kaffir Queen, who had just won a selling plate, and was knocked down to me for 1,100 guineas. After the auction I tendered my cheque for this amount, which, if for no other reason than the fact of having paid 10,000 guineas for Toddington, I did not for a moment think would be refused; but the late Mr. Weatherby would not accept the draft on my bankers, nor would he give an order for the delivery of Kaffir Queen to me. Never before had I been faced with a refusal of my cheque on any racecourse or by any official the world throughout. I quickly cleared up the difficulty by producing three £500 notes, and on asking Mr. Weatherby for the change the boot was on the other leg. He offered to give me a cheque for the difference, and assuming his attitude towards me, I declined to accept it; but I extended to him some leniency by saying that " he could give me the change any time he liked when it was convenient." This I received the following day; but why every kind of petty obstacle, emanating from certain quarters, was always put in my way I have never been able to comprehend.

It was at this meeting that Diamond Jubilee was very nearly beaten by Chevening in the Newmarket Stakes, when he only won by a head over a distance of 1 mile and 2 furlongs. each carrying 9st. I had formed a very high opinion of His Majesty's horse, and I watched every inch of the race. Sloan on Chevening rode one of those extraordinary, inexplicable races which have been so frequently associated with his success. After the race there were many ready to decry the merits of Diamond Jubilee, but I was convinced that Chevening would never get so near him again. The result of the race gave me a better opportunity of backing the King's horse for the Derby, and I supported him well whenever the top odds were on offer, and amongst other bets I booked 14,000 to 8,000 and 12,000 to 8,000. Though I was a good winner at this meeting, I again lost a large sum by fielding against Good Morning, the winner of the Bedford Two-Year-Old Stakes.

At this time I was playing a good deal of cricket, and had laid down an excellent pitch at Toddington, and had supported the game throughout the county of Bedford. I was the means of resuscitating the county club, which had long ceased to exist. I arranged some very good matches, which gave a zest to the game throughout the countryside, and cricket flourished to a much greater extent than it had ever done before in South Bedfordshire. Dr. W. G. Grace kindly came down, and with W. L. Murdoch (ex-captain of the Australians), A. O. Jones (captain of Notts), Charlie Robson (captain of Hants), Lockwood, Hayward, poor old Davenport (who has, alas! lost his wicket in this life), poor Bill Yardley ("Bill of the Play" of the "Sporting Times"), who made the record highest score for 'Varsity matches when he played for Cambridge, Atfield, "Little" White of Herts, and a host of others, helped to give the game a new life in Bedfordshire.

The many matches I played, and the active part I took in cricket, caused me to miss several race meetings, which I should otherwise have attended, and it was not until the Epsom Derby Meeting that I again found myself on a race-course. Here I won the Ashtead Plate with Crarae, which enhanced Toddington's trial to no small degree, for Orris Root, who finished second, ridden by Sloan, subsequently won many races for Mr. George Cottrill. As an instance of the great decrease there is in betting to-day as compared with that of only five years ago, I had £7,500 on Crarae, and my money averaged over 2 to 1, yet he started at 7 to 4 against. Then Toddington cantered away with the Woodcote Stakes, which he won by four lengths, and, with odds varying between 5 to 2 and 3 to 1 laid on him, I won £4,000 on the race.

Fate had not yet once frowned on me, and the larger sum I had on a horse the easier he generally won. The following day was the Derby, and I played up no small amount of my winnings, in spite of the previous bets which I had booked in favour of Diamond Jubilee. The history of the race is common knowledge. The King's horse won cleverly by half a length, and though the excitement did not reach that pitch which it had done in Persimmon's year, it was no less a sight to be remembered. The following day (Thursday) came the Great Surrey Foal Stakes, and that bogey to me, Good Morning, started favourite at evens for this event. Though I had lost many thousands by laying against him previously, I did not attempt to retrieve my fortunes, but again opposed him, though to a much smaller amount. In this race he was left at the post. Immediately after the event there were those ever ready to assume that I "knew something." The air was rife with all sorts of rumours, and I believe—I'm speaking entirely from memory—that Rickaby, the rider of Good Morning, requested the Stewards to hold an enquiry. That he was exonerated from any blame was demonstrated by his subsequently riding Champ de Mars in the Epsom Cup on the same day. Personally, I have always regretted that I did not ask the Stewards to kindly hold an enquiry with regard to myself, but later in the year an opportunity afforded itself to me of being able to show the Stewards my book with regard to the other races Good Morning had run in, and as it proved conclusively that I had lost, as I have already stated, many thousands of pounds by laying against this horse previously, and only won some £1,500 when he was beaten, any explanation from me was quite unnecessary.  This incident goes to show how rife scandal is at times on the Turf, with no foundation whatever to support it.  As the financial result of this meeting I won over £53,000 on the week.

It was at this meeting that the late Mr. Charles Greenwood asked me to run Toddington on the Saturday at Kempton Park.  Being a great believer in running horses in public, I consented.  The horse did not canter to the post with that freedom I had expected, but that anything was wrong with him I did not for an instant imagine.  I had already some £5,000 on him, and he won only by a neck from Royal River, conceding him 7lb.  Among the beaten lot was Volodyovski, who finished fourth with 8st 12lb.  In this race I succeeded, with my win in the Woodcote, in getting back my purchase money, but I would willingly have lost as much as I had won sooner than Toddington should have broken down, as he did through breaking a small bone in the near hind pastern. After calling in more than one veterinary surgeon, I tele graphed to Mr. Peard, of Dublin, and he came over, and was the first to locate the injury.  This necessitated Toddington remaining in the stable for some six weeks, and not being able to train him for a considerable time, he developed roaring, and, being a big horse—he stood over 16 hands 2½— this infirmity increased as time went on.  He never won another race in England, and Mr. W. Allison, of the International Horse Agency and Exchange, finding me a customer for him in America, I sold him to go there as a stallion.  That he was a most brilliant horse, and a game 'un into the bargain, his success at Kempton under such difficulties proves beyond doubt ; while his trial with Crarae so early in May is one of the best I can recall.  That he would have won the Derby the following year there can be no manner of doubt had all gone well with him.  But such is the fortune of racing.

## CHAPTER XXIV.

### THE PURCHASE OF SCEPTRE AND OTHERS.

HE following article, which I contributed to the " Badminton Magazine " in January, 1903, relates to my purchase of Sceptre, whose doings will be fully referred to later on : —" When I first picked up the catalogue announcing the sale of the late Duke of Westminster's yearlings in 1900, a pang of regret took hold of me, and I sat feeling that a central, if not the central, pillar of the Turf had been removed, hoping, but with little confidence, that it would be befittingly replaced. My hopes have not been fulfilled, which rather goes in praise of the late Duke than against his survivors ; for he stood out alone, a unique ideal of a successful scientific breeder of horses, and it may take a generation or even more before the Turf is graced by his like again. During this period of thought I was perusing Messrs. Tattersall's announcement. I felt that the chance of perhaps a lifetime presented itself to a man devoted to the horse and the sport, and that, had I inherited Bond Street, or even one side of it, or to be more modern, were I a nouveau riche company promoter, or ' something in the City,' I would go to the sale ring and buy at any price, not one lot, but the whole lot. Stern reflection convinced me that

I had none of the above redeeming qualifications—and they redeem one from many things unconnected with horses. So I drew a cheque for £20,000 and took the notes with me to Newmarket.

"The following morning I spent several hours inspecting the Eaton yearlings in the company of my late trainer, Charles Morton, and Mr. Peard, the celebrated veterinary surgeon from Ireland ; and let me here thank them both equally for the pains they took on my behalf.

"That evening I saw Mr. Somerville Tattersall at his office at the Rutland Arms ; and explaining that I had seldom bought anything at auction, and that, in a business sense, I was comparatively unknown to him, I produced the twenty thousand pound bank notes, asking him to take them as a security, for I thought I might be a likely bidder the following day. It was after banking hours, and Mr. Tattersall politely suggested that my proposal was quite unnecessary ; but I waived this gracious remark and handed over the £20,000 cash, which I have always felt Mr. Tattersall took with some timidity, as he observed he had no safe place wherein to deposit it.

"The ringside was crowded with perhaps the most representative collection of sportsmen that has ever been gathered together at one time under the auspices of the most famous of auctioneers, and I took up a little corner to myself immediately under the rostrum. The second lot brought in was a chestnut colt by Orme, out of Console. This I secured for 700 guineas, when a sudden feeling of fear took hold of me as I realised that I must be careful and resist temptation, reserving myself, or rather my purse, for the filly by Persimmon out of Ornament. Mr. Peard's characteristic enthusiasm must not, I felt, lead me away, for the filly was last but one on the catalogue ! The bay colt by Orme, out of Gantlet, since known as the Duke of Westminster, was greatly fancied by Charles Morton, and, sharing his opinion, I bought him for 5,600 guineas. I made no bid for the brother to Flying Fox, but ventured an attempt for the colt by Orme, out of Kissing Cup, since known as Cupbearer, who in my humble judgment was one of the best-looking yearlings that ever entered the sale ring, except for one characteristic which forcibly struck me—he gave me the impression that he knew 'too much,' and my trainer agreed that he might be 'tricky.' John Porter bought him for 9,000 guineas for the Duke of Westminster, and, as I anticipated, he turned out a rogue. At last the filly since known under the name of Sceptre was led in. There she stood, what I can only describe as a mass of perfection, even to the merest tyro or a captious critic. Such a mare as perhaps for many years would not be offered for sale again, or could be matched the world throughout, sired by the King's horse, Persimmon, the dam a full sister to the mighty Ormonde, she walked round the ring comprised of millionaires—and others—ready to become the property of the man who would bid most for her ; and I felt I was that man. The value of money was lost in admiration ; any commercial view of the situation never entered my mind ; I fell in love with her! Her prospective qualities, either on the Turf or for the stud, appeared flawless. If one could possibly find the semblance of a blemish it was her inclination to be a little straight in front. She was at once a racehorse and a machine. A bold Persimmon head, his hocks and characteristics, she was her sire all over to look at in all but sex.

"I opened the bidding at 5,000 guineas, to which John Porter added 100. 'Six thousand' from me, 'One hundred' from Porter, 'eight, nine,' and, bidding 900 guineas each time, at ten thousand she was knocked down to me. I was dubbed by some 'an ass,' by the majority as 'mad,' while a few kindly referred to the proverb of 'A fool and his money.' I should have gone much higher, for I had determined that Sceptre should be mine."

Of all who were present, only two bid for Sceptre, John Porter and I, and though she fetched the record price of 10,000 guineas, exceeding by 4,000 guineas that previously given for any other yearling, the bidding for her was quicker and of less duration than that for any other animal sold that day. I then bought the only other filly offered, by Trenton–Sandiway, for 5,500 guineas.

Two days earlier I had bought the brood mare St. Ilma, by St. Simon, with a bay filly-foal by Crafton at foot, and covered by Minting, for 1,300 guineas; also Chimera, by Sheen, with a brown colt by St. Angelo at foot, now known as Thunderbolt, a most excellent performer, for 860 guineas. She was covered by Sainfoin. Both these mares had belonged to Mr. J. A. Miller, and they turned out good bargains, as I afterwards sold St. Ilma to Mr. Croker for 1,500 guineas, I retaining the produce, and for Chimera I received £2,000 from Mr. W. Bass, and £2,000 for Elston—one of her sons by Donovan—and £1,000 for Thunderbolt. These deals showed a profit of 4,140 guineas, with her Sainfoin filly thrown in.

At the following July Meeting I again attended the sales, but I saw nothing which took my fancy except a filly by Persimmon—Ornis, bred by Captain A. Greville, which I bought for 1,500 guineas, and this I called Egg Plum. She never ran in my colours, as I sold her in the spring of the following year; but as I have determined to deal with my different transactions in succession as they happened, I shall have cause to refer to her again.

Apart from the great opportunity of being able to buy the Eaton blood, the fact that the sale of these yearlings took place in July was greatly in the purchaser's favour. As a rule, not that it was so in regard to the late Duke's yearlings, the breeder subjects his produce to a process which is styled "getting them up for sale." This in truth means preparing to help to break them down. Doncaster excels in this respect, and taking into consideration the lateness of the year when these sales take place, it is a pity, and I express my opinion very mildly, that breeders, or their stud grooms, should get their bloodstock up rather for the show than the sale ring. It is unfair to those who want to buy, hard on the trainer who is expected to deliver them fit at the post, and even visits the

vendor himself, for many horses—yes, pretty well the majority
—are ruined by being over " done," and never see a racecourse
in consequence. The good reputation of a stud farm must,
in the first instance, be founded on the blood, and after that by
results. How many good yearlings have been rendered practically useless by being locked in the stable and fattened for
sale, like a prize pig being got ready for the Cattle Show. The
month of September leaves little or no time for the buyer
to turn his purchases out and let them, by the aid of nature,
return to their normal selves. Nearly all the Doncaster
yearlings go straight into the hands of the trainer. Instead
of an animal in a natural hard condition, fresh from the
paddock, he has a soft, heavy youngster to take home. He
is forced to get the fat off at the expense of its legs. Legs in
a racehorse are everything. The work they have to stand
is more than many realise, and the fact that horses break
down is, apart from any faulty conformation, more often due
to the pace they go than anything else. Bad horses do not
often break down, for the simple reason that they cannot go
fast enough. Therefore it would be better for all concerned
if it were made a practice that yearlings should be delivered
in the ring in their natural condition, as that great breeder,
Sir Tatton Sykes, sends up his stock annually.

At the Doncaster Sales of 1900, after having launched out
at those of the July week, I need hardly remark that I was
sought after by all those who had horses figuring in the catalogue. Had I listened and believed all I heard it would be
reasonable to assume that I should have bought the lot! As
a matter of fact I purchased hardly any. Mr. Kennedy, of the
Straffan Stud, co. Kildare, sends up his yearlings in natural
condition, and after Doochary, by Milford—Monday, had
passed out of the ring without a bid being made for him, I
bought him privately for £150. He turned out a real good
two-year-old the following year, and won some valuable stakes.
With the exception of two others, for which I gave respectively
100 and 45 guineas—the cheaper one winning a race—I did not

increase my stable of horses. It might be worth consideration whether it would not be advisable to hold a yearling sale on a much larger scale in July annually at Newmarket, and thereby ease those held at Doncaster. The Cobham Stud very sensibly sell during this month.

I had not betted so largely as before, nor had I attended the race meetings so persistently. I won an ordinary handicap at Kempton Park with Crarae; certainly he brought home something like £5.000 along with the prize, but the added money in this country is so small that an owner is compelled to make up for this deficiency somehow!

Then I found myself at Newmarket again, where I bought Leonid for 400 guineas, Madame Rachel for 710, and the best two-year-old I ever owned, Lavengro, for 700. How good this colt was in his early career I cannot say, for he won all his trials and his races with such ease that it was impossible to estimate what he had in hand. But I shall give the trials and the weights carried by all these horses as I progress.

At the Newmarket July Meeting I had bought the filly St. Louvaine, now the dam of Lovania, out of a selling race. She showed good form, and except that she had very shelly feet would have taken a position in racing high up in the second class standard. This particular season was a dry one, and provided little opportunity for giving her the necessary work, and on running her at Sandown she flinched at the hard going, and on account of this only finished second. Under the circumstances, I had to wait for the rain, and this arriving, Morton was able to give her a few gallops to put her straight, for she was due to run in the Vauxhall Selling Plate at Kempton on October 6. The book said she could not lose this race, and being confident that she would be a strong favourite, I got as much money on her as I could at starting price early in the day. So far from making this a starting-price coup, I saw some friends who I knew were in a position to get £500 each way on a horse, and asked them, without any secret, to do this for me. They all agreed, and I also interviewed four commission agents, not telling them my previous arrangements, and they also each agreed to put me £500 each way on St. Louvaine, so I found myself with £3,500 each way on the filly, and everybody was aware of the bets I had long before the race. Nothing can better demonstrate the susceptibilities of the racing man than what happened.

When I saw Morton in the paddock he advised me not to run the filly, his reason being that she had got loose from her boy and galloped a mile and a half over the Downs the day previously. I gave instructions that the filly should be brought into the paddock, and I would then decide whether she was to run or not. In due course she arrived. St. Louvaine was on her toes, looking fresh and well, and was fly-jumping all over the place. She did not give me the impression that her canter across the Downs had in any way upset her, and I concluded that I would run her. Her trainer, Morton, would not have a penny on her, and the story of her having got loose soon became common knowledge. The fact that I had so much money on her was treated as nothing, and though she opened favourite at 2 to 1, she was quickly supplanted by Irish Lass, the mount of L. Reiff, and drifted out until at flag-fall her price was 7 to 2 against. Ridden by Sam Loates, she won in a canter by a length and a half, and I was very fortunate in being able to buy her in for 280 guineas. This only shows what small things will prejudice backers of horses against carrying out their previous resolves. Had St. Louvaine not got loose, or had Morton kept this fact to himself, St. Louvaine would probably have started at odds on ; but, speaking of punters generally, they are as restless as grasshoppers, and will hop from one place to another without the faintest idea where they are going to land next. A rumour adverse to a horse is, generally speaking, believed without comment, whereas, no matter how straightforward the owner may be, let him state ingenuously, almost publicly, that he expects his horse to win, and though the man may not be doubted, his judgment will be severely criticised. I

14

think I can say that my horses ran reasonably up to their form, and were accepted as being triers when they carried my colours. Yet, though I told everybody I met that I considered Sceptre was a certainty for the St. Leger, the more I spread the report the longer the price she stood at in the market. This has been so with many other horses I have owned, and my experience is not unique, for almost every owner who took up a similar position on the Turf to mine has experienced the fact that the nearer the truth you are in speaking of your horses, the bigger fibber you are put down to be. On this line I must have been looked upon as Ananias.

In this same month King's Courier, by Kingston—Stylitene, winner of the Doncaster Cup, was advertised for sale "to dissolve a partnership," which to my mind stood for " a Yankee syndicate," and I bought him at public auction for 5,200 guineas. By this time I had collected what might be called a very representative stable of horses, and every morning I had somewhere between sixty and seventy thousand pounds worth of horseflesh cantering on the Downs. Before the season closed I had won a small handicap with Crarae, and St. Louvaine also secured a nursery, while Leonid, later on a trial horse of Sceptre and Duke of Westminster when two-year-olds, and Merilla concluded my successes of this year.

\*    \*    \*

During the last few seasons which I have touched upon the English Turf was infested with what I can only term an invasion of the scum of the States. Tod Sloan's remarkable success in the saddle was no doubt the attraction which, like a magnet, drew these men to our shores. Not that they were acquaintances of Tod Sloan, or that he was in any way directly responsible for their undesirable presence. About this time Lester Reiff was at the height of his success, perhaps I might say financial success, and, taking the surroundings generally, our racecourses more resembled the outside

Southern tracks of America than an English course. While they lasted, the way these Yankee adventurers played battle- dore and shuttlecock with the Ring, or, for that matter, with anybody and everybody when an opportunity arose, is marvellous to look back to. They would stand in a cluster, or, as they would themselves term it, a "bunch," until the numbers for a race were hoisted, and then would step down and back indiscriminately with every bookmaker they could get credit from, such horses as Sloan or Reiff rode. The price was no object to them! If it was even money they betted in thousands; if it was good odds against, then they would descend to hundreds. But one hundred in America is but £20 in English money, and it is possible that these individuals may have got mixed in the matter of exchange! This lasted during the period of the phenomenal successes of Sloan and Reiff. An investment on their mounts would show a profit for a considerable time. But the day of reckoning came, and after a most disastrous week, so far as figures were concerned, the American "bunch" failed to come up to time on the Monday, and taking their large gains, went their several ways, some returning to the land of "Stars and Stripes," others being dispersed over the Continent. This is another instance of the credulity, or hospitality if you will, of the racing world. Personally, I confess I took a strong dis- like to these people *en bloc*, and extended this dislike to the jockeys themselves, and I must admit that, even to this day, that prejudice still exists. Generally speaking, I am not in favour of the American jockey or his monkeyship. I in no way apply these remarks to Lucien Lyne or those who hold licenses at the present moment under Jockey Club Rules. During the American boom there were, among others, a couple of men who were received with open arms, and they were given the entrée to all the club enclosures without exception. It was not long before I came to the conclusion that they knew the chances Lester Reiff possessed of winning or losing as well as he did himself, for, apart from

backing him when he won, they often stood aloof
and did not bet at times when odds were laid on
his mount; but on these occasions he was never successful.
Being determined that I would satisfy myself in a practical
way that this was so, I resolved to endeavour to bet with
either or both of these men at such times as I deemed
necessary to attain my object. It was not long before I had
the opportunity of putting my conclusions to the test. It
was on the occasion of a race at Newmarket in which
Americus ran. On the book it looked a certainty for this
horse, but by degrees the odds demanded by the bookmakers
decreased, in my opinion always an ominous sign, more
especially when the connections in this instance are
considered. One of the two persons I am referring to entered
the club enclosure and inquired of one or two bookmakers
at the top of the rails the price of Americus. As much as
2 to 1 had been laid on this horse previously. When the
individual arrived the offers to take odds were not quite so
rare as they had been, and they now asked for odds of 6 to 4.
He refused to bet. I felt I had read the situation, and going
to the rails just where Mr. Benjamin and Messrs. Millard
stand, I said to him, "If you want to back Americus I will
bet you an even £5,000 he does not win." He half turned
towards me, but apparently on second thoughts, he walked
away, pretending he had not heard me. This in racing
colloquialism is styled "cocking a deaf 'un"; but I have
been blessed with good lungs, nor am I often at a loss for
a word, and being perhaps over-anxious to achieve my ends,
I shouted "Americus does not win for £5,000! An even
£5,000 against Americus!" until the gentleman posing as an
American plunger had walked out of sight, if not out of
hearing. I then tried to back Sonatura, the only other runner,
but I could not get on any way. Bookmakers have a peculiar
instinct! They possess an extraordinary faculty! They are
past-masters of understanding songs without words! Though
Americus is returned in "Ruff's" as having started at 6 to 5

on, anybody could have got 6 to 5 against him on the Q.T. The result of the race was that Sonatura beat Americus all ends up by four lengths, and for the first time in my memory there was a general public hooting at Newmarket. I was satisfied. My convictions were correct.

Americus was then the property of Mr. Croker, but that he was a party to these proceedings, or previously knew that the horse was unlikely to win, I do not for an instant believe. On the contrary, I am in a position to state that when this gentleman's horses were successful he was frequently not on them, while this was not generally the case when they were beaten. But the extraordinary result of the course I had adopted was that at certain dinner tables in the evening it was stated that I must be connected with the Yankees! The question was asked, "Why was I offering to bet these large sums against Americus?" Fortunately, however, for me, shortly after this episode 1 was able to dissipate these impressions. As I have always looked upon this occasion in a private rather than an official sense, I feel bound to withhold the facts which brought this opportunity about. If further evidence were needed of the correctness of my conclusions, what can be stronger than the fact that with the warning off of Lester Reiff these men returned whence they came, and have not been seen since, except on one solitary occasion, when one of them paid this country a second visit for about a fortnight's duration, and betted in infinitesimal sums compared with his previous transactions. I have referred to these matters at some length because they came into my life, and because I have always, as far as in me lies, endeavoured to uphold the traditions of the Turf.

## CHAPTER XXV.

### BOBSIE, LAVENGRO, AND OTHERS.

 HORSE that I had as much affection for as any I have owned was Bobsie, by Oxlip, out of Doctrina, bred by that enthusiastic sportsman, the late Dr. Kennard. It may almost be said that a halo of romance surrounded Bobsie. We had been practising the two-year-olds at the starting-gate at Wantage, when Mr. Edward Robson, who trains there, rode up on his hack. The horse struck me at once, and, taking a liking to him, I asked his price. Mr. Robson replied, "£120." "He is mine," I said, and, entering the house. I wrote out a cheque for him forthwith. He had a couple of formidable splints, and on this ground some "vets." would not have passed him; but I was satisfied that they in no way interfered with him, and that to all intents and purposes he was perfectly sound. Every inch a blood 'un, he was full of life, while his colour, bay with black points, showed him off favourably. As a matter of fact, I purchased him for a lady who was in want of a hack, and I had, in my opinion, not seen a better one than this for many a day. In due course he arrived in London, and the lady rode him in the Park, but he was not quite the staid animal that she required for taking exercise on in Rotten Row! On hearing this, I was covetous enough to feel a little pleased, and I had him sent down to Toddington. As far as I knew, he was a blood hack pure and simple. As such I rode

him. His manners were perfect. He gave one a good feel, and the rider at once knew he had something underneath him. 1 rode him about the estate, and, as occasion offered, popped him over a small ditch or so. One day, in the winter of 1902, I had just finished lunch, when the hounds ran across the park at full cry. The temptation was too great to remain indoors, and, making my way to the stables, I had Bobsie saddled, and it was not long before I was following in the wake of the hunt; nor was it long before I caught them up. At first picking my way, 1 soon discovered that Bobsie was one of the finest natural jumpers it has ever been my good fortune to cross, and passing the stragglers I was soon in the thick of it. The scent was breast high, and hounds were running strong. How I admired the old horse I shall never forget. I was more pleased than surprised. At the end of the day I was quite convinced I had ridden a horse that was certain to win a steeplechase. The Oakley Hunt 'Chases were shortly to come off, and I entered him for the Cup to be run for at Kimbolton. The country is a stiff one, and would serve as an example to clerks of courses of some of our suburban meetings, where the fences are gradually but surely becoming less difficult every season. Ridden by Mr. J. Dover, a farmer on the Toddington Estate, he won by a distance, and the second to him shortly afterwards secured a race in another part of the country. I came to the conclusion that my estimate of Bobsie was correct. As he had been a hack since a two-year-old, I did not subject him to a rigorous training, such as I would have given the ordinary steeplechaser, and as a result of a light preparation he won the first four steeple-chases in which he started without a loss. Following his success in winning the Oakley Hunt Cup, he won the Burwood Steeplechase at Sandown Park by a distance in a field of three, and opening at 5 to 1, I backed him down to 9 to 4, and netted a good stake. He then won the Hampton Steeple-chase at Kempton Park, starting at evens, and four days later secured the February Handicap Steeplechase at Hurst

Park, starting equal favourite with Drumcree, who, conceding him 15lb, finished third, being beaten ten lengths. Taking into consideration that Drumcree won the Grand National Steeplechase at Aintree three months later, this was an excellent performance for a hack! When the weights appeared for the National, and taking this running as a guide, I came to the conclusion that Bobsie had an excellent chance for the Cross-country Blue Riband. I had got him what I was pleased to term hack-fit, and had galloped him well enough to cause me to support him to the extent of £500 each way for the National. Early in this year he had won a steeple-chase at Kempton and a smaller event at Folkestone. At this time I was training my own horses at Shrewton, which establishment I will deal with later on. Having to go to Lincoln with Sceptre, I left Bobsie behind, with instructions as to what work he was to do. His final gallop at home was arranged for Tuesday of the Lincoln and Liverpool week, he being due to leave on the Wednesday for Aintree. My disappointment may be imagined when I received a telegram, just after Sceptre had been beaten for the Lincolnshire Handicap, stating that the boy had allowed Bobsie to get away with him, and the horse, running out of the gallop, had fallen over a heap of stones and injured himself to such an extent that it was inadvisable to send him. Such are the misfortunes which owners and trainers have to bear. I was sorry for him, for I am convinced he would have made a bold bid for victory in the Grand National of 1903.

On my return I found the old horse had a leg, but by hacking him throughout the summer I succeeded in getting him sound again. However, it was not until the January of the following year that he won another race, and this was his last success on the Turf. With 5 to 4 laid on Hidden Love, who had been winning several steeplechases in great style, Bobsie started at 3 to 1, second favourite for the Open Steeplechase at Hurst Park. I made it no secret that I thought I should just win, and after Hidden Love had made the running for over two miles, the old horse took the lead, and, clearing his fences like a stag, won amidst considerable cheering with a few pounds in hand. As a winner of an ordinary steeplechase, the reception the public gave to Bobsie went to show how popular he was; indeed, apart from a Grand National, I have never heard such hearty cheering on a racecourse under National Hunt Rules. True, I should like to have kept him, but with racehorses one's sympathies must not override common-sense, and I sold him at public auction for 500 guineas. One of the finest jumpers I have ever seen or ridden, he died in harness, for, over-jumping the water-jump at Birmingham, he fell and broke his back.

I have gone somewhat ahead so that I might deal with Bobsie straightaway, and now I must hark back to 1901. My two-year-olds, Sceptre, Duke of Westminster, Lavengro, and Doochary, together with the older horses, had all wintered well. Toddington, who, as I have already stated, became a confirmed roarer, would perhaps hardly have succeeded in winning a selling race. Leonid had just won a selling race at Lincoln, and I bought him in for 350 guineas, and early in April I discussed with Morton the advisability of trying some of the two-year-olds with Leonid, who was then five years old, as a trial horse. I was anxious to see how Sceptre and Duke of Westminster went, and the following were the weights I tried them at :—

### Five furlongs.

| | Years. | | Weight. |
|---|---|---|---|
| Leonid | 5 | | 9st |
| Sceptre | 2 | (W. Lane)... | 8st |
| Duke of Westminster | 2 | | 8st |
| Kaffir Queen | 3 | | 8st |
| St. Louvaine | 3 | | 8st |

They got off to a fair start, and about two furlongs from home Lane let out Sceptre, who was followed by Duke of West-minster, with the old 'uns riding, and she won in a hack canter by half a dozen lengths, with "The Duke" finishing two

lengths in front of Leonid, Kaffir Queen and St. Louvaine a
long way behind. That Sceptre would have beaten Leonid
at even weights both Morton and I were convinced; indeed,
if any question had arisen, it would have been, with how much
could she have presented the old horse? I then tried
Lavengro, Consort, by Orme—Console, Merilla, and Jam Jar
at the following weights:—

### Five furlongs.

| | Years. | Weight. |
|---|---|---|
| Jam Jar | 4 | 9st |
| Merilla | 3 | 8st |
| Lavengro | 2 | 8st |
| Consort | 2 | 8st |

They got off together, and Lavengro, jumping into his bridle,
won by a distance, with Jam Jar second, Merilla close up,
and Consort tailed off. Sceptre's previous gallop was striking
enough, but the way Lavengro accomplished his task from flag-
fall, and the consummate ease with which he did it, I cannot
easily express in words; even Morton could not hide his
astonishment. I also galloped a few other horses, and the
result of these trials told me two things: on the one hand that
I had some excellent horses, and on the other that I should
have a sale. I then made arrangements with Messrs.
Tattersall, and the sale took place on May 2 at Newmarket. With the exception of Sceptre, I sent all my horses
there, but the majority did not reach those reserves which I
knew they were well worth, the following being a list of those
which were sold:—

|  |  | Gs. |
|---|---|---|
| Merilla, b f by Sir Modred—Cottage Girl, 3yrs...M. Frants T. Olsen | | 100 |
| Leonid, ch g by Prism—Variety, 5yrs..........................Mr. C. Wood | | 300 |
| St. Paulus, br c by St. Florian—Polonel, 4yrs.........Lord Carnarvon | | 800 |
| Kaffir Queen, br f by Lactantius—Cheerful, 3yrs............Mr. J. Hall | | 300 |
| St. Louvaine, b f by Carnage or Wolf's Crag—St Reine, 3yrs | | |
| | Mr. W. Raphael | 1200 |
| Crarac, b c by St. Angelo—Neruda, 4yrs...............Col McCalmont | | 1150 |
| King's Courier, ch h by Kingston—Stylitene, 4yrs...Lord Ellesmere | | 5500 |
| Egg Plum, b f by Persimmon—Ormis.................Mr. A. M. Singer | | 1050 |
| Consort, ch c by Orme—Console.............................Mr. G. Faber | | 2000 |

Perhaps the greatest surprise of the sale was the price given for Consort, for I had the previous July bought him out of the late Duke of Westminster's lot for 700 guineas, and now John Porter purchased him for 2.000 guineas on behalf of Mr. George Faber. Considering I had the opportunity of trying him, not to mention the fact that I found him useless, this did not present itself to me as a bad deal. Although they fetched 12,400 guineas, not one of them won a race on the flat, with the exceptions of King's Courier and Leonid, the latter securing one or two selling races. That King's Courier was a good horse over a mile or less I am convinced, but he could not stay, even though he is recorded as the winner of the Doncaster Cup. The year that he was successful the race was run at a crawling pace, and he was never really extended. Adding to this that he had the assistance of Lester Reiff, who was then riding in tremendous form, these can be the only reasons why King's Courier was ever returned a winner of a race over a distance of two miles. Nevertheless, this victory would naturally mislead any trainer or owner into whose stable this horse went until they had got to the bottom of him. Crarae, though he had done me good service, should, in my opinion, have won races, but this he failed to do in the colours of the late Colonel Harry McCalmont. St. Louvaine cannot now be called a dear purchase to Mr. Raphael, as she is already the dam of Louvania, who was a very fair two-year-old indeed. Nevertheless, 12,400 guineas represents more value than the performances of the lots which I sold justified.

Having weeded out what in racing parlance is styled the "undesirable," I turned my attention to the campaign of 1901. Sceptre looked a good thing for the Woodcote, but previous to this I had won a race with Jam Jar at Chester, while Doochary and Lavengro pulled off a double for me on my birthday, May 30, at Manchester. The former was an unsexed son of Milford, and as a two-year-old was a real good colt. I had tried him quite top of the second class, and therefore I was not surprised when he won the John o' Gaunt Auction

Plate in a canter by five lengths on his first appearance on a
racecourse. Although there were only three runners, he
started at 11 to 10 against owing to the American support
accorded to Chicago II. I managed to buy the winner in for
340 guineas, and as his subsequent performances will show,
his repurchase was not a dear one. His next outing was at
Lingfield, where he had to meet Mr. Prentice's bogey, Pekin,
His Majesty's Pole Carew, and four others. The net value
of the stakes was £1,169, and Doochary secured them in a
canter, winning by three lengths from Pekin, who the following year was presumably backed for the Derby to win more
than one fortune. Remembering that Doochary only cost
150 guineas after being passed through the sale ring without
eliciting a bid, and that after showing stylish form at Manchester I was enabled to buy him in for 340 guineas, the
Lingfield Great Foal Plate was a real nice race to take with
him. But his vein of success continued, for in his next
outing he won the Staffordshire Breeders' Foal Plate at
Wolverhampton, value £437, and giving weight away to
everything in the race (thirteen ran), he romped home the
easiest of winners. He was bred by Mr. E. Kennedy at the
Straffan Stud, co. Kildare, and prospective purchasers might
do much worse than buy this gentleman's lot *en bloc* each
year, for he always sends up a useful one or two out of the
few he offers for sale annually at Doncaster. Though Mr.
Kennedy sells at this meeting, his yearlings are, as I have
already said, not fattened and stabled up for sale, which to
a great extent accounts for the success which has attended
his stock.

Having won the first race of the day at Manchester, and
having in reserve that brilliant colt, Lavengro, for a race
later in the day, I felt I was spending quite a happy birthday.
Again Eugene Leigh thought he had a good thing in
Omaha II., and he was made favourite at 7 to 4 against.
Lavengro opened at 6 to 1, but playing up my Doochary
winnings, he is returned as having started at 3 to 1, a price

unobtainable at the rising of the gate. The American contingent made no secret of their belief that Omaha II. was the fastest horse out of the gate they had ever seen, but I also had an opinion in this respect regarding Lavengro. He was at this period of his career the fastest and best two-year-old I have ever owned. He was, if possible, even quicker than Toddington out of slips, and all observers of racing will remember how good *he* was. On the rising of the barrier, Lavengro jumped off in front, and making every inch of the running won all the way by a length and a half. The crowd cheered. Why? Perhaps because they admired a good horse. Perhaps because there was never any mystery connected with my stable, for I had no secrets, nor did I ever mislead a single man as to the merits of my horses, during the whole period of my racing career.

We had now reached the Epsom Summer Meeting, or, as it is more generally styled, the Derby week. Sceptre was to make her début on a racecourse in the Woodcote Stakes (six furlongs), always run on the first day. She had "come out," or made her first bow to the world when I bought her in July of the previous year. The mere fact that she cost 10,000 guineas, and held the record for price as a yearling, would in itself be sufficient to create considerable interest, and when she was on view in the paddock previous to the race, I think I am right in saying, this at once turned to admiration. Sceptre was all over a racehorse. She had a fine broad head, which resembled more a colt's than a filly's, with those big ears which so many good judges like to see, while her neck was fitted on to perfection. Her shoulders were perhaps the best thing about her, though it would be hard to say what part of her anatomy was better than another. From hip to hock she showed great striking power, and she was ribbed up with symmetrical completeness. She could not but impress anyone having ordinary knowledge of a blood 'un with the fact that she combined those two great qualities—she was both a racehorse and a machine. Her one fault was that she

was a bit straight in front, and one of her toes was inclined
to turn in, but the latter slight defect made no difference to
her whatever. Her straight forelegs were a different matter,
and in her early career, and once as a three-year-old, gave
serious trouble, not to mention anxiety. Her feet, though
moulded to perfection, were inclined to be fleshy. Her
straightness created a weakness in the knees, always discernible after galloping on hard ground ; but I will now go
straight on and deal with her record career. It is almost
needless to remind my readers that she was made a hot
favourite, and, opening at 5 to 4 against, she stood at that
price throughout the market operations. never deviating a
fraction. Csardas, a good two-year-old, figured second in the
list at 9 to 2. They got off to a good start, Sceptre being the
first to break the line, and she made play on the rails. Just
before reaching Tattenham Corner she appeared to hold the
field, but on Sam Loates taking a pull at her to negotiate the
sharp turn, she went back to her field so quickly that her
trainer, Morton, who was standing next me in my box, cried
out, "By gad! she's beat!" But no sooner had he spoken,
than they were heading for home, and once again on a straight
stretch, the filly quickly showed the field her heels, and won
in superb style by four lengths from Csardas. She received
a most gratifying ovation. In all her subsequent races she
showed her dislike to racing round turns, and always lost
ground when these had to be negotiated. Full of courage, she
wanted to gallop straight on. She was never beaten at Newmarket, where, the St. Leger excepted, she showed her best
form, form which will live long after we have run our race in
this life. But the race touched her weak spot. The going
was on the hard side, and the sharp descent at the start is
a severe test to the legs of any horse. The next day she was
lame in front from concussion. The trouble was principally
in the knees, though she had slightly bruised her fleshy feet.
This stopped her fulfilling her Ascot engagements.

For the latter meeting, Morton and I decided that we would

only take Lavengro, who was engaged in the Forty-Fourth
Biennial, a race worth £1,160, run on the first day. This he
won in great style by three lengths, starting at 6 to 5, and I
had a fair plunge on him. St. Windeline, Friar Tuck, and
Punctilio (winner of the Acorn Stakes) were unplaced. I met
Morton in the off-saddling enclosure, when he at once and
without the least hesitation, said, "This is the best horse we
have seen since Ormonde."

How good Lavengro was we ourselves did not know, for
he had answered every question, both at home and in public,
by winning with consummate ease and in most decisive fashion.
After he had been seen to and despatched to the stables,
Morton and I discussed the advisability of sending for Duke
of Westminster, who was engaged in the New Stakes, due to
be run on the Thursday. He had not been an easy horse to
get ready, Morton's particular trouble with him being that he
would eat next to no hay. This accounted for his shelly appearance, and though every kind of hay had been tried, including
American and Australian, he could not be induced to take
"bulk." For a horse to live on oats alone is equivalent to a
man living solely on meat, without vegetables, bread, or any
accessory to aid digestion. Sweet hay is the salt of a racehorse in training. But in spite of Lavengro's very taking
performance in the Biennial there was another presumable
obstacle : he could give the Duke a stone and an easy beating!

Weighing the public performance of the big son of Ladas,
I decided to send for Duke of Westminster, and Morton
telegraphed instructions that he was to be sent to Ascot the
following day, Wednesday. He arrived fresh and well.
Flying Lemur, who, with Game Chick and Robert le Diable,
was engaged in the race, was voted a certainty, and stories
were rife as to the trial he had won at Kingsclere. Nor were
the other two referred to unfavourably ; on the contrary.
Always a nice race to win, the New Stakes was worth £1,732,
and before the horses had gone half way Duke of Westminster
had won it, and he passed the post three lengths in front of

Game Chick, an excellent performer subsequently, with Flying Lemur unplaced. As I saw the Duke striding home I marvelled what sort of colt was Lavengro!

Doochary was not far behind Duke of Westminster, and with Sceptre and Lavengro I possessed four such two-year-olds as no man has owned for many a year, and such as few have ever possessed since the days of horseracing commenced.

Before I proceed further, a brief description of Lavengro may be interesting. He was a herculean giant. A rich bay with black points, he stood not quite 16 hands, with over nine inches of bone below the knee. No ordinary racing girth was large enough to fit him, and girths had to be made specially for him. I cannot call to mind any two-year-old so deep, and I do not except Minting. Behind the saddle he had any amount of power, and though sickle-hocked, this was only a blemish to the eye. Duke of Westminster was a colt of quite an opposite stamp, being light of frame and lighter in colour. The next race Lavengro ran in was the Hurst Park Foal Plate, value £1,135. Game Chick had arrived, but for some reason, perhaps judicious, she did not run. The big colt had to give her a stone, and through the Duke, would have beaten her for certain. Odds of 3 to 1 were laid on him, and though he had nothing to beat, the style in which he accomplished his task was a treat to see. Yet he was within an ace of not running! When being plated in the early morning he had been pricked, and when Morton met me at that excellent hotel, the Mitre, at Hampton Court, he broke the unwelcome news to me. We visited his box together, and on taking the poultice off, to my relief he trotted quite sound. After he had won, I was so pleased with my trainer, and the natural anxiety he had displayed, that I presented him with a cheque for £500.

Then came the "Julys" at Newmarket, and Sceptre, though not entirely sound again from her Epsom jar, won the July Stakes, value £1,530. The turf on the July Course is exceptionally good. and resembles more that of the Wiltshire Downs than that of any other racecourse, Goodwood always excepted. Goodwood is the Queen of Racecourses! The race did Sceptre good; in any case, no harm. It was only an exercise canter for her, no more than she would have had to do at home, and though odds of 10 to 1 were laid on her it was a remunerative bit of exercise. Lavengro a fortnight later won the Chesterfield of £850, which he ran away with, and 20 to 1 was betted on him doing it.

With four such youngsters, not much heed was paid to those of lesser degree in the stable, and it was not until Goodwood came round, that I won another race. This was the Richmond Stakes with Duke of Westminster, who was again opposed by Game Chick and Flying Lemur. Odds of 7 to 4 were laid on him, and Danny Maher, who rode, taking matters somewhat easily, only won a head from Game Chick. the brother to Flying Fox finishing third two lengths away. By not a few it was contended that the filly ought to have won, but on consulting Maher, he confirmed my reading of the race, and said he won very comfortably indeed. There was some talk of a match being made, but my offer to run again for £1,000 a-side was not accepted.

I later on won a small race with Barberstown, and with this exception my stable was very quiet until September, when I received a rude shock, and experienced one of the greatest disappointments. Sterling Balm had just won the Gimcrack for that excellent sportsman, Major Joicey, and John Watts, who trained her, had a very high opinion of the filly. So had I of Lavengro! They were both engaged to run in the Champion Breeders' Foal Stakes at Derby and 7 to 4 was laid on my colt at the start. I had a very large sum of money on him. To my astonishment he ran slack, if not currishly, right through the race, and was beaten easily by Sterling Balm; in fact, he only just beat Battle Song for second place, and that something was wrong was manifest, for Doochary had beaten this same colt in a canter at Wolverhampton not long before. The reason for this defeat I could not imagine, and a watch

15

was kept on Lavengro after his returning home.  As a result the cause was soon discovered, and it was found that he had resorted to those abuses which have cursed the career of many a good colt inclined to the stallion stage.  Every precaution was resorted to—electric batteries, American contrivances of all kinds, shields of every description ; but all to no purpose, for if the remedy was successful one way, he would sulk and refuse to lie down.  I have had him standing for six days and nights, getting more savage every twenty-four hours.  In the end the cure was, if possible, worse than the disease. My admiration for him turned to disgust, and, except a selling race, he never won again.

Lavengro, from being the best two-year-old seen in England for some considerable time, had rendered himself next to useless for racing.  From being worth any amount he had, as it were, turned sovereigns into pence.  His promise at the stud had been prematurely dissipated.

Sceptre in many ways was an extraordinary filly.   One peculiarity with her was that as a yearling she got her winter coat in the early autumn, the hair being of abnormal length. This was also the case as a two-year-old in a modified degree, but only as regards the mass of hair.  As early as September she had got her " overcoat " on, and so she appeared at Doncaster to run for the Champagne Stakes.  I had not seen her for some time, though Morton had told me how she looked, but he stated that she was well in herself.  My admiration for Sceptre was so great that, even had I thought she was unlikely to win, I should have been compelled to support her, and before seeing her in the paddock I had already given instructions to my commission agent.  Had I not been somewhat precipitate, I certainly should have varied these by a great reduction, for when she came into the paddock I hardly recognised her.  Her coat, long and shaggy, was staring. She had been hunter clipped along the belly and on the legs. Though never a good walker, she appeared in this respect worse than ever.  I sent in to stop my commission, but the ring at Doncaster is not an easy place in which to discover a person, and when my man was found the bets on my behalf had been made. An owner cannot be too careful! He should always see his horse before deciding to back it. The race was run, and Sceptre led to the distance, when she failed, in my opinion through weakness, to keep her place, and Game Chick beat her by a length and a half, and Csardas, whom she had beaten pointless in the Woodcote, just finished a head in front of her for second place. It is possible that owing to her abundance of premature hair, Morton had refrained from giving her that work which ninety-nine per cent. of Persimmon's stock require ; for after a gallop she would, in the condition she was, naturally sweat much more than under normal circumstances. Hence, had she done the requisite work, she must of necessity have become weak. As it was, she carried no muscle whatever. So luck continued, for Duke of Westminster fell slightly lame, and could not fulfil one of his valuable back-end engagements. The only other race I won that year was with Madame Rachel, but she was of jades the jadiest, and though starting at the nice price of 5 to 1, I won very little over her victory, Morton refusing to back her for a penny.

Before going further, it may be interesting to relate how I endeavoured to keep Sam Loates at the head of the list of winning jockeys for the season of 1900. At this period there was no little rivalry between the American jockeys and those of the old division. I had strong feelings on this point, and keenly favoured the hope that an Englishman might head the list. At the beginning of the last week of the season it was a race between Sam Loates and Lester Reiff. They stood at 135 and 137 wins respectively.

It was a tough task that Sam Loates had in front of him, for a lead of two and only the last week to go, was a formidable one. Leonid and Merrilla both possessed fair chances of winning at Folkestone, and I took them there, Sam Loates riding at this meeting, while Reiff went to Warwick. Luck did not favour Sam, for though he got Leonid home on the first day, he also rode two seconds in Bogatir and Lyddite, and a third in Baccalaureat, while Lester Reiff tied this one success by winning on Waltzer in the Midlands.   On the second day Sam could only get second twice, on Merrilla and Miss Biddo, while Reiff went one more ahead by the aid of Karnak.   In the hope of gaining another bracker for Sam I sent Leonid on to Manchester.   This turned out disastrous, for with odds of 11 to 8 betted on him, Reiff beat him a short head on La Figlia ; but I have an idea Sam rode a little too confidently on this occasion.   This put the result of the race for winning mounts almost beyond hope, but I did not despair, for though Reiff on Orris Root beat my filly St. Flora later in the day, Sam scored on La Lune.   Then Wax Toy, a Yankee horse I had bought, could only get third to Billow, the mount of Reiff, and riding Spectrum in the Final Plate, he landed himself at the head of the list for the season of 1900 with six to spare.   My effort to help Sam Loates to pass and beat the American jockey cost me a very considerable sum, but it was quite a sporting battle ; we lost, and there it ended.

Though I had won £11,171 10s. in stakes in 1901, I had not had a good season.   No one except him who has gone through it, knows the enormous amount which is absorbed in forfeits, fees to officials, and railway charges, to say nothing of the training bill by one running some thirty to forty horses.   I mention this because unless an owner continues to be extremely fortunate he is compelled to reflect on the colloquialism, " I've had some ! "   My training bill alone came to something over £100 weekly, while the forfeits, fees, and railway charges, with the boys' and trainer's fares and their expenses, not to mention my own, reduced the winnings in stakes to nil, and left me on the debit side for the season. Being under-capitalised having regard to the stable I was keeping, I realised that something would have to be done to raise the wind, and as the only machinery to set this in motion was a sale, I made it known that I was prepared to part with any horse I possessed providing a price could be agreed. It is true that J. B. Joel, after her success in the Woodcote, offered me £10,000 for Sceptre "and chance it," but as I had chanced these figures, except that they repre-sented guineas, when she was a yearling, I did not quite appreciate "the chance" so seriously as Joel appeared to do.

As was only natural, John Porter, on hearing of the possibility of getting the Eaton-bred two-year-olds into his stable, was anxious to accomplish this, and it was arranged that he should meet me at Wantage and see them, together with Lavengro and the others.

After inspecting those horses which he wished to see, Porter asked me to put a price in writing on both Duke of Westminster and Sceptre, and to leave the offer open for a day. I put a stiff one on the former, asking 25,000 guineas, while I purposely offered Sceptre too cheaply, which doubt-less caused a slight suspicion about her—the Turf is ever sceptical. I risked asking so little for Sceptre, believing it would create a doubt that something was wrong with her, and having no desire to part with her, I took a big chance. The "Duke" being a colt and unbeaten, was taken away, and I was left with 21,000 guineas and the filly. I certainly believed that Duke of Westminster was the best colt in England at the time, but I had no doubt—and I frankly admit it—that I would beat him with Sceptre the first time they met.

## CHAPTER XXVI.

## A CHANGE OF STABLES.

WAS quite contented with my trainer, but with all men carrying on business, weight of money must tell. This presented itself in the person of Mr. J. B. Joel, who made Morton a very lucrative offer to become his private trainer, and from a commercial point of view Morton was perfectly right in accepting this. He waited my convenience, and after due deliberation I determined to train my own horses. With this in view, I took over Elston House, Shrewton, from John Porter, whose son George had trained there for Mr. Keene, Mr. Gretton, and others. Shrewton presented itself as an ideal training place, for, apart from being healthily situated, with about forty-eight acres of land at my disposal, there were four distinct training grounds lying north, south, east, and west. How good these Downs were is borne out by the fact that during the two years that I trained my horses I only had one of the whole lot who ever broke down, and that was Jam Jar, who has since won races.    At Lavington there were two gallops of one and a half miles and one and a quarter miles respectively, of the finest turf that can be found on any Downs in England.    On Mr. Hooper's farm I had a gallop of one mile straight, which turned into a crescent-shaped gallop of about a mile and a quarter.    The home Downs consisted of one mile straight and another of six furlongs, and a horseshoe gallop of a mile and a half, while the Alton Downs gave me a gallop of two miles and a half, the first mile and a half perfectly straight, then, rising out of the valley, a little on the collar, and, taking a wide turn at the top, running on for another mile straight. In the winter, or in the wet season, these grounds were never used, as Salisbury Plain can be galloped over anywhere during those periods.

The principal thing in a training stable is summed up in one word—detail. I believe I left nothing undone. I had my boxes built not in the shape of a yard, as is usual, but in straight lines of from eleven to thirteen scattered about the place. I also had isolated hospital boxes, and in these I always put fresh horses, that I might have bought out of a selling race or elsewhere, before I permitted them to join the string. The hay of Wiltshire is renowned, and it grows in every possible kind. My oats I got from several places, but have great pleasure in stating that those of Messrs. Elsey, of Lincoln, were by far superior to those of any other dealer. I had my own forge and blacksmith on the place; in short, when I had completed my arrangements and my horses were at Shrewton I do not believe my stable lacked in anything.

The great essential in the construction of stables is ventilation. For this reason I am against the stereotyped yards which are generally in use in the larger—and, for that matter, the smaller—training establishments in England. True, they give a neat look to the place and are pleasing to the eye, but the eye is not the pulse of health. In building my boxes I favoured wood against bricks, having all the roofs thatched, which I secured by a covering of wire netting of a fine mesh, which formed a protection against birds and vermin of all kinds. Thatch keeps a stable cool in summer and warm in winter. Each box had its ventilating pipes, which ran into larger ones in the roof, where the current found a vent. The doors were in top and bottom halves, and the top part could be left open at any time, the horse being then secured by the closing of a strong gate of stout zinc wire. This gave him more air, more sun, and an "open door" to his surroundings. Had the boxes been built in the narrow compass of a yard, it would have been the invariable practice of the horses to have watched their opposite neighbours through these gates, possibly leaving their feed for this purpose and seldom resting. But by having my boxes built in one line and scattered about the place, not one set of boxes being within view of the other, I could give my horses all the air, sun, and liberty obtainable, without any chance of the retarding effect I have referred to. Nor was this the only advantage gained by the method I adopted. Horses, at least in one respect, are very nigh human. They have their Don Juans and their Hebes among them. Let the former face the latter, with only a gate of thick wire and the space of a yard between them, and—did not someone once swim the Hellespont?

Nearly all the boxes had chalk floors. These are particularly healthy, and can be dug out and refilled as often as deemed desirable. Bricks can, to a limited extent, be kept clean, but they are porous, and therefore must retain a certain amount of insanitary matter. Chalk is a filter. There is never the suggestion of a disagreeable smell in a stable where the chalk floor is properly kept. The daily scraping takes off a thin layer from the surface; in other words, the horse has a "clean sheet" to lie on every night.

The boxes all contained long, narrow windows level with the eaves, back and front. These were primarily used to assist the ventilation. They were never both completely closed down at any time. It may not appear smart to the eye, but in a stable cobwebs should never be swept away. They catch the fly. The fly is a pest. Keep your stables sanitarily clean, and the rest will take care of itself. Let the decorations fail to please the critical eye if you will, but do not allow the boxes to offend the nostrils, or your stable will "come undone."

Having completed my establishment, I was advised to obtain the services of a man who possessed the qualification of an American trainer to take charge of my horses. This may sound as if I had been infected with the then raging craze, or desired my horses to be tuned up to a Yankee Doodle concert pitch by the aid of a few double octaves in dopes ; but such was not the case, and, generally speaking, I do not think it would harm a stable to be saved from either or both. Anyway, I engaged one.

## CHAPTER XXVII.

### SCEPTRE AND SOME OF HER RACES.

SCEPTRE was now being prepared for the Lincolnshire Handicap (1902), and was doing gentle work, preparatory to the more arduous gallops which she would later on have to undergo. Some four weeks before Lincoln I was called away to Paris. The horses were then left in complete charge of my American trainer. On my return I found, to my dismay, that Sceptre had gone off her feed, which was quite strange for her, and she appeared nervous, restless, and upset. I soon discovered the cause. She had been galloped a mile in company with Lavengro at racing pace, before she had been got properly ready to undergo so severe a task; the following day she had gone the same distance with two fresh horses; the next morning she had been sent a mile again with Lavengro, as fast as he could bring her along; and on the fourth consecutive day she was set to beat the whole lot at a mile, giving away lumps of weight. Then she had been locked in the stable for a rest! Little wonder that she had been off her feed! I was never so near committing a breach of the law in my life; and as I write I can with difficulty restrain the expression of my feelings. But the miracle was that, except for feeding badly, the filly stood it all; she was as sound as ever, and her legs were as clean as the day she was foaled. True, she looked tucked up, and was dry in her coat, but the courageous spirit was still there. The abnormal tasks which had been set her had not killed this. Walking her on the Downs the morning following my return, she was actually anxious to go! I had already written striking her out of "the Lincoln," but in view of the way she went that morning, and remembering that she held a prominent place in the betting, I deferred the posting of my letter to Messrs. Weatherby. There were but some fourteen days to run prior to the race, and I took over the feeding of her entirely, and supervised her exercises—I cannot call it work, for of that she had had more than enough. It was now a delicate and anxious task to get her to eat at all. She ate mostly out of the hand, with an occasional apple or piece of carrot to entice her; but all my endeavours and resources could not get her to eat more than a measure and a half of oats, which in weight would come to about 5lb 4oz a day. By way of contrast, throughout her St. Leger preparation she consumed six measures a day, about 21lb, never leaving an oat, a difference of 15lb 12oz per diem!

With patience and assiduous attention I succeeded by degrees in getting her to take three measures a day; she improved steadily, and gained strength; and being fully aware of her capabilities and marvellous constitution, together with the fact, as I have said, that she held a prominent place in the market on the Lincolnshire Handicap, I decided to run her. I backed her for a large stake, and should have won over £30,000 by her victory, exclusive of the money I had put on for many of my friends, not to mention some of my acquaintances. Not getting off too well, she joined the front rank too early in the race, ultimately being beaten a head by St. Maclou, 7st 12lb. She started a strong favourite at the short odds of 11 to 4. There were a good many who, ever ready to form hasty opinions, adversely criticised Hardy's riding of Sceptre, some even going so far as to say that he had thrown the Lincolnshire Handicap away. These people have no consideration. They do not for a moment make any allowance for apprentices during the early period of their career. True, Hardy made great use of the filly, and it is possible he was over-anxious to get home on her; but this is only too reasonable to imagine would be the case, and light weights, as a rule, have not had the experience of heavy ones. This is known to the owner and the trainer before the boy is put up, and it always has been, and will be, a handicap against the light division. These irresponsible criticisms, which were passed by equally irresponsible persons, even before Hardy had returned to the paddock with Sceptre, annoyed me, and prior to his dismounting, before everybody present, I thanked Hardy for the excellent race he had ridden on her; and, though I had not won the large sum I had backed her for, I endeavoured thus to express my dissent from the gratuitous opinion of a few men who possibly ought to have known better. In racing there are all sorts of chances to contest against before the winning-post is reached, and it is, in my opinion, unfair that the younger generation of jockeys should be so often blamed, when no more could be expected of them before they were given the mount. With these feelings I entered the weighing-room, just as Hardy was taking off the colours, and, before the whole of his brother professionals, I pointedly thanked him again for the race he had ridden for me, and I hope it gave him some encouragement. I believe it did. If so, I succeeded in carrying out my views, which were that the youngster should not be severely censured because he had got so near, yet not quite near enough. I was not inclined to treat my transatlantic trainer with extenuating consideration, and having lost the Lincolnshire Handicap, I brought off a double event by seeing that I also lost him.

In taking over the full charge of my horses I found myself in very good company with Sceptre for a Queen, and having the "Thousands" in my eye (not yet in my pocket), I started on my self-imposed task. It has been stated "in print" that Sceptre was in training the whole of the season, and, though

I do not expressly deny this, I must at least qualify the observation. After Lincoln the filly had a sound rest, trotting and cantering for as short a period as possible in the early morning, and going out in the afternoon, sun and weather permitting, to walk and eat grass. Her appetite returned, and her work slowly began to keep time with its increase. She had done more work of a most erratic kind than any three-year-old had ever before been asked to do, and, being a filly, I nursed her.

The day preceding her departure for Newmarket she did a fine performance on my trial ground, Randall being in the saddle, and being half the size again that she was at Lincoln, I left with her for "headquarters" rich in confidence; and there my riches ended. One hears of a shoe pinching; in my case, I frankly admit, it was the pocket.

Taking her into the paddock on the day of the Two Thousand Guineas caused her instantly to burst into a profuse sweat, so, removing her clothing, I at once sent her out on the Heath. She was so full of courage that it took no little time and precaution to saddle her; but, once Randall was on her back, she cooled down to business in a marvellous way. How she won the Two Thousand is common knowledge, beating with consummate ease such horses as Ard Patrick, Rising Glass, and others, in the then record time of 1min. 39secs. Duke of Westminster also ran, it was his first appearance since I sold him, and he shared favouritism with her, but, as I anticipated, she beat him pointless. On the following Friday she won the One Thousand. I have no hesitation in saying that on that day St. Windeline was a good filly, and here again Sceptre made a time record for the fillies' race. In saddling her at the starting-gate she twisted a plate, and the blacksmith not being at his post, as had been arranged, it took all my strength, and a good deal of the skin off my fingers, to wrench it off. I had reason to know that Sceptre was not the only one who perspired before a race. Of the One Thousand I only saw the start. Sceptre got badly away, but being ridden patiently, and allowed to warm to her work, which she always wanted to do, she by degrees gained on the leaders. Difficult as it is to follow horses when they are running from you, I could see her creeping up in the style I knew so well, and was confident she had won. The cheers from the stands confirmed this. Short of a front plate, which must have taken at least one or two inches from her each stride, and getting badly away, this was a better performance than most people were aware of.

In the winter I had backed Sceptre to win the Derby, and the first bet that was obtained for me was one of 1,000 to 30 against. Just previous to the running of the Guineas I gave instructions to my commission agent to support her somewhat liberally on my behalf, and on my return to Shrewton I had backed her to win somewhere about £33,000. Giving her a brief rest, I went on with her training for the Derby. This continued satisfactorily until within about ten days of the race, when, after a rousing gallop, I found her lame. She had bruised her foot.

I shall never forget my feelings, nor shall I ever be able to express them. Here was I, the owner and trainer of the favourite for the Derby, a filly who had just succeeded in winning both the One Thousand and Two Thousand Guineas, a feat never before accomplished, who was perhaps the greatest public favourite our racecourse had ever seen. I was, as it were, her sponsor, and she was lame! Apart from attending to the injury, the first thing I did was to keep the fact a strict secret; and so far did I succeed in this, that she did not go back a fraction in the betting. Her injured foot yielded to treatment, and after two days I had her trotting and cantering on the Lavington Gallop, than which there is no better in England. Having got her round, with her appetite now set, I was confident that I would win the Blue Riband of the Turf, a race which it is the chief ambition of every sportsman who owns a racehorse to win. The day of the race came round, and I received permission of the Stewards for Sceptre to go to the post the opposite way of the course, accompanied by Barberstown, a mare who always accompanied her wherever she went. She was an even-money chance, and I never hedged a sixpence ; indeed, I had supported her at as short a price as 5 to 2. She exhibited a disinclination to start, and would not go up to the gate, and in consequence got badly away. Another thing which told against her was that she was drawn on the outside. Randall, who had won on her at Newmarket, again rode her, and I am afraid he showed some indiscretion, when he vigorously drove Sceptre up the hill to catch the leaders. In successfully accomplishing this in so short a space of ground and time, her chance must have been greatly jeopardised, and this, in my opinion, is the chief reason why she was beaten, or, in any event, did not finish second. Every excuse was forthcoming for Randall. It was the first year he was riding as a professional. What the Derby is to an owner or trainer, it can be no less to a jockey. Sceptre ran neck and neck with Ard Patrick to Tattenham Corner, and came into the straight looking all over a winner ; but this was only for a moment, and the work which had been asked of her in the early stages of the race began to tell. Changing her legs, she dropped back until she did not even finish third, being beaten by Friar Tuck.

Having seen to Sceptre and despatched her to the stables, I made my way to the weighing-room to consult my jockey. That the race had been a great strain on Randall was marked on every feature, and he was so upset that he could hardly speak to me. None but those riding an even-money chance in the Derby can realise what it means when they are beaten, and I sympathised with Randall. All he could say to me was, " Please come and speak to me later ; I am too upset to talk." He certainly was. Whether the stoppage in her work helped towards her defeat I cannot definitely say, but subsequent events strongly suggest that when she bruised her foot and was forced to stay in the stable for forty-eight hours, it must to some considerable extent have militated against her chance.

On the Friday, starting at 5 to 2, she won the Oaks in a canter, with St. Windeline again second, and Elba third ; but in this race Randall waited with her until Tattenham Corner was fairly rounded, and then, letting her stride out, she won in grand style. The reception she received was one which will not be readily forgotten, nor can I call to mind any heroine of the Oaks who has ever been the recipient of so great an ovation. The cheering continued for long after the race, even in face of her defeat in the Derby on the preceding Wednesday.

After Sceptre's stylish performance in the Oaks, I have since learned that there was a miserable minority which assumed that she did not try in the Derby. One person in particular—but never within my hearing—continually trumpeted this, and he. I believe, never saw the Derby of that year. Any man who has owned horses, or has any knowledge of racing, should have known better. And such an aspersion was nothing more or less than the cry of a coward, the yelp of a cur.

I had won the Oaks. Sceptre and I had been cheered to the echo. The ovation was unanimous. I had lost the Derby with the same filly, and though I have never made it public property before, I had lost so much money over Sceptre in that race that I had to visit the offices of Messrs. Pratt and Co., of 9, George Street, Hanover Square, on the Saturday, and request them to advance me the stakes I had won over the Oaks to enable me to settle the bets at the Victoria Club, on the Monday. They obliged me by advancing the amount I required. Hence my winnings on the Oaks did not fully liquidate my losses on the Derby. So much for the *canard* which one man in particular was ever ready to spread about, and who, when challenged, could only muster sufficient courage to deny that he had spread it.

# CHAPTER XXVIII.

## THE GRAND PRIX, ASCOT, AND THE ST. LEGER,
### 1902.

AVING already referred to Shrewton, I feel I cannot pass this pretty little sleepy hollow by, without further notice. What I call Shrewton was, and, correctly speaking, still is, comprised of five old hamlets, namely, Shrewton (town of Shrews), Maddington, Rolleston, Orcheston St. George, and Orcheston St. Mary. In the good old days of yore, these parishes consisted of a few cottages, more or less scattered, but it is quite conceivable that St. George and St. Mary of Orcheston may have had an eye to the future. Anyway, the increase of population, for which Shrewton and its environs have very rightly gained a most deserving reputation, has caused these five old parishes to link themselves together, with the result that without the different districts being explained to the stranger, he would look upon the whole as the village of Shrewton. I say this with a full apology to Rolleston, which boasts eighteen parishioners all told—mostly children!

This chain of five hamlets makes up a fairly pretty village, on one side shops and houses of varied sizes and shapes, on the other old trees and a river without water. The "river" is fed by the springs which only rise about four months in the year, except during very wet seasons, when they hold out accordingly. Furthermore, the many military wells which

16

have been sunk on Salisbury Plain have been the cause of diverting a great deal of the water. The bottom is gravel, so that when dry it is quite inoffensive to the nose. Taking it altogether, Shrewton is perhaps more quaint than pretty. The main street, in other words the village itself, runs snake-like, in curves, and is studded with old timber.

Generally speaking, the tradesmen, like their shops, are quite up to the standard, and a more respectable or better lot it would be hard to find. I was agreeably surprised to see how advanced they were, not alone in their business, but outside it. One great drawback to the progress of the place is that there are no gentry in the neighbourhood. And yet poor little Shrewton has to face an even greater drawback. It has five churches and five parsons!

Yet from what I saw of the inhabitants and the parsons I should unhesitatingly say the former were far in advance of the latter. One parish, as I have said, musters in all but eighteen souls, including babies. The result is that one, or at the most two, make up the congregation. I have, solely out of compassion for the vicar, often sent my children with their governess to Rolleston church, and they not infrequently have been the sole occupants of the place. Are not these five churches and five parsons helping to hold religion up to mockery? The world is more enlightened now, and Shrewton in this respect is far from being behind the times. Surely one, or, say two, well-filled churches would leave a better impression than a sprinkling of congregations here and there. If Shrewton and its district, not forgetting the camps pitched on the Plain close by, only require two policemen, they cannot possibly want five parsons!

Thus sermons abound in Shrewton, and perhaps for once, to reverse the order of things, it might not be entirely uncalled for to ask these five gentlemen of the cloth to listen to one. For that matter these remarks may equally apply to the dear ladies, and one or two of the sterner sex, who control Shrewton society!

About a couple of years ago the Postmaster, who had held

office at Shrewton for pretty well half a century, died. He had been a faithful, obliging servant, and was identified with the place. His grave remained rough and uncared for, as the gravedigger had left it. Not one came forward or made any attempt practically to recognise in the only way then possible, the many obliging acts which the old Postmaster had performed in his lifetime. Strange, and had it not been for an unworthy racehorse owner, no memorial stone would have adorned the uncouth mound of earth which marked his resting place. Not that this owner of horses, and trainer to boot, was an old inhabitant—on the contrary ; but he had this mark of esteem erected in the village churchyard solely out of respect for grey hairs—and as a sermon in stone.

Harking back, there are few men, if any, who have won the Two Thousand Guineas and have been served with a writ for a paltry amount within an hour of its accomplishment. This happened to me, and strange as it may sound, the writ was issued at the suit of an inhabitant of Newmarket, namely, Gilbert the saddler. I had only a few minutes previously subscribed fifty pounds towards the Newmarket Coronation festivities! Nor had I forgotten Shrewton in this respect, having placed £200 in the hands of the five parsons, which sum 1 insisted was to be spent to the last farthing in honour of our King. One of the clerics was a solid teetotaler, and there were some rare old ructions in committee as to whether the beer to be provided should be malt or ginger. This knotty point was submitted to me, and I quickly put the matter at rest by writing across the question in red ink " Both."

We now know that the running in the Derby improved Sceptre to such an extent that she won the Oaks in a canter, and as she kept fresh and well I determined to dispatch her to France. Though it was a long time since England had taken the spoils of the Grand Prix, I felt that a good chance existed of again bringing the prize home to England. This policy has been frequently condemned, but to criticise is an easy task, whilst to train is to be subjected at times to unfair criticism. I left her at Epsom under the charge of Mr. Goodgames, and preceded her to Paris, so that I might have everything in readiness for her reception. Some few days before the race was due to be run Sceptre was boxed at Epsom at 7.30 a.m., and was swung on and off the boat without being changed from the van she travelled in. During the journey she ate her hay, corn, and green stuff with avidity, arriving at her quarters in Paris just before 11 o'clock that evening. She stepped out of the van showing no signs of fatigue. M. Halbron, who generously places his stables at the disposal of all English owners running horses in France, was there to receive her, and I again take this opportunity of thanking him for his kindness and for the interest he exhibited in the welfare of us all. I know of no similar reciprocity of courtesy to French horses and owners on this side of the Channel.

The Grand Prix is an international contest. Unlike most of the French races, it is open to the whole of the world, and horses of almost every nationality are entered for it. Now that the *entente cordiale* is so thoroughly established, would not this be an opportune moment for the French Jockey Club to throw the whole of their races open to the world, or, as a distinctive mark of amity, to England? To a man with any sporting instincts, the attempt to win an international race is a great temptation, more especially when linked with such a chance as I believed I possessed in Sceptre. I could not help remarking the courtesy which was extended to me, and I can only compare it with the ovation which was accorded Monsieur Blanc and Val d'Or, when he won the Eclipse Stakes at Sandown Park.

A steward of the French Jockey Club very courteously asked me if I had a reserved seat from which to view the race, and on my replying in the negative he gave me a ticket for a private box; but this was found to be overcrowded. Immediately, and without the least hesitation, he invited me into the Stewards' box, and from this point of vantage I saw the

Grand Prix run for. On the smaller events preceding the Grand Prix, I had won about 26,000 francs, and this is the sum I had on Sceptre. Randall, who had had the mount both in the Derby and Oaks, came across to ride her. Whether he suffered from the nervousness he had displayed at Epsom, or took extreme precaution on account of his riding in a field of strange jockeys I cannot say; but he left on me the impression, and this has never been removed, that he did not display that nerve which one likes to see in a jockey about to contest a great race. True, it is common knowledge that Continental riders are ever ready to bustle and jostle the visitors, and in a race like the Grand Prix this does not add to the jockey's confidence. I may recall the extreme precaution enforced upon M. Cannon when he rode Matchbox in this race. It was much the same with Sceptre, except that apparently the precaution to resist foul play was in her case still greater. At this period that mechanical contrivance called the "starting-gate" was not in vogue in France. Nevertheless Randall took things quite leisurely, and when the flag fell did not get well away. Starting in the middle of the course, Sceptre was permitted to remain outside everything all the way, which in itself would account for a very considerable distance of ground. So they ran, the filly always going well within herself. When rounding the final turn near home she held a position so far on the outside of her field that she actually appeared to be in front of those going the nearest way, being still covered by the angle of the rails. Shouts went up for Sceptre, but when they came into line it was seen that instead of being in front she was some lengths behind, and favouring the stand side of the course instead of that of the winning post. It was a desperate race between the first three, Kizil Kourgan winning by a head from Retz and Maximum, who ran a dead-heat for second place, Sceptre finishing about two or three lengths behind the winner. I am as certain as it is possible for a man to be that Sceptre went at least 200 yards further than the victor. The

Stewards of the French Jockey Club had cautioned the jockeys prior to the race, and this was not likely to add to the comfort of the visitors, for it practically admitted the existence of unfair and foul riding.   I do not for a moment wish to detract from Randall's capabilities as a jockey and a horseman; on the contrary, I am sure that when he relinquished the amateur for the professional grade, he did so with ability on his side, and the improvement he has wrought in himself by constant practice has placed him among the foremost in his business.   The race did Sceptre no harm, she ate up as usual, and having several engagements at Ascot, I shocked those owners and trainers who keep their horses in glass cases by deciding to run her, and she left La Belle France on the day after the Grand Prix and proceeded to Ascot.   On Wednesday I ran her in the Coronation Stakes, when, getting away badly, she failed to concede Doctrine a stone.   I shall always look upon this race as one of her greatest performances.   Left many lengths behind, when the horses came into full view one might reasonably have thought that she had broken down, or had met with an accident; but no!   On she followed, a rearguard to the stragglers behind.   Then suddenly Randall appeared to realise his position, and, as though by magic, she swept round the turn almost as wide as in the Grand Prix, and resolutely galloping up Ascot Hill drew almost level with the leaders.   Here the race hung in the balance for some strides, but the gigantic effort, the terrific speed she must have put in, carrying the full penalty of 9st 10lb, giving away a stone, and in some cases 21lb, told its tale, and nature could not withstand the strain.   How she ever got into such a hopeless position in the early stages of the race I did not take the trouble to inquire, but I learned afterwards that she had fly-bucked at the post and unseated the jockey.   The Anglo-American seat may have its advantages, but in cases such as the above the rider frequently finds another seat, that of *terra firma*.   In this case I believe it was a blackberry bush!   When Randall returned to scale he did not report to me that the mare had dislodged him at the starting-gate and got loose. Under the circumstances he never rode Sceptre again.

The following day, with this gallop in her, she, with Hardy up, won the St. James's Palace Stakes, easily beating Flying Lemur, Rising Glass, and five others. This conclusively points to Sceptre's extraordinary nature. In my opinion, had the races been reversed, she would have lost the St. James's Palace Stakes, and have won the Coronation Stakes on the following day. Had Sceptre ever run a dead-heat, I have no hesitation in saying that the run-off would have been an absolute certainty for her. Inconceivable as it may appear, she would, I fully believe, have run better in the run-off than on the first occasion. Had I run her in the Hardwicke Stakes on the Friday, I believe she would have won this more easily than when she beat Flying Lemur. Were proof needed, her subsequent Goodwood running fully confirms what I have stated.

After Ascot I eased her up completely, but with what result? No sooner did she cease to do her usual work than she began to feed less; in short, extraordinary as it may sound, work was to her an appetiser. Her first engagement at Goodwood was in the Sussex Stakes, in which she was beaten two lengths by Royal Lancer, conceding him 6lb, in other words, 9lb at weight for sex. It was this race which fully convinced me that if Sceptre did not regularly have abnormal work she was useless. After this race she pulled up so blown and stuffy that there were critics ready to assume she made a noise, and this was hinted in more than one paper. Happily nature had provided Sceptre with legs to withstand the extraordinary training she required, though it must not be forgotten that during 1902 and 1903 our summers were wet ones, and the going generally on the soft side. The day following her defeat in the Sussex Stakes, I shocked the majority of the Goodwood early birds by sending her, with Hardy up, at first six furlongs sharp, then, after walking her about, a

mile and a half at good three-quarter speed, and on the following morning, she being due to run that afternoon in the
Nassau Stakes, I sent her a sharp mile as quickly as she could
go. She had to give heaps of weight away all round. She
won the race in a canter by four lengths, Elba finishing second,
receiving no less than 17lb, with Ballantrae beaten a distance.
Had Royal Lancer met her that day I do not think he would
have fared any better than did the rest of her opponents.
It was my experiences at Goodwood which won me the St.
Leger with Sceptre that year.

I had from five to six weeks before me prior to the St.
Leger, and, returning home with her, she thrived daily on long
gallops of all distances, eating her hay and corn with the same
precision as her matchless action, putting on muscle, revelling
in her daily work without intermission, and stumping up a
horse a week!

Not long before the St. Leger, I was approached by Mr
Horatio Bottomley with a view to Sceptre having a gallop
with his horse Wargrave, who had just won the Ebor Handicap. The idea of the proposal, I understood, was to discover
the merits of Wargrave with a view to the Cesarewitch, the
filly's subsequent running in the Doncaster race to be the
guide. I acquiesced, and in due course Batho arrived at
Shrewton with Wargrave and the stable jockey.

The order was secrecy, and Wargrave was stabled at a
farm about a mile away from my place, while preparations
were made to "dodge" the tout by starting the following
morning before the day had fairly broken. In the grey mist,
before the reflection heralding the rising sun had spread its
crimson carpet in the sky, Sceptre, Wargrave, and Silverhampton were making their way across Salisbury Plain to a spot
known as "Newfoundland." Here Laodamia, Comedy, and
many other good horses had been trained in times gone by,
while the old village folk can rattle off the names of several
Derby winners who have done their final gallops in the neighbourhood of Shrewton. It was my desire to try them on the

straight two miles gallop known as "Alton," which runs
on a ridge above the Knighton gallop in the valley below, but
the going was inclined to be hard here, so I determined to run
on the lower ground, which is two miles and a quarter in
length with one turn. The first mile and a half is straight,
rising out of the valley until the collar is quite as severe as
the finish at Ascot. At the top of this is a turn with a dead flat
run-in. The jockeys received instructions to pull up at the
mile and six furlongs post, or two furlongs beyond the turn.
I expressed my doubts about this gallop, as Sceptre had
done regular work here, and had never once been asked to go
beyond this turn, having, indeed, always begun to pull up
before reaching it, and being so well acquainted with her pecu-
liarities, I was afraid she might stop here according to her
custom. Sceptre and Wargrave were at even weights, with
Silverhampton carrying a "feather." The latter—on book
credentials useless, but at home a very good mare—started at
the far end of the valley. The horse got some two lengths
the best of the start ; Silverhampton, spinning away as was her
wont when not out racing, came along a cracker, Sceptre
pulling over them for the first six furlongs, when, against all
orders, the boy let her have her head for a second, and in a
stride, as it were, she was leading them some three or four
lengths. The change of places was magical, it was so
instantaneous. I muttered a brief word, not for publication,
and, turning to Batho, added, "She will never take the turn
with nothing to bring her along." On she sped pulling double,
and Wargrave, I may say, was well behind her.

On they came at a smashing pace, Silverhampton fading
away. The crucial point was being neared. Would she round
the point with nothing to lead her? She passed the last
furlong post before the bend. In a second she began to look
about, and in less time than it takes to clap one's hands she
slackened down, apparently, to those who did not know her,
beaten. Wargrave consequently caught her at the turn, and,
with Silverhampton, passed her ; but Sceptre had done her

usual gallop on this ground, she had reached her destination, and knew the "pulling up post" too well from past experience. She had Wargrave well beaten, and was merely cantering when she stopped. To all intents and purposes she had won the gallop, and personally I was quite satisfied.

"Spider" was the sobriquet of the boy who rode and "did" Sceptre, and good and honest lad though he was, the temptation to show off and beat the stranger ridden by a professional was too great, so, disobeying strict injunctions, he let Sceptre out instead of waiting to be led round the turn. Had that been accomplished she would then, I am sure, have gone on in the manner already described in the earlier stages of the gallop. Poor "Spider" was very sorry for himself, and candidly admitted the mistake, pleading over-excitement, while he was no less outspoken as to "what she'd a' done if she had only known of the turn."

I there and then impressed on Batho, to the best of my ability, that he should take no notice of the gallop, that it was all wrong; but sooner than disappoint him and Wargrave's owner I would gladly give them another trial after the St. Leger. Being convinced that my estimate of the gallop was correct, I felt I could make no fairer offer, and no more straightforward or sporting proposition. But Mr. Horatio Bottomley and his friend dissented from my view of the trial, and, guided by what they incorrectly considered the true state of things, laid against Sceptre for the St. Leger. My commission agent took one large bet of £5,000 from their representative, but even this did not convince them, and they continued to lay against "the old lady," as they now know to their cost.

That the field for the St. Leger was a good one, and above the average, is certain, for Rising Glass, who ran second to her in the race, did not know defeat afterwards that season, and he beat, amongst others, Templemore, giving him a year and 6lb. Templemore in turn vanquished Black Sand, the winner of the Cesarewitch, who subsequently defeated William

the Third, winner of the Ascot Gold Cup, at the last Newmarket meeting of the year.

Perhaps the most extraordinary circumstance in connection
with the St. Leger was the betting. I had supported Sceptre,
and up to flagfall backed her on every opportunity; all my
friends and the majority of my acquaintances—and the
latter would make a goodly number—had likewise freely
supported her. There was no secret, and I had publicly
expressed my sanguine conviction that she was well and
would win ; but in face of her well being, the more money
that went on her the worse favourite she became ; she was
shuttlecocked about in the market in an alarming manner,
amply sufficient to create a suspicion of a screw being loose
somewhere. I could not discover the screw nor its insecurity,
but it made my responsibility for the St. Leger favourite no,
less, for I had, in losing, *all* to lose.

It is not for me to describe how Sceptre won the St. Leger,
to comment on her great "reception," nor to say how much
I shall ever cherish my pride in her.

## CHAPTER XXIX.

### SOME REMARKS CONCERNING SCEPTRE.

CEPTRE'S last race this season was in the Park Hill Stakes at Doncaster, which she lost, attempting to give Elba 12lb forty-eight hours after the St. Leger. After she had lost, it was a matter of regret that she started; but it looked a mere walk-over for her, and this was a general view, proved by the fact that 4 and even 5 to 1 was laid on her winning. But her severe St. Leger preparation, the great task she accomplished (see Rising Glass's subsequent form) in heavy going, had left its effects, and they told against her beyond my judgment or belief. This I shall always deplore; but that the St. Leger of 1902 was a severe one, much more so than was generally appreciated, is further endorsed by the running of Rising Glass on this same Friday afternoon, for it took him all his time to beat an indifferent horse like Perfectionist, the race being in the balance at the Intake turn. Wednesday's struggle had left its mark behind on one as on the other, but unfortunately for Sceptre, carrying the welter weight of 9st 8lb, she had to meet Elba, fresh and perhaps better than she had ever been in her life, with 8st 10lb up, while Rising Glass, after a fair fight a couple of furlongs from home, beat Perfectionist at even weights with the reasonable impost of 8st 12lb. As to the respective merits of Perfectionist and Elba, the filly has since proved herself vastly superior to the colt.

Furthermore, Elba carried more muscle and looked better on this particular day than she ever did' before. The only time she has since approached being anything like her former self, was when she won the Great Metropolitan at Epsom, and it was solely on account of her "rejuvenated" appearance that I backed her for this race. In the Cesarewitch following Sceptre's St. Leger she looked tucked up and fretful, but had she been the Elba of the Park Hill Stakes day she must have won the long-distance handicap of the year in a common canter. Her running at Ascot and Doncaster with Sceptre fully proves how well she was at the latter place, no matter what excuses may be made for the St. Leger heroine.

It may be of interest to describe here the winding-up gallops I gave Sceptre prior to the St. Leger. As I have already mentioned, taking the filly to Goodwood won me the race. That she was, if anything, a stayer, I had fully satisfied myself. It had been a wet season, and having ascertained that the going on the Town Moor was good, I took the mare to Doncaster, accompanying her myself, on the Saturday preceding the race. I had arranged that Hardy should come on there after racing that day, and be ready to ride her on Sunday morning, Mr. I'Anson having kindly consented that the chains should be taken down, and that I should have the use of the course.

She travelled well. On the Sunday morning, with Hardy up, I sent her the full length of the St. Leger course, a little over one mile and three-quarters. The following day she went six furlongs sharp, followed at an interval by a mile at racing pace. On the Tuesday, *the day preceding the race,* she again negotiated the full course, being brought along by three different horses, stationed at successive distances of about five furlongs from each other. I told Hardy that if he did not beat each one in succession he would not ride her in the race. I had two solid reasons for this. Firstly, the enormous amount of work the filly required in the last forty-eight hours of her winding-up, and secondly, the common practice among jockeys, who too often assume the position of trainer, and ride horses in gallops according to their own views, rather than in accordance with the instructions given to them. Not that Hardy ever took this course. On the contrary, a better-behaved lad in this respect I have never met. He obeyed my orders to the letter.

On the morning of the race I had the " old lady " out early, long before the majority of the onlookers were about, and, after a sharp canter, sent her a mile and a bit, the last six furlongs as sharp as she could go. On returning to the stables she had about two pulls of water and a double handful of corn. The normal quantity given to a horse due to run eight hours later would have left her stuffy. I merely recapitulate these facts to show what some horses require. That she would have won the great race of the North had she not been subjected to the two last gallops I have referred to, I do not for an instant believe. In my opinion the St. Leger was Sceptre's greatest victory. Anyway, the cheers which accompanied her home are ringing in my ears as I write.

She did not run again that year ; nevertheless, in a letter which the "Sportsman" thought fit to publish it was suggested that I left her in the Cambridgeshire for an ulterior motive and then scratched her. I have nothing to say upon the point beyond the fact that the writer died in a mad-house some few months afterwards. This will in no way surprise those who have the misfortune to be acquainted with the general run of letters which from time to time appear in the daily sporting Press.

Adverting for an instant to the "Thousands," I must not omit to record that I refused two bona-fide offers of 38,000 and 40,000 guineas for Sceptre. The latter offer came from an American millionaire, or, rather, his agent, and on my declining it he asked me to put a price on the filly. I replied : "Well, we'll start with New York on account." Though I had to borrow to help me settle the bets I lost over her in the Derby, I stuck to her as long as the sinews of war held out; but nothing melts quicker than money when it once starts on the liquid course. Quicksilver is a baby to it.

I had won a few small races with one or two others in the stable, and at the end of the season 1902 headed the winning list of owners, £23,686 being the amount placed to my credit in prizes. To the uninitiated this may sound a large sum of money to win. But to those who have had to support a large stable such as I kept up, on the best possible lines, such a sum is almost entirely, if not quite, absorbed in expenses and forfeits. If this is so in a successful year, what must be the loss in a bad one? I am referring only to owners who keep up a big string and run their horses as sportsmen. That racing can be run on commercial lines and made to pay is abundantly proved. That times are not quite as "simple" as they used to be goes without saying, and for this reason more than one commercial house has threatened to "chuck it." The sooner they carry out their threat, the greater welcome it will receive. Nevertheless, my experience tells me that some consideration will, sooner or later, have to be extended to the owner, or he will slowly but surely become extinct. It is impossible, under the present state of things, that an owner on a large scale is ever likely to receive that encouragement which he may possibly consider he deserves. Forfeits, fees which are little else but taxes on stakes, &c., &c., will, sooner or later, submerge him, and once he begins to go under there he will stop until he is drowned. Always providing he has a limited capital; also that he is a sportsman. The authorities hate reforms, but the day has surely come when the revenue required to support racing should be derived from the companies of gate-money meetings. When this change from the open meetings first came into force the owners should have been relieved, and the executives of the different dividend-paying racecourses made to bear a portion of their expenses. Difficult it may be to carry into effect, but I say in all seriousness that unless the owner receives some relief from the many expenses he is now mulcted in, he will be compelled to throw up the sponge, or resort to those tricks which handicap the handicappers, and at times play havoc with the public.

Though I had achieved with Sceptre the unprecedented feat of absolutely winning four classics out of the five, and though I trained and owned her, and was the first trainer ever to head the List of Winning Owners, the expenses of the upkeep of such a large stable as I had gathered together, clearly showed me that, even with apparent success, I was under capitalised —I was rich in horseflesh, but poor in pocket. To offer racehorses, no matter how valuable, to one's bankers as a security is about as useful as waving a red rag before a bull. It was after a hard struggle that I was forced to send Sceptre to the sale ring in the December of this particular year. I could not help myself. She was, as it were, the asset of the establishment. Only those who have owned and loved a great horse will appreciate my feelings. Only those who have gone through the whirlpool of financial troubles will understand my position.

Arrived at Newmarket, I put a reserve of 24,000 guineas on her. In the stable she looked perfect, even with her long coat, which she annually grew, but which with age came less each year. It was a horrible moment when she stepped out of her box on her way to the sale paddocks at Newmarket. Even the name of Tattersall at that moment had no pleasant sound for me. It was a cold December morning. No sooner had she started on her way than the east wind caught her. Her coat, a few minutes before all gloss, had turned, and she looked, to the everyday critic, a different creature. She entered the sale ring. Mr. Somerville Tattersall put her in at her reserve, namely, 24,000 guineas. There was a silence. I can distinctly call to mind Mr. Chaplin trying to infuse some animation into one or two rich men to bid, almost suggesting that he wished it was all happening twenty years ago; how he would then have bid and bought. I think I heard him ejaculate, " Go on, bid up." But no one displayed either the pluck or the judgment, and, embarrassed as I was pecuniarily, I felt, as she walked out of the ring, much more relieved, much happier, if possible, in my enthusiasm at retaining her; much richer than had she gone.

The inexperienced may be under the impression that winter is the hibernating season of those engaged in training horses for flat-racing. It is quite the reverse, that is if the trainer is a man who attends to his business by superintending it. The yearling is the foundation of the racehorse. Too much care cannot be devoted to it. Its breaking-in in its baby days is, in my opinion, the most intricate and important detail of a racing establishment. The trainer has not only successfully to discover the temperament of the yearling, but he should also have a shrewd knowledge of the temperament of the lad who he has decided shall "back" this colt or that filly. An impatient lad may easily cause irremediable evil, heavy hands will create a "heavy" mouth, a few intemperate strokes with the cane will probably cause chronic nervousness, commonly dubbed excitement. Without a perfectly all-round balanced lad, the yearling may quickly favour hanging to one side or the other, and in this respect once get him "fixed," neither good St. Archer nor St. Fordham could get him right again. Not even that jockey who possessed the best hands of them all, Tom Cannon, and he is not yet a saint I am pleased to record, could reclaim a youngster who in his early days has been given a bad mouth. But having successfully got over the stage of the breaking-in of the baby, and having taught him to walk straight without sidling about on the sight of this or that; in short, having accustomed him to the "probabilities" of an everyday life, he has yet to learn to gallop. At this point the lad in charge is apt to become over-zealous. He is "busting" to jump him off and show the rest what he can do. Stable lads vie with each other in this respect, with much greater zest than do some jockeys when riding in a race!

The difficulty the careful trainer has in keeping the boys in

17

hand is incredible.    The young horses, full of courage, are ready to run away on the least inducement ; and there is a great difference between running away and galloping.    Very few lads appreciate this, and there are trainers who allow this grievous mistake to occur year after year, venting their "private dictionary" on the lads after the mischief is done. The legs of many a valuable yearling have been damaged for ever at this stage of his schooling.    As a baby learns to walk, so a yearling should learn to gallop—by degrees.    He should be so broken and *encouraged* that, led by the head lad's hack, or any similar slow, sober old gentleman capable of setting a good example, he can be ridden as a hack, before attempting to start him galloping upsides the rest of the inmates of the nursery.    And always have a gelding to lead him.    Patience, we are told, is a virtue ;    in the breaking and training of youngsters it is an absolute essential.    Not the least detail must be missed.

Then comes the final part of his education, one which appears to be opposed to all sporting instincts, though commercially it may save time.    The baby has to be brought under the barrier of the starting-gate.    This is possibly the most crucial period of his early days, and there are not a few whose tempers are ruined, or at least injured, at the circus-like business which has to be gone through before they can be accustomed, if they ever are, to this artificial adjunct to sport.    True, there are some youngsters who take to the gate almost at once ; but there are others.    We are so inclined to look to the successes that we often take no heed of the failures.    But the gate has come to stay, and that being so, I can do no good by here dwelling on its bad side—stern fact says, there it is, take it or leave it.    I think I have now established what I wished to explain to those unacquainted with a legitimate racing stable, namely, that the winter season is no holiday, but a busy and most anxious time for any trainer worthy of the name.

So far as the owner is concerned, the great obstacle he

has to face is that there are no prizes to be run for during this period, and he has to pay his training and other bills, with no possible chance of anything coming in, unless he descends to the fast-languishing sport under National Hunt Rules. Once a sport in which many a good man indulged, and an open field for the amateur, it has for the past few years drooped and drooped to such an extent, that unless somebody comes to the rescue it will soon to all intents and purposes become extinct. It wants the support of aspirants to Grand National honours, either as owners or amateur jockeys. In the eighties and earlier there were many. Where are they to be found to-day? The best men I ever knew—I am speaking of all-round sportsmen—are now passing the meridian of life, or have, alas! passed it, and their deeds in the field and on the Turf are now but pleasant reminiscences. I can see no youngster to-day likely to follow in their footsteps. This is the knell which has been sounding the gradual decay of a most glorious sport, full of traditions, full of ceaseless adventures and stories, full of those chances and risks which the youngster of the present day appears only too anxious to avoid.

## CHAPTER XXX.

## THE SALE OF SCEPTRE.

RATHER from necessity than choice, I was compelled to continue running horses during the close season on the flat, and with Barberstown (Bobsie I have already referred to) and a few others I managed to win some races, and succeeded in what I believe is the prevailing spirit of 'chasing nowadays—I refer to the new school, not the old—I made it pay.

By the aid of this I was enabled to hang on to Sceptre. and as a final shot, whether I was to retain her or not, I took Hobson's choice, and ran her in the Lincolnshire Handicap. Financial matters were in a critical state with me—that is, unless I sold, and creditors who had displayed reasonable patience, for which I sincerely thank them, were beginning to "place the matter in the hands of my solicitor."

Lincoln is not a galloping course, and I can imagine none more unsuitable to the "old lady"; but there it was—win, and I could retain her; lose or not run, and she must go to meet the just demands made upon me. The rest of my horses had done little, and would not have realised their value, much less sufficient to meet my liabilities. Therefore the Lincoln of 1903 had to decide a lot for me. I got her well, but the length of the course, an easy mile, was all against her, and I was more than doubtful, indeed, I was certain, she would not strike the ground quickly enough to be in it with them in the early part of the race. I had not backed her for a large sum, though she was a good favourite, but merely for sufficient to carry me over the stile if she won.

She cantered to the post full of that fire which I liked to see her display, and before long "They're off" re-echoed in the stands. My opinion was confirmed. Sceptre had not begun with her field, and was not to be found among the leaders. Over Norton, always nicely placed on the rails, took up the running a long way from home, and won comfortably, with Portcullis second, Ypsilanti (7st 9lb) third, Sceptre (9st 1lb), easing up, being placed fifth, a head behind Cliftonhall, who had only 6st 10lb. The falseness of the race is proved by the position occupied by Ypsilanti, not to mention Cliftonhall. In any case, Sceptre had been set a formidable task, as the form subsequently proved.

It was my last chance of retaining a mare I had more than an affection for, and I accepted the inevitable.

No sooner has a man a horse for sale, than a certain set start a scandal as to its well-being, soundness, or something or other. The prevailing *canard* in connection with Sceptre was that she made a noise. "Bob Sievier would never sell her if she was all right." How little did they know what Bob Sievier had gone through, and the struggle he had made to hang on to her as long as he had done! The outsider is a poor, suspicious mortal—even impecuniosity must carry with it some motive!

It so happened that Mr. Arthur Chetwynd was due to stay with me at Liverpool for the National week. At that time he managed Mr. Bass's horses, and that gentleman can never look back with regret to the deals which Mr. Chetwynd made on his behalf, at my suggestion. No sooner had I put the fact of Sceptre being for sale before Mr. Chetwynd than he cabled to India. Asking the price I put upon her, I replied 25,000 guineas. He inquired if the shillings were for him as commission, this being customary in deals where a middle-

man intervenes. I answered in the affirmative. He said:
"Then I shall cable £25,000, for I could not accept anything
out of the transaction." The next morning the answer came.
and Sceptre was no longer mine.    I had sold her on the
spot, but at the subsequent request of Mr. Chetwynd I agreed
that she should pass a veterinary examination. Mr. Leach,
of Newmarket, as excellent a vet. as he is good-natured,
duly arrived at Shrewton.    Knowing how thick-winded
Sceptre was, I gave her plenty of work preceding his arrival,
and she passed without much difficulty.

Then Alec Taylor came along to take her away—well, I
bore it very well, all things considered, and I do not wish to
look upon the scene again.

During her two-year-old career Sceptre won two-thirds of
her races, and as a three-year-old won half.    The whole of
the latter, with the exception of the "Thousands," were run
on good or soft going, an important feature which some of
her captious critics have always overlooked.    Had the going
been hard, she would undoubtedly have missed some of her
minor engagements, but fortune favoured her in this respect.

Sceptre's various records for races, apart from the nominal
records of being the highest-priced yearling ever sold, and
being trained by her owner, an amateur, are as under:—
Winning the Woodcote Stakes, Epsom (for two-year-olds),
6 furlongs in 1min 10 3-5sec ; the Two Thousand Guineas,
one mile in 1min 39sec ; the Nassau Stakes, Goodwood, one
mile and a half in 2min 40sec ; and the record for "classics"
in absolutely winning four of the five great races.

I have been often asked my opinion as to which was the
better, Sceptre or Pretty Polly. My answer has invariably
been, "They were both too good to be compared."

There have been so many incorrect statements in regard
to the prices realised by the different horses which I bought
at the sale of the late Duke of Westminster's yearlings, that
I will put all contention at an end by stating the exact figures.
They are as follows :—

## PRICES PAID BY ME AT AUCTION WHEN YEARLINGS.

£

For Sceptre, by Persimmon—Ornament ...................... 10,500

For Duke of Westminster, by Orme—Gantlet ............. 5,880

For Sandflake, by Trenton—Sandiway ....................... 5,775

For Consort, by Orme—Console ............................... 735

Total .... ... £22,890

## PRICES RECEIVED AND STAKES WON.

£

Duke of Westminster (bought by John Porter for Mr. George Faber) ................................................. 22,050

Consort (bought by John Porter for Mr. George Faber) 2,100

Sandflake (bought by the International Horse Agency on behalf of Mr. W. Bass) ............................... 1,680

Sceptre (bought by Mr. Arthur Chetwynd on behalf of Mr. W. Bass) ................................................ 25,000

Stakes won by Duke of Westminster ........................ 2,645

Stakes won by Sceptre ......................................... 25,650

Total ......... £79,125

The result of the deal in these four yearlings shows a profit of £56,235, exclusive of expenses, an item which would shock the uninitiated. It is not uninteresting to note firstly that Duke of Westminster more than paid for the lot; secondly, that Sceptre won in stakes more than this sum; and thirdly, that her sale price also more than covered it. Hence the original outlay was regained by the aid of any one of these three different results, and those who at the ring-side on that warm July morning stigmatised me as a fool afterwards recalled their mistake like sportsmen, or viewed me with the jaundiced eye of jealousy. The latter feeling is no less prevalent among the ordinary general run of those on the Turf, than it is among professionals on the stage, in the law, and;

for that matter, wherever success predominates over the failure of those who stand still.

With the departure of Sceptre, Shrewton lost her Queen. The village folk—and I shall always look upon them with no small esteem and regard—were as loyal to the old lady as if she *had* swayed a Sceptre. After the "Thousands" the little hamlet was bedecked with flags, and the local brass band turned out to a man and everyone rejoiced—except the local bookie!

A kingdom without a crowned head is a barren waste, and Shrewton had no further charm for me—at least until my children returned home for their holidays. Until then there had been a kind of vacuum about the place. But time passes very rapidly, and is a great healer, and with it we leave the past troubles of life behind.

Among other horses I bought at auction was the American Scotchman II. I gave 240 guineas for him, and may say I bought him partly out of curiosity. That he must once have been a real good horse I have no manner of doubt, but when I took him over he had been puncture-fired, while his neck, in places, where the hypodermic syringe had been inserted, showed the "puncture" scars, almost as plainly as those on his legs! Had Scotchman II. been treated and trained according to English principles I fully believe he would have turned out a second Ypsilanti.

There is no question that many of the horses running just before this time were subjected to the nefarious practice of what in America is called "the dope," and when in later years the history of the Turf is written, this period could not be better described than as the successful epoch of the Yankee Alchemists.

This wretched American practice, which, be it said to the honour of the New York Stewards, is punishable to the extent of "ruling any offender off the track," was, with all its attendant tortures, insidiously introduced into this country. The agonies the thoroughbred suffered from the unnatural administration of the drugs, which went to make up " the dope," were only too apparent on our racecourses, and those subjected to this brutal treatment went to the starting-gate like mad animals. By the aid of the dope, forsaking and eschewing all the honourable traditions of sport, a certain section of notorious Americans succeeded in ruining many good horses, at the same time playing havoc among the bookmakers. There was neither art nor science in their methods; it was sheer brutality.

In time the cruelty was detected and fully exposed. A rule was passed by the Jockey Club forbidding such practices, and the pirates have since departed for Columbia. In my opinion there is no more reprehensible offence against the canons of racing than that of resorting to the trick of doping —not even when a man descends to methods which effectually stop a horse from winning.

## CHAPTER XXXI.

### SOME ANECDOTES.

URING 1903 I won some small races with Boycot, St. Joie, Thunderbolt, Snowdrop, and others, my best winner being Heronry, who secured the Acorn Stakes at Epsom, and I sold her at Doncaster that autumn for 3,000 guineas.

I possessed nothing above the useful class, but I had a very nice-looking lot of yearlings, and their running has substantiated my estimate of them. They were Brother Bill, Cherry Ripe, Potash (a good winner in South Africa), Elston (half-brother to Thunderbolt), King Duncan, and others. As an instance, and a very pronounced one, of the "glorious uncertainty," King Duncan, by Ayrshire—Amphitheatre, came out on his first home gallop one of the best two-year-olds I ever tried, and was at the time a long way in front of both Cherry Ripe and Brother Bill; but it must be said for the latter that he had not thus early got his strength. I tried them first in the latter part of February, and now that their respective merits on a racecourse are known, their early trial may be the more interesting.

Trial, February 26, 1904, four furlongs:—

|  | St | lb |
|---|---|---|
| King Duncan | 7 | 11 |
| Value, 3yrs | 8 | 4 |
| Cherry Ripe | 7 | 4 |
| Brother Bill | 7 | 0 |
| High Treason | 6 | 10 |

They finished as placed, King Duncan winning easily by a length, and his style much impressed me. Cherry Ripe ran like a stayer, beaten two lengths, Brother Bill finishing well in front of High Treason. A more satisfactory gallop at this early period than King Duncan's could not be imagined, and except that Value was a thorough genuine bit of stuff for about four furlongs, and had nearly always led her field in every race she had run, I should have doubted the gallop. Nor must it be overlooked that Value won a selling race this same year at Brighton (1904). In the middle of March I had Hardy down at Shrewton, and fully to satisfy myself I tried the same lot again at exactly the same weights, except that I put 4lb more up on King Duncan. Hardy rode him, and he won just as easily, the gallop being a reproduction of the former one except that Brother Bill finished neck and neck with Cherry Ripe. He was gaining strength and coming on. King Duncan was engaged at Liverpool, and I felt I had something to bet on. I made no secret of his usefulness, and he started a good favourite. He had eaten and done well since leaving home. On the rising of the barrier he jumped off and led his field to the turn. At this point the rest were riding to keep within hail of him. As much as 100 to 5 was offered on him, but no sooner were these long odds shouted than he stopped —I can offer no reason—and was not even placed. On returning home I tried him again, and this time put the three-year-old St. Joie in the gallop as well as Value, leaving the two-year-olds out. Again the result confirmed his home merits ; he won in a canter. I believed I possessed one of the best colts I had ever owned, though his Liverpool performance was an enigma ; but up to the time of writing these lines he has never won a race ! I sold him to Mr. W. Bass, and I have no doubt now that he will not finish his races in public. What he can do at home I have no idea. This is at least a vivid picture of the " glorious uncertainty." Both Brother Bill and Cherry Ripe have turned out smart—the former a stayer, the latter a sprinter—and I am only too pleased that they are both owned by a good sportsman. Elston, the half-brother to Thunderbolt, also promised well, and perhaps, like the brown son of Chimera, he wants time, though I believe he has turned out a disappointment. Then Perpetual won a nice lot of races, and Colonel Wozac, even after leading Rock Sand in his work, showed he had not lost his form. Boycot, Yankee Duchess, Twin Cherry, and Snowdrop have also brought grist to the mill, and taking them collectively they would have made up a fairly successful string for any one man to own and train.

Although I have already briefly explained the natural advantages of training on the Wiltshire Downs, the great galloping area, and the many gallops adaptable for the various seasons of the year, Salisbury Plain has also its humorous side.

I remember a sham fight, and it was indeed well-named, which took place between different contingents of volunteers. Some of these aspirants to military honours, as soon as they are under canvas, perambulate with stilted step, throwing out their chests to such a degree as almost to suggest they have "bought the Plain." No sooner do some of these young scions of Mars put on the King's uniform than suddenly, as if by magic, they imagine they are better men in all respects than when engaged in their ordinary humble, everyday occupation. Opportunity makes the man, but I fail to see why a uniform should, any more than a wig and gown must necessarily make a good counsel!

The sham fight I have referred to was arranged to take place, the whole being set down according to military red-tape rule, and there was nothing in these preliminaries to suggest that the opposing force had anything to meet except a host of ingenuous friends! As "enemies" they were of the courteous description, effusively so. Each side knew where the other was, their numbers, &c. At a stipulated hour bugles sounded in both camps with the same punctuality that Big Ben announces the time of day. Without the semblance of fear or responsibility the men fell in, the majority with a picnic smile on their countenances. They one and all treated the fear of death with the utmost contempt, though it is possible the romance attached to the Victoria Cross did to some extent appeal to their wild imaginations. It was a glorious holiday. To the martial strains of " The Girl I Left Behind Me " (I have often wondered whether the girl always wasted her time all this while) on came the noble " Death or a Night in the Canteen Brigade," while from an imaginary hiding place " on the skyline " the enemy awaited them with blank cartridges, a fair portion of which had already " gone off " by accident as they lay in deadly ambush awaiting the onslaught. There is little or no cover on Salisbury Plain, and all plantations are declared out of bounds, hence the ambush disclosed the enemy silhouetted against the sky! To hold a hidden position on the top of a hill would be an overwhelming advantage, but when this proves to be an unprotected and fully-exposed position, it may be questioned if with the aid of modern weapons, the picture might not be quickly transformed into a dissolving view! But these are not conditions seriously taken into consideration at all sham fights, more especially what I may excusably term "amateur" ones, so the opposing forces gradually but surely got nearer and nearer without the loss of a man, but not without the loss of a lot of powder. In view of the progress the fight had made it was strikingly extraordinary how exceedingly well the men had retained the polish on their boots! Nearer and nearer these boots brought the foes to closer quarters. Then things appeared to me to get into a hopeless tangle, my past experience of active service was of no use to me; possibly the advancement we have made since those days is beyond my comprehension. Suddenly the retreat sounded, and all was over. The umpires met and made their award. Which side won I never could exactly understand, but one thing was clear to me—there had never been a change of bowling during the whole match.    The only bit of "active service" I witnessed during the whole of the "march" dubbed manœuvres, was a handful of over-zealous volunteers chasing a hare with hatchets.

I do not wish it to be thought that I in any way desire to depreciate our Volunteers ; on the contrary, but what I do think is that it would be possibly better all round if, in their sham fights, they were opposed by regulars.

On one occasion, just before the St. Leger (1902), I was out with my string of horses earlier than usual when I came across a picket of Volunteers.  They had been "on watch" all night, and were sleeping peacefully under the shelter of some bushes.  I aroused the sergeant, and as he was rubbing his eyes I ejaculated peremptorily. "Consider yourself under arrest!"    He was wideawake instanter!    I had "formed fours" with my string, and they were "marching" on peacefully towards the training ground.  The picket fell in, and I marched "the prisoners" off in the direction of the gallop. The sorry faces of the men almost drew an expression of compassion from me, but I kept up the joke.    Having reached our destination, I sent Sceptre a clinking gallop, led by Doochary and Scotchman II.   The "prisoners" appeared highly delighted, and ordering them to fall in, I addressed them thus : "You have seen Sceptre, the best filly in the world, do a real good gallop, and my advice to you is, always to keep your eyes open, and back her for the St. Leger. Attention! Right turn! Dismiss!"

Later in the season I received a very pleasant letter from that sergeant thanking me for arresting them, adding that all the prisoners had had a good win.

I once had rather a funny experience with two subalterns who had just joined the gunners, and were "recruited" to Bulford Camp.  They came across me on the Plain, and had evidently lost their way.   The open country, its general appearance and stillness, with not a thing moving to be detected as far as the eye can reach, appears to inspire some of these youngsters with a military zeal, more imaginary than real. Riding up, they inquired the way to Bulford. To direct strangers across country, over what to all appearances can best be described as the open veldt, is no easy matter, for it can only be done by travelling from one landmark to another. Being familiar with the country, I explained these to the best of my ability, and sent them on their journey. Shortly afterwards I noticed they came to a halt, and one of them, taking what appeared to be a map from his pocket, they consulted it. It was not long before I observed them riding back towards me at a gallop. Pulling up, one of them accosted me as follows: "Look here, when we asked you the way to Bulford we did not desire to be put on the wrong road."

I replied that I had directed them the right way, but if they, thus early, practically understood the military map better than they did plain English it was useless for them to inquire. Then the other youngster chipped in, and producing the map, said something to the effect that they were not going to be "spoofed." I observed that if they knew anything of the game of spoof they were acting the part of their own markers. At this juncture they again consulted the map, and leaving me with a look of swaggering contempt, rode off in the direction of Lavington, the exact opposite way to Bulford!

That evening, at stable time, two young men rode up and inquired of one of the boys the way to Bulford Camp. I fancied I recognised the voice of one of the youngsters I had met in the morning, and leaving Sceptre's box, sure enough I confronted my two friends. They gave a sheepish glance. I at once put them at their ease.

"Your horses look a bit knocked up. Don't you think you might give them a rest before continuing your journey —and come and have a look at Sceptre?"

".Sceptre?" they ejaculated simultaneously. "Are you Mr. Sievier?"

"Yes. Come into the house, and if you care to stop to dinner I will ride over to Bulford with you afterwards."

The lads put up their tired nags, and late that evening I rode over to the camp with them. I have met them since, and the lesson they received that day was not inferior to any they learnt at Sandhurst.

A better lot of sportsmen than the officers regularly quartered at Bulford I do not wish to meet. Without exception they preserved the gallops, and did all in their power to promote the welfare of the trainer. It was always a pleasure for me to show them over the stables, and I do not remember on any occasion of their visits one of their number asking my opinion of the chance of any horse I had engaged in a race. This was not the general custom with the Militia!

During my residence at Elston House, which was the name of my place at Shrewton, I trained a few horses for Lord Fermoy, an Irish nobleman who possessed a charmingly sanguine estimate of their merits, not to mention their value! My only regret in this connection was that for all practical use his calculations were so much at fault. Then I sold Thunderbolt to Mr. Herbert Sleath-Skelton on the understanding that he did not leave the stable, and having won a very useful race with him, I induced his new owner to purchase Happy Slave at the sale of Mr. "Joe" Lewis's horses for 1,500 guineas. The horse was as sound as the proverbial bell except in temper, and in consequence of this latter curse, so prevalent among thoroughbreds, was a very peculiar horse to train. I took great pains with him, studied his temperament, watched him, and kept a strict eye on the boy who "did" him. Happy Slave frequently and emphatically demonstrated that work was the last thing he cared about, and that he infinitely preferred slow paces to fast. There are some human beings not entirely lacking in these qualifications! With considerable patience and care I got him to my liking. Then I tried him. As a result of this trial I told Mr. Sleath-

Skelton that the Newmarket October Handicap (1903) was a
real good thing for him. He was allotted 6st 12lb, and with
Butchers up could claim the 5lb allowance. When I say he
was a stone and a beating in front of Thunderbolt (3 yrs), who
had won a fair race at Salisbury in a common canter by two
lengths, a similar event at Hurst Park, and that in the gallop
Snowdrop and Colonel Wozac were beaten off, I do not think
I was exaggerating my description of his chance. Both
Hardy and Butchers rode in the trial. As the race was run,
Happy Slave had the winning of it at any point, and how he
was ultimately beaten by a neck by Gourgaud I can only
leave his jockey to explain. Both his owner and I had a
large sum on him, and his subsequent performance in the
Duke of York Stakes amply shows how easily he should have
won.

Mention of the Duke of York Stakes recalls one of the
most extraordinary experiences I have had in racing. Happy
Slave was engaged in it with 6st 6lb, inclusive of the apprentice allowance, and Sceptre, then the property of Mr. Bass,
was handicapped at 9st 4lb. On the day of the race, about
a couple of hours before the start, Lord Berkeley Paget and
Mr. Arthur Chetwynd came to me in the paddock at Kempton. I noticed they displayed no little anxiety, and the
reason for this soon appeared, when they stated that Sceptre
was lame. Alec Taylor, who was standing close by, was
called up, and he explained the symptoms. I knew exactly
what was the matter. I had gone through the same experiences with the "old lady" myself. She had a knack of
going superficially lame. To all appearance she would at
these times undoubtedly be pronounced lame. But after
walking for less than a minute she would shake it off, and
trot, canter, or gallop perfectly sound. I explained this,
adding that if she were mine she would run, "but"—and I
addressed myself to Lord Berkeley Paget and Mr. Chetwynd
—"if you do not run I shall win with Happy Slave; but run
her, it will not harm her, nor should I advise you to run if I

18

for an instant imagined it would be detrimental to her future." I was fully aware what a good thing it was for Mr. Sleath-Skelton's horse with Sceptre out of the way. I had backed him to win about £10,000 at long prices, not for an instant thinking I could beat my old mare, and had a good round sum on him for a place, which I looked upon as a certainty. It was ultimately decided to start Sceptre, and I believe I am right in saying that had I opposed the idea of her running, both Lord Berkeley Paget and Mr. Chetwynd would, under the circumstances, have acted on my advice. From a pecuniary point of view it was greatly to my interest that she should not take part in the race.

Naturally, I was fully aware of all Sceptre's little failings, not the least of which was her dislike to come round a turn. As soon as her jockey took an " easy " at her she always hung, and was inclined to stop. The only way to ensure her keeping up her pace, so that she had not to be set going again after rounding a turn, was to let her run wide outside her field. This I knew Madden would not attempt. I was in a peculiar position, only made peculiar through my devotion to Sceptre. I had Mr. Sleath-Skelton's interests primarily to consider, and this I did. I gave Butchers, who again rode Happy Slave, strict injunctions to get a good place at all costs before reaching the bend for home. I further impressed upon him that at this point he had to come on for all he and his horse were worth, and, if possible, to " shoot " his field. He carried out my orders to the letter ; indeed, he rode as good a race here as he had ridden a bad one at Newmarket, and I cannot give him higher praise than this. Just before reaching the home turn he secured the rails, and coming on he was clear of his field, and dashing up the straight, led by at least three or four lengths. Nor had I forgotten that Sceptre always went freer for Hardy than for any other jockey, and on this occasion Madden had the mount. He brought her round the turn on the rails in the rear of the field, and she had to be shaken up as soon as she got straight for home. This, as I have stated, I was sure would happen, and it was this and nothing else which I knew was the only possible chance Happy Slave had of winning. For seconds it looked as if she would never get through, but Madden at last emerged from what looked like an impossible position, and *then* it was seconds as she began to get nearer and nearer to the leader. Madden made a feint at trying to get up on the inside, but, thank heaven, he changed his tactics, for if he had pursued them, Butchers most surely would have squeezed him, with the chance that she might have been the victim of an accident. Butchers was but an apprentice. Suddenly placing her on the outside, Madden made a determined effort. Sceptre responded. It was a great race ; they had passed the number-board opposite the stand ; they were close home ; Happy Slave still led. With a grand determined effort Sceptre appeared to lay herself down level to the ground, and they passed the winning post locked together. The excitement was intense, and the judge's verdict was, "Sceptre by a short head."

Immediately after the race Mr. Arthur Chetwynd sought me, and, holding out his hand, shouted in the midst of the excitement that prevailed, "Well, Sievier, by God, you're a sportsman ! "

## CHAPTER XXXII.

### SIEVIER v. DUKE.

AM now approaching a period which may probably be considered the most interesting of my life to the public from the mere fact that, generally speaking, they are already acquainted with its outward aspect, though to a great extent they are ignorant of the actual facts. I say "ignorant of the actual facts" in all its meaning and with all its force, for the miscarriage of justice in the slander action, Sievier v. Duke, could only find its fellow in the criminal case of Adolph Beck; and it is not a little significant that Mr. Justice Grantham presided as judge on both of these occasions. In the latter case this judge allowed "expert" evidence as to handwriting to be received as though it were a mandate from Above, which, after Adolph Beck had been found guilty, proved to be absolutely unreliable; indeed, utterly untrue. On the other hand, Mr. Justice Grantham disallowed certain questions which would at once have established the innocence of "the prisoner," and after a severe and adverse summing up, the jury were inevitably compelled, through the misrepresentations made and allowed, and through the suppression of evidence which would have broken down the prosecution, to bring in a verdict of Guilty against a man as innocent of the crime with which he was charged as the judge himself.

This case is notorious for its gross miscarriage of justice, and is fresh in the minds of all ; indeed, it can never be eliminated from the black pages which record these terrible—I might say tragic—facts. My sole reason for mentioning it is, as I have stated, that Mr. Justice Grantham, the judge of Adolph Beck, was also the judge in the case, Sievier v. Duke.

In dealing with Sir William Grantham and these legal proceedings I shall be compelled to refer to several matters already dealt with, so in this respect I must claim my readers' indulgence and forbearance, but justice cannot be done without here and there harking back.

That I had no fairer hearing than Adolph Beck a very large majority of the British public have fully testified ; and were proof required I might quote the many letters which appeared in the daily Press at the time, the judge's extraordinary misdirection to the jury, and last, but not least, his permitting the reception of evidence which no other judge on the bench would for an instant have tolerated, and which subsequently caused a question to be asked in the House of Commons, when the Solicitor-General, in reply, stated in effect that he deprecated that any such statements as those complained of by the hon. member were permitted by the judge, and that similar " evidence " would not be allowed in civil cases again.

Therefore, I wish it to be fully understood that I am not penning these lines with any idea of vindicating myself. I have more friends to-day than I had then. Many men who at that time were only nodding acquaintances shake hands with me now. I do not believe that any unbiassed man would assume I had a fair trial, and this being my conviction I will proceed to prove it beyond reasonable contradiction.

I preface my remarks with these observations, so that when I reach the evidence which was adduced at the trial, with the questions and the answers—indeed, the whole case, as represented by my counsel and misrepresented by Mr. Justice Grantham—my readers may be able better to appreciate the true state of things.

Throughout the whole proceedings a mysterious something

—I think I could give it a name, but I will not—appeared to pervade the atmosphere of the court, except perhaps when Sir James Duke was in the witness-box. It laid hold of the unprofessional listeners as might the insidious, sleepy sickness of the desert; and those who have not listened to a *cause célèbre* lasting over several days have no idea of its subtle influence, how infectious it is, and its inevitable damnation to the party it attacks.

Nor must my readers overlook the fact that Mr. Justice Grantham is deaf. This may account for everything—or anything. If " what the eye does not see the heart does not yearn for," then truly what the ear does not hear the brain does not trouble about.

Now that my readers are enlightened on some preliminary points let me proceed with the story. I regret that in certain instances I shall be compelled to give names, but when I feel I can in justice to myself suppress them I shall certainly do so—not that I see any reason for this, except that some people are but cowards when brought before the critical eye of the public. I have had some practical experience of this!

It was the Second October Meeting at Newmarket, the year Grey Tick won the Cesarewitch, 1903, and several of us made up a very jolly party at the Rutland Hotel, composed of Major Sellar, Mr. Arthur Chetwynd, four other members of the Raleigh Club, and myself. It is not an uncommon thing for cards to be played after dinner, and this has been known to have taken place in the most exalted circles! At the previous Newmarket Meeting, when Sceptre won the Jockey Club Stakes, I had lost a little amongst pretty well the same friends and acquaintances; on this occasion I won. The game played was baccarat. On the first night nothing very sensational occurred. At times I was losing within the region of four figures, and the game fluctuated until it closed for the evening, when I was merely a hundred or so out. After it was over, two of the players—whom I need not name— certainly had a royal duel, one owing the other something like

£12,000 at one time, but it eventually ended in their going double or quits—a most childish and ridiculous arrangement. On the third evening I took the bank—we had most of us had a go at it—and had one of those lucky runs which sometimes favours one side or the other, the banker or the punters. With the exception of myself, every man present was, as I have said, a member of the Raleigh Club. I mention this because the members of the Raleigh are no fools, and are generally considered capable of looking after themselves. When the game ended Major Sellar owed me something like £7,000. I gave him—and those who were present will fully endorse this—every chance to get out, but my luck was in; I could not do wrong, and my opponent could not do right. I had no wish to win so much, and I felt that my attempt to reduce the amount by giving Major Sellar these chances, had only been the means of increasing it. Hence, the next morning I spoke to one of the party, expressing my feelings on the subject of my winnings, and in the end, on my own proposition, it was arranged that instead of £7,000 I would call it £3,000 that I had won. For one gentleman to make this concession to another, under the circumstances, is merely an act of courteous generosity; on the other hand, I believe it is unheard of for a card-sharper to forego any portion of his gains when the money is at hand to liquidate his claim. On our arrival in town from Newmarket, on the Friday, I had occasion to call at the Raleigh to see a friend who was there. On entering the hall, I saw him in the now famous gazing-room, and, not being given to hanging about, I went in to him. Several members were present, all of whom I knew. I was asked to have a drink—not an uncommon act of hospitality at any club—and I had one. I noticed someone prowling about the doorway, and, as he passed to and fro, glancing into the room. It was the now "immortalised" Sir James Duke. On the following afternoon Major Sellar called at the Carlton Hotel—where I then stayed whenever in town— and handed me his open cheque for £3,000. After doing so he informed me that had he believed what he had been told, he would have been perfectly justified in refusing to settle. We were then walking up Regent Street, and I suggested that he should take me into the Raleigh and explain what he meant. He said he was sorry, but he could not take me into the club. He was perfectly friendly towards me, but I was quite satisfied there was something wrong somewhere, and I then and there demanded a reason for his statements. He refused, but the more he declined the more insistent I became, until at last, seeing that I was resolved, and would not accept any refusal, he was compelled to tell me what had occurred.

The idea may have got abroad that Major Sellar, after hearing what Sir James Duke had to say, ran like the gossip of the day from him to me, and repeated everything in breathless haste. It was not so. Naturally, he was very much perturbed at what he had heard, more especially when it is remembered that he did not believe it. Nevertheless, I had to force him to repeat the statements which had been made, and it was with evident reluctance that he told me the story. I need not state the exact conversation which took place between us, but will condense it by taking the words bodily from my counsel's brief:

"That on the 16th of October, 1903, Sir James Duke was in the Raleigh Club in the society of Major Sellar, and he informed Major Sellar that the presence of Mr. Sievier in the club was objectionable.

"That on the day following, Major Sellar asked Sir James Duke, in the presence of Mr. T. Lushington and Mr. Arthur Chetwynd, who it was who had complained of Mr. Sievier, and it was under such circumstances that he uttered the slander as follows:

"'It is a great pity you should have anything to do with the sort of man Sievier is. His reputation is known, and he is a card-sharper, thief, and murderer. I have seen Sievier thrown from a boat into the sea for cheating at cards, and a man was once found under his window, in Australia, murdered, and it was common repute that Sievier murdered him.

"'Sievier made money by Sceptre being beaten in the Derby of 1902.

"'Sievier was ordered out of the Jockey Club Stand at Newmarket, and was turned out of it, and this was done at my instigation ; I unmasked him to the Stewards. He was also turned out of Boodle's Club.'"

Had I been a murderer, or ever been charged with so heinous a crime ; had a man ever been found murdered under my window in Australia ; had I been a cheat at cards, and thrown into the sea in consequence ; had I been a thief, and unmasked by Sir James Duke to the Stewards of the Jockey Club ; had I ever been turned out of Boodle's or the Club Stand at Newmarket ; had 1 made money by Sceptre being beaten in the Derby, I knew all or any of these could be easily proved. Had I been guilty on any one count—my life has been a thoroughly public one—I leave the merest stranger to imagine whether I should have been fool enough—I might say mad enough—to have brought an action in the public courts !

A more vindictive lying statement has never been uttered by any man against another, and my first impulse was to chastise Sir James Duke in the manner he well merited. But the whole thing was so outrageous, so utterly false, that I determined to seek the "JUSTICE" of my country.

1 did not remember Sir James Duke ever speaking to me but once in his life, and that was after Success had won me a selling race at Brighton. He said, to the best of my memory —and it certainly is more accurate than the "noble" baronet's —"Well, you might have told me to back it." I did not know him, and took no notice, but, turning to an acquaintance, inquired who he was.

"That's Duke," was the response.

"Who's Duke?" I asked further.

" Sir James Duke ; he's a Steward here."

" What ! the fellow who received a mixed reception at Lewes, when he rode in one of the amateur races ? "

" Yes."

" Oh ! "

And I passed on ; and from that day to the time when I learnt of his foul accusations I had never heard of him again. He might have been dead.

That he had uttered the slander, there was no manner of doubt, for, apart from Major Sellar, it was confirmed in a letter to me from Mr. Arthur Chetwynd, which ran as follows :

<blockquote>
" Raleigh Club.

" Dear Bob,—David (i.e., Sellar) has told me about matters. The party has said the same thing to me, and I will stick to you both.—Yours,

" A. C. CHETWYND."
</blockquote>

What Mr. Chetwynd meant by sticking to one, I soon realised was not quite in keeping with the spirit of his letter. When asked to call on Sir George Lewis to confirm his note to me, he shuffled out of it, and in the end I was unable even to put him in the witness-box.  Not quite a legitimate return for the advice I gave him to run Sceptre for the Duke of York Stakes, when she beat the horse I trained by a short head !

Mr. T. Lushington made no statement, no promise—and kept it !

I consulted Sir George Lewis, a writ was issued, and the usual legal preliminaries were gone through.  I had arranged a trip to India, but this I was compelled to forego.

Shortly after this, at the Liverpool Autumn Meeting, I lost £6,000 to a member of the Raleigh Club at baccarat.  At one time during the play I was a good winner.  There were only three players, the other one being also a member of the Raleigh.  It may appear strange that if there was any truth or foundation for the slander I am dealing with, that after being a good winner I did not possess sufficient skill to retain my gains ; but, on the other hand, left off a very heavy loser.

The defence set up was the usual farcical denial, and it is only the " alternative " part of a defence that ever need be taken seriously.

The defendant having denied slandering the plaintiff, then goes on to explain how and why he did so, if he did so, and so on, and so forth.   In this case, as I have observed, he denied the slander and alternatively claimed privilege on the ground of being a member of the committee of the Raleigh Club.

Prior to the hearing of the case all sorts of rumours were afloat.   It was common report that, win or lose the case, Mr. Charles Gill had stated that I should afterwards be prosecuted for perjury, and the defendant and his followers repeated this *ad nauseam.*   As we proceed we shall find this threat was carried out to the bitter end, except that my traducers ignominiously failed to substantiate' even a *primâ facie* case against me.   Of this anon.

In May, 1904, the case was likely to come on at any moment, and when it was discovered that Mr. Justice Grantham was to be the judge I immediately consulted my counsel, Mr. Eldon Bankes, K.C.   I had previously retained Mr. Rufus Isaacs, but he was also engaged upon a long and complicated case, in which he represented the Brighton Corporation, and which came on in another court at exactly the same time.

We were alive to the fact that Mr. Justice Grantham and the defendant were Sussex neighbours, and I asked Mr. Bankes to apply that the case might be removed from his court. Needless to say, he did not jump at my proposition.   Anyhow, he later on gave me to understand that he had seen Mr. Justice Grantham in his room, who assured Mr. Bankes that I should have an impartial trial.   God save us !

## CHAPTER XXXIII.

### THE HEARING OF THE CASE.

N connection with legal practice and its formalities there are many things which are incomprehensible to the layman, and perhaps one of the greatest enigmas in connection with the law is that high-falutin, misleading term, "special jury." The very qualification "special" at once suggests that a jury is specially got together to try a particular case—men of special ability or standing. No such thing. Many an ordinary jury consists of men of far better standing and intelligence than this very incorrectly styled "special jury." Take the "special jury" which had been collected together to try my case. The members were drawn from the neighbourhood of St. Pancras, the foreman being the keeper of a small public-house situated in one of the dingy back streets abutting on Tottenham Court Road; another was an alien lodging-house keeper living in the vicinity of the notorious Percy Street—and so on. There was not one who had the slightest pretensions to be a knowledgeable man, who could have had any familiarity with the mode of life of those engaged in the case. The whole of these twelve men—good and true, no doubt, in their proper places—as the case proceeded, were nothing more nor less than astounded. That there could have been so much money in circulation bewildered them; and how this bewilderment was whetted by the judge's observations, the admission of prohibitive

evidence, and his ultimate summing up, will amply demonstrate itself. Then, again, in the face of protests by my counsel Mr. Eldon Bankes, Mr. Charles Gill was permitted to continue his asides to the jury throughout the hearing, and I will especially point to these as occasion arises. Get twelve men lost in astonishment, and what may not happen?

It was doubtless a case which should have been tried by a Hawkins, or a Russell, or a positive lawyer such as Mr. Justice Channell.

The first witness called was Major Sellar, who proved the slander and the uttering. In cross-examination it was attempted to prove that Major Sellar had not paid me the £3,000; and to many of his answers to Mr. Lawson Walton's questions Mr. Charles Gill, in a most unwarrantable and certainly unjust manner, loudly ejaculated such remarks as "Now you have him," "Ah! now you've got him," with the palpable intention of biassing the jury, beneath whose box he sat. A more unfair procedure cannot be conceived, and yet, in the face of my counsel's protests, it was not checked by the judge. Perhaps he did not hear Mr. Eldon Bankes— everyone in court heard Mr. Gill! During the luncheon interval the cheque Major Sellar had given me was produced, and this set aside the false issue the defence were trying to prove, rather by the aid of "asides" than by the evidence then being given on oath. Major Sellar also swore that the slander was spoken in a most vindictive way. The whole of the cross-examination was based upon the assumption that I had lent Major Sellar money, that he had not discharged his debt of honour, and was, as it were, in my power, for which there was not a tissue of foundation. If the defence honestly believed their slander, why not have asked Major Sellar if he thought he had been the victim of foul play?

I then entered the witness-box. I took a long breath in the hope of inhaling a portion of the "impartial" air of the court, with a view of invigorating myself—but I found none. It took no observer of men to know which way the weathercock pointed. Somebody appeared to have made a fixture of the indicator, no matter which way the wind might veer.

I denied the slander in its entirety. Mr. Lawson Walton cross-examined me. Mr. Charles Gill was next him, and my answers were subjected to the same critical comments —I may without exaggeration say sneers—as had been those of Major Sellar. The first assumption was that I had swindled Mr. Ernest Benzon at cards in Australia. This I denied, nor was my evidence once shaken, nor were any documents produced to refute or weaken it. Since the case Mr. Benzon, who was not in England at the time of the trial, has written me a letter, which I have published in the WINNING POST, and which denied the allegations made by Sir James Duke. But my answers were never taken as evidence by the judge. He accepted the *questions as facts*, no matter what my reply to them, for in his summing-up—I style it such out of compulsory respect—he referred to this suggestion of swindling Mr. Benzon in deprecatory terms, without a tittle of evidence to justify him in so doing. Indeed, he adopted this course throughout. My answer on oath was no more received by him as evidence than had it been negatived by other witnesses, but none were called to contradict my statements! Why? Because there were none.

Then came the question of the cancellation of my presentation at Court. This occurred in 1888, solely through my having broken the cordon of social rules by becoming a bookmaker in Australia. No other reason has ever been officially or unofficially suggested. In support of this the official letter addressed to me was produced at the trial:—

"Heralds College, February 24, 1888.

"My dear Sir,—I beg to acknowledge the receipt of your letter of yesterday's date. The causes which have led to the cancellation of your presentation are shortly these :—

"Immediately after levée several people came forward and testified to the fact that you were engaged on the Turf in Australia as a bookmaker, and that in such transactions you took the name of Sutton. . . . The best that can now be done is to help me in getting clear evidence that you were not engaged on the Turf as I have mentioned, and then I am sure the announcement cancelling your Presentation would be removed.—I am, &c."

What could be plainer? But Mr. Justice Grantham shrugged his shoulders at the letter, placed it among a bundle of papers, and there it slept until the case was over. The fact that my presentation was cancelled was hurled at the jury, and in his summing-up Mr. Justice Grantham even made the extraordinary statement that "Her Majesty would rather give up her throne than be addressed by such a man." This must have conveyed the idea to the jury that I had been guilty of some heinous offence against my country. Would it not have been more in accordance with what an Englishman accepts as justice if his lordship had read to the jury the letter, which clearly sets out the facts? The suggestion that our late revered and beloved Queen, rather than be addressed by me, would have vacated the Throne of England may possibly, by the aid of a powerful imagination, be deemed judicial, but to the every-day man of the world it can only commend itself as the merest clap-trap.

I was then questioned concerning an episode with which, under the circumstances, I have been reluctantly compelled to deal at some length in my autobiography, and with which my readers are now fully acquainted. It is that of Lord Deerhurst. I see no reason to refer to this matter again in detail, and it is no fault of mine that it was ever brought up again. In this respect Lord Deerhurst has no one to thank except Sir James Duke, and how easily it might have been allowed to pass in silence is shown by the fact that Lord Deerhurst was in England at the time the case was heard, but was not even subpœnaed by the defence. We were both young men, and it is now over nineteen years ago since we both made this stupid mistake, and the defendant might have had the good grace to let the affair sleep in the peace which the fulness of time had granted it. More especially do I say this as the facts would have assisted, rather than have militated against me.

I was next cross-examined with regard to an action which I brought in 1892. Mr. Gill asked that the defendant's name should not be mentioned, and the judge allowed this, as he did in every similar instance on behalf of the defence, but on the one solitary application of my counsel that a certain lady's name should be suppressed Mr. Justice Grantham refused. I have refrained from mentioning the names of the gentler sex throughout, and I shall, as far as possible, continue to do so to the end. But in justice to myself I cannot refrain from publishing the facts, together with the names of the parties concerned, in the case referred to. I was asked to dinner at a certain house in Ashley Gardens, and I there met Mr. Charles Henry Farrer, the defendant in the action upon which I was being cross-examined, Mr. Arthur Finch Kemp. both members of the Raleigh; Mr. Walker (known as Hookey Walker), and Mr. Cameron. I may here observe that, with the exception of Mr. Walker, whom I have not since met, the others to this day remain acquaintances of mine. The party consisted of several, all of whom it is unnecessary to name; all played roulette, and after a time this game was forsaken for baccarat. At a reasonable hour Mr. Kemp left. I had been keeping the bank, and owed him £45. I also owed various sums round the table. The luck fluctuated, and when it came my way Mr. Farrer played against the run and lost £2,000. He then said he had lost more than he could afford to pay. This must also have applied to "Hookey Walker," for, as I have said, I have never seen him since! I had a private conversation in another room with Mr. Farrer. He explained what I believed was his position, and I agreed to accept a payment of half in settlement of my claim. After this interview we returned to the company, chatted for, say, another hour, when I left. He had promised to give me a cheque at Ascot the following day, but when I asked him for it, made an excuse about having forgotten it. The fact was, he had not the amount of his losses at his command. Later on I heard he had made certain statements, and my solicitors, Messrs. Lumley and Lumley, on June 27, 1892, wrote to Mr. Farrer demanding an apology, claiming payment of the agreed reduced amount, or the name of his solicitors, to whom they could send process for acceptance of service on his behalf. No answer was received to this letter, and on July 4 a further communication was sent to Mr. Farrer informing him a writ had been issued against him for slander, and it was ultimately served upon him personally. There may be some significance in the fact that he answered none of these letters.

In the meantime Mr. Kemp very rightly wrote to me asking for the £45 I owed him over play on this particular evening. Anyone who knows Mr. Arthur Finch Kemp must be fully aware that he would never ask for a debt of honour to be paid if he was not quite satisfied that everything was straight and above board. I handed the letter to Messrs. Lumley, and at an interview at their offices Mr. Kemp, who was Mr. Farrer's friend, voluntarily signed a proof of his evidence regarding that evening, and I here reproduce a pertinent extract from it:—

"During the time I was playing baccarat at ——'s house I did not see any cheating at cards there."

The case was set down, and after weary waiting was due to be heard. On the eve of the trial Messrs. Lumley received a letter from Messrs. Chester and Co., dated November 23, 1893, which was as follows:—

" 36, Bedford Row, London, W.C.

"23rd November, 1893.

" Dear Sirs,

"*FARRER ats SIEVIER.*

" When Mr. Farrer made the charges upon which this Action is founded he believed them to be true, but he is now advised that they are charges which he cannot justify or substantiate, and as he cannot substantiate them he feels, as an honourable man, that he must withdraw them.

" Having therefore withdrawn the charges it follows that Mr. Farrer must pay the sum agreed as the amount which he lost to Mr. Sievier, namely £1,000.

" He has already paid 1/3rd of this amount to Mrs. ——, thus leaving 2/3rds for which he is prepared to send you a cheque on behalf of Mr. Sievier.

" You will be good enough to write us a letter that the Action will thus be at an end, and in due course to forward us for signature the necessary consent for its removal from the List.

" Mr. Farrer has authorised us to write this letter upon the advice in conference of his Counsel, Mr. Lockwood and Mr. Marshall, that it is the right course for him to take.—Yours faithfully,

"CHESTER & CO.

" Messrs. LUMLEY & LUMLEY."

With the whole of the charges unreservedly withdrawn, backed by the advice in conference of such honourable gentlemen as Mr. Frank Lockwood, Q.C., and Mr. Marshall, Q.C., what more could any man capable of accepting a retraction expect? I agreed to the terms, and in doing so forgave and forgot. I should mention that the hostess had a third share of the bank with me, which will account for this amount being paid to her. Thus the affair ended, except that my solicitors could not obtain payment, presumably on the same score that caused the slanders to be uttered—it was not convenient to settle! In reply to many applications for payment Messrs. Chester and Co. wrote, on December 22, 1893:—

> "We have sent a copy of your letter to our client and urged his immediate attention, and we hear this day that he is, and has been, taking active steps to procure the sum agreed to be paid by him to your client. . . . We can only ask your indulgence for a further period."

Still no financial settlement arrived. On January 13, 1894, Messrs. Lumley and Lumley were compelled to apply to the Divisional Court that the sum due be paid within seven days, and this brought about a final settlement soon afterwards.

Some few years ago I was at the Empire Theatre, and Mr. T. Earle, a mutual friend, came to me and asked if I would speak to Mr. Farrer, as he wanted to apologise to me personally. I agreed. In expressing his regret, which I then deemed quite unnecessary, but no less an act of courtesy, Mr. Farrer admitted he had made unfounded charges, and had been disgracefully egged on by a man whose name I forbear to mention. To all this I swore in Court, and the papers were put in. Mr. Farrer lives. If there was anything he had to testify to against me why was he not called? Until the summing up, not even my enemies could have hoped that this episode could have been put in against me. Yet it was. Indeed, the case was proceeding on such extraordinary lines that I began to marvel if his lordship was not possibly going to send for the black cap.

During the early part of my examination in chief, I was asked two questions, which I set out with their answers, for on reading them again, in the light of subsequent events, they appear to me to be strikingly interesting:

"Have you ever been called before the Stewards at all for anything?—Nothing."

"For how many years have you owned horses?—Twenty-

four or five years, in Africa, India, Australia, and England ;
and about none of my horses has there ever been a question
of their running brought before the Stewards at any meeting
I believe there are others who have been before the Stewards."
And I looked in the direction of the defendant.

I will deal now with the two Brighton incidents—that of
Arthur Renton and John W. Taylor—which the defence
suggested were cases against me, but no evidence given in
court supported this assumption in any way whatever, nor was
any called, though the manager of the Hotel Metropole had
been subpœnaed by the defendant.  If he was permitted by
the judge to put the Vine Street constable, Drew, into the
witness-box, as after referred to, the reason for his not calling
other witnesses whom he had compelled to attend the court
must be obvious.

Dealing with the matter of Arthur Renton the facts are
simple, and have never been in dispute.  In 1893—and I must
here draw attention to the distant dates of all the episodes
which the defendant attempted to convert into dishonest
actions—I was staying at the Hotel Metropole. at Brighton.
which at that time, owing to the novelty of these new palatial
coloured glass establishments, was doing a far larger business
than is the case to-day.  I was acquainted with Renton.  I
had been playing pool with him on the evening in question,
and during the progress of the game he introduced me to one
of the players, named Cavanagh.  After the pool was over
Renton came to my sitting-room, and Cavanagh accompanied
him.  It was proposed by Renton that we should have a game
of cards, and, as I had none, a pack was obtained from the
hall-porter, either by Renton or Cavanagh.  Renton said he
would take the bank at baccarat. which he did.  He shuffled
and dealt the cards during the whole of the play without intermission.  It ended in Renton owing me a little over a thousand
pounds.  As he was leaving he asked me to give him a chance
by going double or quits.  Those who know me would be
surprised if I had not agreed.   I have gambled for much

heavier stakes, both on the racecourse and on the Stock
Exchange, not to mention on the several other chances which
help to make life interesting. Besides, I have never been a
mean gambler, and, if winning, have not held the loser in my
grasp without opening my fingers and thus giving him a chance
of escape. We cut the cards, and I won. The next morning
Renton breakfasted with me, and, as is often the case where
liabilities are involved, he hinted that he could not settle.
As it subsequently transpired that he owed the ring a very
large sum, methodically dispersed among its members, when
he sat down to take the bank at baccarat he could have had
no hope of settling had things—as it turned out they did—
gone against him. I merely make this remark *en passant*, for
the man who risks his reputation by playing without having the
necessary funds at his command, and loses, invariably resorts
to the only possible excuse—namely, that something irregular
has taken place. But he does not assert this at the card-table ;
he does not challenge the winner ; he makes no complaint,
but the next day, or the next week, as his position of a
defaulter makes itself felt, then, and only then, he suddenly
imagines *he* must have been " sharped." Did it ever occur to
Mr. Justice Grantham—if it did he kept it very dark—what
sort of a man is he who will risk incurring a debt of honour
without having any hope of paying if he loses ?

Renton having introduced me to Cavanagh, I was not a
little surprised that later, on the following day, he should
attempt to connect me with him, though I was fairly
acquainted with the contemptible schemes to which a man
who cannot pay will resort. The manager of the hotel saw
me, and said he could not allow the licence to be jeopardised,
and—very rightly—politely asked me if I could leave before
any scandal got abroad. As I was leaving that evening it
made no matter, but under the circumstances I certainly should
have left in any event.

On the Monday following, I had an appointment with
Renton in town, at the Hotel Victoria, and he arrived with

a friend and a solicitor by the name of Mr. Popham. Needless to say, this ended in a deuce of a row all round, in the middle of which up turned Cavanagh! In the end I brought an action for slander against Renton ; but, having previously made inquiries which assured me that Cavanagh was a man of ill-repute, and commonly known as "one of the boys," I waived any claim I had against Renton on account of the card-playing. Throughout my evidence I was continually cross-examined by Mr. Justice Grantham, and on every possible occasion he asked me many questions, which, if shorn of their answers, as was palpably the case in his summing up, must have misled any ordinary jury. As an instance, with reference to the play during this particular evening, I quote the following : —

"Mr. Justice Grantham : Let me see. The date of this incident was almost simultaneous with your bankruptcy ?—Yes, it was.

"And presumably you had no money to lose ?—I had not a great deal of money.

"And how would you have paid if you had lost ?—I would not have lost.

"I see. A sort of heads I win, tails you lose game ?— No, my lord. I mean I would not have lost more money than I had with me. I had money on the table, and I played in a normal way.

"But what if you had lost ?—I would not have continued to play after losing my ready-money. You are assuming, my lord, that I would have played whether I had money to pay or not. That is not the case."

Whether such ejaculations as "I see. A sort of heads I win, tails you lose game" are unbiassed and likely to leave a just impression on a jury, I leave to any fair-minded person to decide.

I swore to the fact that Renton had subsequently apologised to me, that we had shaken hands and dismissed Cavanagh from our minds; and, further, that I had introduced him to my wife, and he had lunched with us at Epsom. This being so, I believed that the heat and passion which had been displayed on both sides were amicably ended. To corroborate my statement, I publish the following letter, addressed to Renton's solicitors :—

                    " 37, Conduit Street,
                         " Bond Street,
                              "London, W.
                         " 10 January, 1894.
" Messrs. Boxall and Boxall,
      " 22, Chancery Lane, W.C.
" Dear Sirs,
          " SIEVIER & RENTON.
" We thank you for your letter of the 8th inst. The papers have recently come into our hands, and on perusal thereof we gather that your Client had already withdrawn the slanderous allegations, and under the circumstances we have advised our Client, as the matter is only a question of costs, to give Notice of Discontinuance, which will enable you to take out a Summons to tax your Costs, and there is therefore no necessity to agree terms. A formal Notice of Discontinuance shall be served in the ordinary way.
          " We are, dear sirs,
               " Yours faithfully,
                    " LUMLEY AND LUMLEY."

Messrs. Lumley and Lumley in another letter again set out the fact that Renton had apologised, that I subsequently introduced him to Lady Mabel Sievier, and we had lunched together in my box at Epsom.

Messrs. Boxall and Boxall must have been aware of this, and the matter thus ended.

In face of the above, on the advice of such excellent and well-known solicitors as Messrs. Lumley and Lumley, Mr. Justice Grantham addressed me as follows, and I append my answer : —

"Mr. Justice Grantham : But you must really see that when this matter comes before the jury it must impress them very much, when there are two cases (one Farrer's, who withdrew everything and paid in full) in which you are charged with being a card-sharper and you do not go on with the action, but pay all the costs—I am speaking of the action against Renton.  Does it not strike you that this jury would have very great difficulty in giving you any damages after you have allowed such proceedings to end in this way ?—No. my lord, because my action was stopped, Mr. Renton and I having made the amende honourable ; we have visited together, we have broken bread together, we have drunk together, and he died a friend of mine."

Some time after this matter was concluded, as Messrs. Lumley and Lumley state in their letter, I met Renton, and in the course of conversation explained that I had paid his costs, which was hardly "cricket." He stated that he had quite overlooked the matter, and, insisting on paying mine as well as his own, wrote me a cheque for £100 in his rooms in Jermyn Street. That cheque I endorsed, and it was paid through my account in the usual way. But not one of these facts, sworn to in the box and uncontradicted, was ever mentioned in the judge's summing-up. Arthur Renton is since dead, and his body was made bankrupt.

Taking the chronological order of things, the next "incident" was connected with Mr. John W. Taylor. During the Sussex fortnight—which is the time during which the Goodwood, Brighton, and Lewes race meetings are in progress —I was staying with my wife and some friends at Brighton, while Mr. and Mrs. Taylor and Captain Baumann (the Ship-wreck) were located close by. Mr. Taylor came round to my house (I had rented one on the front) and explained that he had had a very bad week, and asked me to introduce him to Mr. Porter's club, a well-known resort in those days (1893), frequented by many prominent gentlemen on the Turf. Baccarat was played there every evening; and Mr. Taylor, not being in a position—as he explained and afterwards con-firmed in a letter to me—to meet his liabilities on the fatal Monday, desired to take a chance at winning. Accompanied by Mr. A. Cox and Captain Baumann, both mutual friends of some years' standing, we repaired to Mr. Porter's. There the game of baccarat was played, counters being handed to those who paid for them, while some favoured few could be supplied with them on credit. It was not long before Mr. Taylor lost his "ready-money" supply, and he then began betting with me "on the nod." I frequently requested him not to bet so high, and once asked him to stop altogether. In the witness-box I made a mistake in the amount, and stated it was £3,500 which he lost; and, after so great a lapse of time and the many transactions I have had, I think this may be considered excusable. In reality it was £6,000 which he lost to me, at what might almost be called public play in a public room, during this particular week. Mr. Justice Gran-tham, living in Sussex, must surely have heard of Mr. Porter's Club. I had lost £2,000 the previous night to Mr. Wynne, a solicitor, who has since sought clients in a new sphere. At the break up of the evening, or early morning, we—Mr. Cox, Captain Baumann, Mr. Taylor, and I—walked home together. Such evenings were common enough in those days. So far from there being a suggestion of anything wrong I here repro-duce a letter from Mr. Taylor written to me on the following day :—

"Hamblin's Hotel,
"Brighton,
"August 6, 1893.

"Dear Sievier,

"Only just got your note, as I have been out for a drive. I am very C.D. to-day—and no wonder after sitting up so late. I think I can square the account with the Ring, as no doubt one or two will wait a bit. Many thanks all the same for offering to help me. I will see the cheque to Porter is met, though I am a bit pushed.—Yours truly,                    "JOHN W. TAYLOR."

This gentleman confessed to being so pressed that he made a point of letting me know that he would meet the cheque he had given for counters and the charges levied for taking the bank, doubtless because I was morally responsible for him. In my evidence I was reluctantly compelled to state that Mrs. Taylor had herself written asking me to let her husband off as lightly as I could, and an appointment was made for me to meet Mr. Taylor at the East India Club. On my arrival I found a note awaiting me, as follows:—

"Cox's Hotel,
"Jermyn Street, S.W.

"Dear Sievier,

"Came up to see you. Have just had a wire from my wife. Would you mind coming round here and seeing Captain Baumann for a few minutes, as I may not be back in time, not knowing what she wants to see me about.—Yours truly,

"JOHN W. TAYLOR."

This was a device to enable Baumann to intervene and prevail upon me to accept as small a sum as possible, and he pleaded so well that, after agreeing to accept half in bills at Mr. Taylor's convenience, I further reduced the amount by

£500. It was arranged that I should lunch with Mr. Taylor at the East India Club a day or so later, which I did, and there I received the bills and his thanks. Shortly afterwards he served me with an injunction, obtained ex parte, not to part with the bills, and alleged all kinds of things against me ; but, unfortunately for him, I had met an old friend of his, who told me that Mr. John W. Taylor would wriggle out of anything if he could. How true his friend's estimate was Mr. Taylor has amply demonstrated by wriggling out of the Stock Exchange by the aid of the hammer! I had quickly discounted the bills with Sam Lewis, and I heard no more of the matter until ten years afterwards, when this was made a "charge" against me. Mr. Taylor's affidavit in support of his injunction had not, indeed it could not have been refuted, as the application was ex parte ; but it was put in as evidence against my denial in the box, and Mr. Justice Grantham accepted it, in face of my swearing that "This man has been kicked out of every club in London, he was hammered on the Stock Exchange, and he is a defaulter on the Turf." If untrue, my statement on oath would be easy to refute, and the penalty for perjury is severe.

To show what kind of person J. W. Taylor is, as I write I have in front of me a cheque dated October 20, 1903, for £474, made out in favour of Mr. J. W. Taylor or order, endorsed by Mr. J. W. Taylor, and payable through the payee's account only. It was paid into the Westminster Branch of the London and County Banking Company. It is drawn by a firm of turf commission agents, whose offices are in Piccadilly. Shortly after Mr. Taylor lost to this firm a small sum—something under forty pounds—and it was only after many months and much pressure, that he was compelled to disgorge this paltry amount, although he had received winnings amounting to £474.

## CHAPTER XXXIV.

### "THE YOUNG MAN HORN."

WILL now refer to the matter of Ernest Horn, on which I was cross-examined. In the 'eighties every man about town was more or less acquainted with the brothers Horn, and they were identified rather by their overbearing swagger than by any other significance. Each of the brothers had a nickname. One was satirically dubbed "Hunting Horn"—his "illegitimate" right to this sobriquet being solely that he was for ever talking of hunting, and "twenty minutes on the grass without a check, boys," without ever having participated in a run except by jogging leisurely along the lanes and byeways. To hunting he was what a small suburban semi-detached villa is to a country mansion! The other Horn was called "Drinking Horn" which Mr. Justice Grantham at once accepted as incontrovertible evidence that Horn was for ever drunk. Yet the "hunting Horn" had never jumped a fence in his life! On these lines his brother, "the drinking Horn," would never have had a drink.

These two Horns were connected with the firm of solicitors, Horn and Francis—not actively, but in many other ways. Horn and Francis acted for them, but at the periods upon which I am compelled to touch Solicitor Horn had blown his last note, and was no more, leaving Francis the sole controller of the firm. Any letters which Francis had written, any affidavit he had prepared, and to which Ernest Horn had sworn, were all pressed by the judge as against me, though without any corroboration whatever, in face of my denial. At this very moment Francis had been struck off the Rolls, and was languishing in one of His Majesty's gaols. After that, whoever refers to Mr. Justice Grantham as being a weak judge must surely be mistaken. It is one of the strongest things I can imagine.

Indeed, so carried away was the judge that in his summing up he referred to Ernest Horn as "this young man Horn," whereas there was no evidence whatever before the court as to his . age, nor was there any possibility of Mr. Justice Grantham being acquainted with it—unless in "Drinking Horn's " lifetime, as in the case of Sir James Duke, they were personal friends. I shall refer to this again when I sum up the judge's summing-up.

It is now about eleven years since Ernest Horn, after the closing of the Casino, entered the billiard-room at the Hotel Metropole at Monte Carlo, and challenged me to play billiards. I may here point out to those who are unacquainted with this rendezvous after the closing of the Casino, that, at the time I am referring to, it was customary for many of us to meet here nightly. The room, a public one, contained two billiard tables, lounges, &c. There were seldom less than fifty in the room from twelve o'clock onwards, and sometimes I have known it to be inconveniently crowded. At the time Horn challenged me there were any number up to a hundred present. We were both well-known men, and the majority of those present were at least acquaintances. A match was arranged, and the interest was such that the second table was not used, but chairs were placed round the room, and when the game started we had quite a gallery. As it was suggested in court that Horn was drunk at the time it does not say much for those present, or for the management of the Hotel

Metropole, that they permitted him to play billiards under such circumstances, even assuming that I am one who would take advantage of a man's drunken condition.   Horn was no fool at billiards.   Our respective merits were well known, and so far from his not being sober, there was all-round betting on the game.   I could name at least a dozen who were present.   But there are some men whose conceit leads them to believe that they can play for money before a gallery, but it has been my experience that, as a rule, the reverse is the fact.   Generally speaking, the man who is solely dependent on himself, and has a fair stake at issue does not play the same game as he does under more normal conditions.   This was exactly Horn's case, for in attempting to rise above himself and show himself off as he so dearly loved, he failed, and, failing, fell.

I gave him a start, which in the second game had been increased according to the correct handicap which the preceding game pointed to.   What could have been fairer or more sporting I cannot conceive—and I mention this rather to enlighten those who are unacquainted with me.   My friends know that I have played billiards, cricket, or any other game on the same lines as I have always run my horses.

So drunk was Horn that the last game was called 98—70 in his favour.   If Horn was drunk I must have been incapable!

Now, there is one significant thing about this, and I shall touch on it later, but feel I cannot let it even now pass without brief reference.   Horn was 98, and required but two points for game.   Mr. Justice Grantham, in his summing up, observed, " He (Sievier) allowed Horn to get to ninety-eight."   Mr. Justice Grantham's acquaintance with indoor games can be no greater than with outdoor sport.   Is it not obvious that if I *allowed* my opponent in a game, upon the result of which £700 depended, to get to 98, when he got to this point he still had another stroke, and if he scored he would win the game?

As a matter of fact, he did not score again, and I won.

The play ended in Horn owing me £700.   After it was over

we sat in the hall of the hotel chatting. On going to our rooms he asked me to his, and, producing his cheque-book—it must not be forgotten that all this time his swagger never left him—he said, in effect, " Fill up a cheque for what I owe you, and I'll sign it." I did so, and being in monetary difficulties, I suggested making it out in my wife's name. He consented without demur, asking me to make one out for £100 which would be paid at sight, and another for the balance, which he would arrange for. The £100 cheque was paid at Smith's Bank, and the larger one handed to them for collection. Like a great many others who have been in a losing position, Ernest Horn ("this young man Horn") evidently began to ponder how he could repudiate a liability, incurred publicly under the circumstances I have described. Many bets had been made on the games by the onlookers; none of these were disputed or left unhonoured.

I am not making a running commentary on what happened, but recapitulating the facts to which I swore. An attempt was made to suggest in cross-examination that Horn was drugged by me and then inveigled into playing billiards! Could anything be more preposterous? How could a man who was drugged stand up to make a stroke in a public and crowded room?

The larger cheque was dishonoured on presentation. It was unlikely I was going to sit still, more especially when Horn, to fabricate some excuse for not settling, gave out that he had been drugged. Unfortunately for Horn, I took the matter up, and it reached such a serious pitch, owing to the lies he told one on top of the other, that I telegraphed to Lord Dufferin, then the British Ambassador at Paris, and wrote fully. The result was that Sir James Harris, the British Consul at Nice, came to see me at Monte Carlo, but Horn, in face of the calumnies he had spread—had fled. He never came to Monte Carlo again. And there the matter ended. So far from my being "shown the frontier," as was suggested, and made to suffer all kinds of penalties, it was not until March that my wife and I left for Paris, where I then resided. I have often visited Monte Carlo since, have shot at the Tir aux Pigeons, and put up at any hotel I felt inclined to. Now, let us descend to the impossible, and assume it is possible for a man to play billiards under the influence of drugs, why did Mr. Lawson Walton ask me the following question?

"Was it not within the knowledge of everybody in the hotel that he (Horn) was in a state of more or less chronic alcoholism?

Answer: "Certainly not."

And if there was any truth in this question, why was I shortly afterwards asked the following, which would have been unnecessary had the former suggestion been the fact?

"Do you know that the manager of the bank consulted the police, and that an inquiry was held to see whether there was sufficient evidence to show that Horn had been drugged?"

Answer: ".I never heard so."

Now, we have it from the other side that the police, at the request of *the bank manager*, who was not present, and was no party to the matter, held an inquiry, which resulted in their not being able to substantiate any such story as that of drugging, concocted by Horn solely to evade payment of a debt of honour. The police at Monte Carlo are for the most part composed of detectives from all countries, and had there been a grain of evidence to be gleaned they would have discovered it. And after this inquiry, what was the end of it all? Horn cleared out from Monte Carlo and I remained.

Mr. Justice Grantham allowed the illegal evidence of Police-constable Drew, then why were not the Monte Carlo detectives called as witnesses?

And, apart from my answers categorically denying the suggestions which the line of cross-examination assumed, I also swore to the fact that Ernest Horn ("the young man Horn," who in this year of grace would have been fifty-six years of age) had been expelled from the Badminton Club for much the same sort of thing. Yet this was never again touched upon, and the judge held Horn up to the jury as a lamb who had been slaughtered, without a thread of fact to support such a contention.

The whole of this fictitious story, in all its incredibility, was launched at me, and though strenuously denied and explained as I have herein explained, the judge discarded the answers and brooded over the questions until he hatched them into fact in his summing-up.

Then we come to the lying accusation that I had been expelled from Boodle's. I produced letters from the Secretary which clearly proved this was false, and I was not even cross-examined on the point. Nevertheless, it was one of the charges embodied in the slander, and the judge never once touched upon the subject in his summing-up—nor was he likely to, judging from his demeanour from the moment the case was opened.

Some thirteen or fourteen years ago there. appeared in a paper called the "Hawk," which very shortly afterwards ceased to exist, a libellous paragraph concerning me, written by Augustus Moore. I consulted Messrs. Wontner and Sons, a firm of solicitors, whose strict probity needs no tribute from my pen, and they sought the advice of Mr. Charles Gill, then a rising junior connected with the police courts and criminal cases. Mr. Blanchard Wontner and I agreed that I should criminally prosecute the editor, and a judge's fiat was obtained. The facts were before Mr. Wontner and Mr. C. F. Gill, but the latter held that my having made a book in Australia, my presentation being thereby cancelled, and my having just been made bankrupt, would form an insurmountable barrier to my obtaining a conviction. Mr. Wontner differed, and I decided to consider the matter. A lady, whom I need not name, begged me not to continue the case, and her mother also intervened. I saw Mr. Wontner again, and he strongly asserted his disagreement with Mr. C. F. Gill's opinion, and offered to engage another counsel. But I had to consider a lady, and felt that I had no other

20

alternative. In the end a compromise was agreed to, on the undertaking of the editor that my name should not be mentioned in the "Hawk" again. I do not wish to put forward any such reason as that a man who has just been visited with financial rebuffs, even to bankruptcy, does not possess that vigour which a full purse so much assists, or any other kind of excuse. I merely state the true state of things as they then existed, and they must go for their value at that. But what I complained of was that Mr. Charles Gill, who was at that time my paid counsel, in other words, my paid confidential servant, who, by virtue of the law, is fully protected against divulging anything placed in his keeping in his capacity as a lawyer, should have given any information to the other side, sufficient to warrant Mr. Lawson Walton stating in public court, "*I have the benefit of Mr. Gill's recollec tion in the matter.*"

If this is to be the common practice of counsel, what litigant is ever safe? As there are matters upon which we consult our doctors which we should not care for them to trumpet from the housetops, so those who consult a lawyer, do so under the strongest impression that the interview or consultation is on the honourable understanding that it is strictly confidential, and hermetically sealed within four walls.

But the gravity of Mr. Lawson Walton's astounding statement that he was benefiting by the prompting of Mr. C. F. Gill's recollection—his recollection of my confidences in consultation with him, for which services he had been paid by me—did not end there, for Mr. Eldon Bankes had at this juncture to rise and appeal to Mr. Justice Grantham, by "objecting to Mr. Gill making running comments on the evidence in the hearing of the jury."

If the Judge heard Mr. Bankes he took no notice of him. I leave my readers to form their own conclusions.

Now let us go to a more congenial clime, and once again turn to Monte Carlo. Horn had long since departed from this world, and his trumpeting was no longer heard on the

Riviera. But it had apparently left an echo behind, and this Mr. Lawson Walton reproduced, as we shall see—but it was a faint blast.

In the face of the false suggestions which the defence had previously attempted to establish, namely, that I had drugged a man when playing billiards and then betted with him while he played! that I had in consequence been "barred" the Principality of Monaco, I was at a later stage asked in cross-examination if I was not again at Monte Carlo in 1901. If I was shown the frontier, as the defence suggested, how could they, in the next breath, reasonably ask me if I was at Monte Carlo a few years later? The particular time in question was the occasion when I met the Duke of Braganza under circumstances which I will fully set forth, and again I must emphasise that during the whole of my review of the case I am merely repeating the evidence, and any comments on it can be taken for what they, in the opinion of the reader, may be worth.

The facts are that I had played in the Club Room of the Casino at Monte Carlo one evening in February, 1901 (I must emphasise the fact that I had uninterrupted and unchallenged entrée to the Club Room in face of the Horn accusations), and had lost my ready money, though I was in a position to borrow had I been so inclined. I did not do so. There were others like myself; indeed, towards the end of the evening this is frequently a case of being in the majority! Mr. Guy Chetwynd—I should have preferred to have withheld his name, but Sir James Duke caused it to be mentioned—the Duke of Braganza, and I were "in the majority," and we agreed to go over to the Hotel L'Hermitage, a most excellent and high-class house, and have a flutter. We were joined by others, one of whom was a Mr. Burns. The game was baccarat, and the Duke had the bank for the greater part of the evening, and in the end he lost a fairish amount. In the Rooms he was a plunger quite of the "break the bank" order. He did not depart from his practice during the play under notice; on the contrary, had those punting staked as heavily as he desired he would have lost thrice as much, or more. After the game was over the I.O.U.'s were totted up, and something like 75,000 francs were owing by the Duke round the table, while others owed to, or were owed by, the rest of the players, as the case might be. Monte Carlo is rather a whispering gallery than a secret place, and the next day the topic of conversation was the previous evening's play. Like the snowball, the story increased as it rolled on, and francs became magnified into sovereigns. A certain cocotte, who has since joined the ranks of peeresses, intimated to one, whom I need not name, that Mr. Burns, who had been one of the players, was a card-sharper. This travelled at such a rate that it beat all records of wireless telegraphy. Mr. Ralph Sneyd, a friend of the Duke of Braganza, consulted me about it. He had previously seen Mr. Guy Chetwynd, who was a slight loser on the evening, and he denied—and in this I concurred—that any cheating had taken place. Further, as the Duke had for the most part during the time he lost, dealt the cards himself, such a statement was only worth the consideration usually given to stories which emanate from— a cocotte. I agreed that the detectives should be set to work, but nothing could be brought to light against Mr. Burns. What he had won I had paid him at the request of the Duke; nevertheless, I expressed my readiness to fall in with anything that might be decided upon. As a result I met Count Batthyany, a Steward of the Austrian Jockey Club, and a gentleman whose honour is unquestioned throughout Europe. Mr. Sneyd introduced me, and we discussed the turn things had taken. It may appear superfluous for me to mention it, but there never had been a suggestion made against me, or that I was in any way connected with any wrongdoing, had any taken place. The whole and sole point at issue was whether Mr. Burns was the man his malicious accuser asserted he was. Nothing could be substantiated, and Count Batthyany, without any hesitation, decided there was nothing left but for the Duke of Braganza to discharge his debt of honour. After this, coming as it did from a relation of the Duke's, I voluntarily offered, and I felt it was only in accordance with what any man should do under the circumstances, to write a letter to the Duke, assuring him I would return him the money I had won, in the event of Mr. Burns ever being proved a cheat to the satisfaction of any one of us. To this moment I have never been asked to refund the money.

After this interview with Count Batthyany and Mr. Sneyd, I received the following letter, produced in Court:—

> "Hotel de Paris.
>
> "His Royal Highness the Prince of Braganza begs of Mr. R. S. Sievier to come and see him at the hotel now, as he wants to settle the matter concerning the payment."

I had quite forgotten to give the Duke of Braganza the "indemnity," but remembering it the next morning, I despatched it by messenger. The Duke had at the same time sent a note to me, and they must have crossed on their way. It ran as follows, and was also produced in Court:—

> "His Royal Highness begs of Mr. Sievier to send the few lines he showed him, telling he would refund 55,000 francs in case Mr. Burns is the man looked for. This *also* was agreed with Count Batthyany and Mr. Sneyd."

In face of this I was asked question after question for which the defence could have no warrant but their own imagination. It was put to me that my "name was known to the Monte Carlo police in connection with card playing with Horn?" Billiards by now was turned to cards, and a different phase put on this or that, as a child engaged in making faces out of putty. From first to last it was an attack with nothing but inference for a weapon, but, as I have said, the questions were

marked down as evidence. But were the documents I produced forgeries? Were my answers given on oath a running
chain of lies? Had either been the case, bearing in mind what
was eventually attempted in another court, the result would
inevitably have been a term of imprisonment.

Just prior to the case coming on, Mr. Guy Chetwynd consulted his solicitors, and on their advice communicated with
Messrs. Lewis and Lewis, who were acting for me, offering
to tender his evidence on oath if it would be of any avail.
This was totally unsolicited, and I must, knowing as I do
the great majority of moral cowards that exist, both thank this
gentleman for his proffered services, and take this opportunity
to eulogise his pluck. I cannot do better than publish the
proof of his signed evidence:—

"I was staying at the Hotel L'Hermitage, Monte Carlo,
and was present when the play took place with the Duke of
Braganza.

"My sister, Lady Anglesey, came out to stay with me either
the day before or the day after.

"Mr. Sievier was staying at the same hotel. I knew him
as a successful backer.

"At Chester races I put £500 on a horse for him which
won, and I sent him a cheque for £4,000. His reason for
asking me was that he, being so well known as a successful
backer, could not get the same price as I could.

"This is the only transaction I ever had with him. I
was in the rooms at Monte Carlo, and lost some money and
was going away when I saw Sievier, who was playing Roulette.

"He asked me if I had been winning. I said 'No.' He
said 'I can't do any good either; let us go out and have a
game of Poker or something.'

"The Duke of Braganza was either sitting or standing next
to me, and he turned to me and asked if he might join us.
I said 'Certainly. Do you know Mr. Sievier?' and I introduced him, because I was going to play with Mr. Sievier.
We walked up to the hotel and went into a room downstairs

which is a reading or writing room. Burns and Mr. ——
joined us. I knew Mr. —— as a pigeon shot. I did not
know Burns.

"We played Baccarat. The Duke of Braganza started by
taking the bank. No money passed, but we gave I.O.U.'s or
cheques.

"When we stopped playing, Braganza said he had not got
any money, but must telegraph to Vienna for it. Sievier said
'Don't trouble ; pay at your convenience.'

"Braganza next day said there was a rumour about Burns
being a sharp, and something about a notice having been put
on a boat about him.

"Sneyd came and said to me there was an ugly story going
about that Burns was a card sharp. I said 'I don't believe
any such thing.' I said the game would bear the strictest
investigation, and it was absolutely nonsense to say that there
was any cheating about it.

"Finally there was a meeting between Prince Batthyany,
Sneyd, and Sievier.

"Braganza didn't want to pay Sievier himself after what
he had said about Burns, and he asked me to pay him and
get a receipt, which I did. I paid £4,000, and there was
£3,000 still remaining. I think there was a condition that
that was not to be paid if Burns proved to be a sharp. About
a week afterwards I went to India.

"The result of my play was I lost to Sievier.

"It was never suggested that there had been any cheating,
but the only ground for not paying was that Burns was said
to be a sharp."

Having made this voluntary statement of facts, Mr. Guy
Chetwynd saw Sir George Lewis, and offered the following
additional evidence :—

"About three weeks ago I was in White's Club.

"Mr. Sneyd was there playing billiards. He said to me,
'Have you been subpœnaed in this Duke case?' I said 'No,'
and he said, 'I am just off to see Duke's lawyers.' Later I

got a message from the porter at White's that Mr. Sneyd wished to see me. I went to White's Club at 6 o'clock to see him. He said, ' I have just seen Duke's solicitors. I am going to give you a word of advice—you had better go and see them at once.' I telephoned and made an appointment for the following morning. The following morning I went there and saw Mr. Wynne. He said ' I want to see you about this game with Braganza at Monte Carlo. Tell me your story.' I told him that I had played there. He said ' Of course this case is very unpleasant. but we must get Counsel to extend his protecting hand over you. We shall keep you out of the box if we can. If you are called you will state all you remember. There was a game. You played and Braganza played, and that is all. and you forget everything else.' I said ' What do you mean by extending a protecting hand over me ?' He said ' Well, this game takes place, a young man is inveigled into a private room.' I said ' That is not true to start with.' He said ' And then loses a large sum of money.' I said ' Have you ever inquired how much he has lost in Vienna gaming rooms ?' He said ' We cannot prove that there was anything wrong about the game. We shall not attempt to prove it, *but we shall try and prove it by inference to the jury.* I said ' In other words, what you want to do is, you want to keep me out of the box, and if I am called you want me to say words which you put into my mouth. I positively refuse to do that which would be unfair to Mr. Sievier.' He said ' Of course you will understand that we cannot prove all this, but it is necessary for us to get as much evidence together as possible to damage Mr. Sievier.'

"I have often seen Mr. Sneyd since, and he has never suggested there was any cheating. He made no complaint against Mr. Sievier, but, on the contrary, he has told me what a good fellow Sievier was."

Without a solitary word of comment I leave the reader to form his own conclusion.

## CHAPTER XXXV.

## LEGAL ELASTICITY.

O matter how petty, every triviality which could be distorted into an incident was theatrically introduced into my cross-examination, with Mr. Charles Gill playing the part of prompter, audible to all in court, except, presumably, the judge. Some thirteen years ago, while my wife was driving through Shanklin, one of those burly, loafing wretches who infest this world, and inflict upon their victims abuse and insult against which the law offers little or no protection, vented his foul language in the presence of my wife to such an extent that I jumped out of the trap and thrashed him on the spot. If every man acted on the impulse of the moment as I did, it is possible these blackguards might exhibit less bravado, or at least not so readily attempt to bully and insult their superiors, more especially ladies. Rather with the hope of levying blackmail than for any other reason, this ruffian summoned me, and the local justices decided that I had taken the law into my own hands, and fined me five shillings! This incident was actually brought up against me, and I was referred to as a man who had committed all kinds of savage assaults! But let us imagine that I had committed fifty similar breaches of the law, what had all this to do with my being charged with the crime of murder, with being a card-sharper, and with causing horses to be pulled in a race?

Why did not the defence rather give us the name of the man who was supposed to have been found murdered under my window in Australia, or the address of the house, or better still, an account of the inquest which must have taken place? Would not any of these have been more to the point? But such evidence was impossible, because the accusation was utterly false, without a scintilla of truth to support it, and was the outcome of the malignant imagination of Sir James Duke.

The questions whether I was a murderer as I had been accused of being, or whether Sceptre had been pulled in the Derby, and so on, were never touched upon by the judge— and possibly, in consequence, were forgotten by the jury— the vital facts that I had been engaged in horse-racing, had betted and played cards, and that my wedded life had not turned out a success, swamped all other considerations. There was no serious question as to whether what Sir James Duke had stated was true or false ; I had knocked my head against Mrs. Grundy's orthodoxy, and that was quite sufficient for me to be accused of anything my accuser chose to invent. On these lines, and none other, the case went on—I refuse to admit that it was tried.

Then my bankruptcies were hurled at me as though I had committed some criminal offence, nor did Mr. Justice Grantham once refer to the evidence that I had, generally speaking, paid all my creditors in full *after I had got my discharge.* Again, what had the vicissitudes of poverty to do with my case which was at issue? But I am mistaken in describing it as my case. I had ceased to be the plaintiff, and was transformed into the defendant!

Then it was attempted to insinuate that I had spent my wife's money. Assuming this to be so, again I ask what had it to do with Sir James Duke's accusations? I sincerely regret being compelled to refer to it, but my wife had an allowance from me of over £1,500 a year at this time. In the case Rex. v. Sievier, which I shall later on refer to, it was proved in the cross-examination of a bank clerk subpœnaed by the Crown from Lloyd's Bank that I allowed Lady Mabel Sievier over a thousand pounds annually. Does this not answer any "insinuation"?

But Sir James Duke left no ladies out of the case, if the introduction of their names was calculated to sway the judge, and, through him, influence the jury. The defendant's solicitor's statement, which I referred to above—"*but we shall try and prove it by inference to the jury*"—is indeed significant. No matter at whose expense, without any regard to the feelings of my wife, private affairs, having no bearing on the case, were mercilessly laid bare with the hope of "*proving by inference to the jury*" that I had cheated my own wife! Whatever husband and wife's private affairs might be, they were foreign to the issue, and with this observation I will leave this cowardly "inference"—cowardly if for no other reason than that it involved a lady and had no foundation whatever.

Nor did the defence refrain from going to any limits in their endeavour to gain an "inference," and even placed a letter in my hands, written by my wife at a period when we were estranged (1898), which she had addressed to Mr. C. S. Pelham-Clinton, then of 4, Wilton Street, S.W. This letter was passed up to me in the witness-box without my wife ever having been consulted, or her consent asked, and such a breach of etiquette, not to say faith, is of so extraordinary a kind that it can hardly commend itself even to my enemies. For Mr. Pelham-Clinton to put Sir James Duke in possession of this letter, and for the latter to attempt to make use of it under any circumstances, without my wife's knowledge or acquiescence, was, to say the least, as ungallant as it was unmanly.

Mr. C. S. Pelham-Clinton had let his house furnished to Mr. Sawyer, a gentleman who the defence inferred was a myth, but who has been proved to exist when witnesses for the Crown swore to Mr. Sawyer's identity in the case Rex v. Sievier.

It was at a moment when I was pecuniarily embarrassed that Mr. Sawyer placed this house, which he had taken temporarily, at my disposal during his absence. Not finding the place in what I deemed a desirable state, I left it at the half term, and any further rent was refused. Instead of suing Mr. Sawyer, Mr. Pelham-Clinton sued me, and because I was described on the writ as " Sievier, otherwise Sawyer, otherwise Standish (one of my Christian names), otherwise Savile," it was inferred, and the inference was accepted by the judge, that all these were aliases of mine! My denial went for nothing, and a writ which could describe anybody as anything, *was accepted as evidence.* Why, I could bring an action against anyone, and place on the writ aliases *ad infinitum*, and we are to understand that JUSTICE would hold that this is sufficient proof, even against evidence on oath, that the face of the writ must be Truth! If so, who is safe!

True, as regards Mr. Sawyer, I had at times acted for him, and in this one respect there were some grounds for the inference set up by the defence. I had written letters on his behalf in his name (though none were produced), and assisted him in his business as a commission agent. He had helped me in many ways, trusted me implicitly, and I in return had helped him in his official affairs. The name of Savile I have never used, and that of Standish belongs to me, though I have never used it as a surname. In Mr. Pelham-Clinton's case I was examined in chambers by Mr. Horace Avory, who would have discovered if I had been really Sawyer, Standish, or Savile. But before Mr. Justice Grantham there was no doubt about it! The face of the writ said so! But before Mr. Marsham at Bow Street the Crown witnesses, in cross-examination, were compelled to swear that I was not Sawyer, and further that they knew Sawyer apart from me. So much for these aliases.

In nearly every instance where I had won at cards the fact had been touched upon, nor had it been hastily passed over; on the contrary, it was presumed I had never lost. Mr. Bankes, in his re-examination, desired to question me in regard to the many times when I had lost—and lost very heavily. But the judge would not allow this, nor would he permit certain papers to be put in and read which would have explained many matters, and which referred most favourably to my conduct in a number of cases, which by inference the jury were influenced into believing were dead against me. In brief, not one of my counsel's objections was allowed, and he was over-ruled upon every point he raised. On the other hand, the defence sailed or drifted where it chose.

Trivial matters were insinuated against me one after another, and except that these should have helped to show the true weakness of the defence, which clutched at every straw, they call for no comment from me.

Then because I sent the sum of £300 to my late clerk in Australia it was implied, and this inference was strongly supported by the judge, that there must have been some collusion between us, and it was even suggested that it must have been an amount owing to him out of the sum paid to me by Mr. Benzon. As I have previously stated, Mr. Benzon's letter has been published denying that anything of the kind could have been the fact. Bookmakers' clerks frequently "stand in" with the book, or take a share in a big bet, or are promised a certain sum in certain events. It is the common custom. But this was pooh-poohed, and Mr. Justice Grantham shrugged his shoulders significantly when I swore this was so. Inquiry could so easily have been made. There are plenty of bookmakers of whom the question might have been asked.

Let me now deal with the statement of Police-constable Drew, which Mr. Justice Grantham allowed, and which afterwards caused a question to be asked in the House of Commons as to whether such testimony was either admissible or desirable. But Mr. Justice Grantham appeared to welcome this forbidden method, and dwelt upon it in his summing up. This police constable swore that he had known me in the West End for the past ten years, and that my reputation was bad. That such "evidence" should be received in a court of Justice in this country is incredible. It is only admitted against a criminal at his trial *after* he has been convicted. But what did he say in the brief—all too brief—cross-examination Mr. Bankes subjected him to? He admitted that for eight of the ten years I had lived in the country! Then my counsel, as would any lawyer with a belief in justice, remarked that Drew might swear the same thing of him, or of his lordship. On this he resumed his seat. But what effect did this irrelevant introduction have on the jury? It was dramatic! Indeed, it was quite a "Gillian" touch, if Mr. Gill will pardon me saying so! If Drew was to be called, why was he not asked if I had ever been charged with a criminal offence, or suffered imprisonment? Would this not have been sounder than his mere uncorroborated opinion? And I would ask any sensible citizen, if he wished to inquire into the reputation of a man living a country gentleman's life, whether he would seek the opinion of a police constable?

Before finally disposing of my cross-examination, I must touch upon the volunteer incident, out of which so much was made by Mr. Lawson-Walton after the pointed observation of the judge. Mr. Justice Grantham said :

"This is the most serious charge which has been made against you. Cannot you tell us what the name of the insurance office was?" I replied: "No, my lord, I cannot. I have a great many details to remember in this case. If your lordship will give an intimation that you think this money is due, I will pay it myself to-day."

This ended my cross-examination, but it was a distinct cue for Mr. Lawson-Walton.

"This is the most serious charge against you." Those were the words and the conviction of the judge. Very well, let us take this seriously. The whole of my evidence has been given and the cross-examination ended. The inferences surrounding the Horn and Renton affairs, the suggestions regarding the Taylor and the Duke of Braganza incidents— everything paled before this serious charge.

This must, at least from Mr. Justice Grantham's point of view, be looked upon as the very worst thing I have done in my life. On these lines, which the judge himself laid down, I ask my reader to follow the facts closely, and having done so, ask himself if this "most serious charge of all" is, as it stands, or even under any circumstances, inferred or real, sufficiently bad in itself to warrant another man to accuse me of murder; of being thrown into the sea for cheating at cards; of drugging a man when playing him game after game at billiards in a crowded public room; of having caused Sceptre to be pulled in the Derby, a mare I loved only too well and clung to until my purse held out no longer.

I had been the means of resuscitating County Cricket in Bedfordshire, and supported all the local clubs throughout South Beds, not to mention several in the north of the county also. I had given £50 to the Luton Football Club, and contributed to the winter game in the same spirit and to the same extent that I had done to cricket. I had sent donations to the local hospitals. I am forced to touch on these matters, for no doubt it was these considerations which prompted my being invited to a farewell dinner, given at the Town Hall at Dunstable, to six volunteers who were about to depart for South Africa. In an after-dinner speech I said I would insure each of these men's lives for £100. I instructed Mr. E. J. Wingfield-Stratford, a gentleman then acting as my secretary, to carry the insurance out, and amongst other sums he in due course received the money from me covering the amount required for the purpose. Beyond this I gave the matter no attention. It appears he corresponded with Sergeant Robert Hamblin, of the volunteers, who was at that time an insurance agent at Dunstable. I was ignorant of all this, and probably should have been so to-day had not the sergeant in question, during the progress

of the case, voluntarily addressed himself to Messrs. Lewis
and Lewis, acquainting them with his recollection of the
matter. He stated that the negotiations were carried on on
my behalf by Mr. E. Wingfield-Stratford, now unfortunately
deceased, and that he was sure the men *were insured through
him*. He had since then moved from Dunstable to St. Albans,
where he now resides, and could not find his books, he having
given up the occupation of insurance agent. The company
he believed he had insured the volunteers in had since
amalgamated with another, and with the short space of time
at his disposal he was unable to discover any documentary
evidence to support his statement. Nevertheless, it was the
statement of an independent witness, of a brother volunteer
of the two men who had died in South Africa. Was it likely
to be untrue?

I had not troubled myself to ascertain with what office the
insurance had been effected, and though I now learn that it
was with one of those companies which sprang up at the time
for this special class of business, I should most probably have
forgotten the name had I done so.

I had forty horses in training, which were valued at something like £80,000; quite enough to keep a man occupied
without having to attend personally to minor details, which
I entrusted to others. The insurance was, I believe, a matter
of £36. And because I, under the foregoing circumstances,
could not trace this identical amount, the judge ruled this
was "the most serious charge which had been brought against
me."

I, who had given 10,000 guineas for a yearling, had jibbed
at keeping my promise for this paltry sum! Though I had
given ten times £36 to the different cricket and football clubs,
had defrayed the whole of the expenses of the Coronation
festivities at Shrewton by handing £200 to a committee formed
to carry out the rejoicings, and supplemented this by sending
a cheque of £50 for a similar fund at Newmarket, apart from
smaller amounts given to the villages in the vicinity of my

home, it was inferred, and by the judge emphasised, that I had failed to pay £36 to insure the six men's lives as stated! If this be so, then no man can ever do a generous act in the eyes of the law, but he can indeed commit a crime. Nor must it be overlooked that I stated in the box, if the judge intimated that he thought the sum the insurance would have brought in was due from me, I would pay it that day. He did not say it was. But he dwelt on the incident in a "national" spirit in his summing-up, and Mr. Lawson Walton took the hint and made it the tag of his speech!

# CHAPTER XXXVI.

## CHALLENGE TO SIR JAMES DUKE.

I ENTERED the witness-box on the 5th of May, and left it on the 10th, which, exclusive of Saturday and Sunday, made four days in all. What was the reason for this abnormally prolonged period? Why was my cross-examination dragged on day after day? Is it not significant?

When I left the witness-box the judge shrugged his shoulders and looked towards the jury in a manner which I cannot describe in any other way than as unjust. For reasons best known to themselves the foreman stated that they would like Sir James Duke to go into the box. After some hesitation he entered it, and was sworn.

I here quote *verbatim* a passage which appeared in the "Winning Post" of November 18, 1905:

> "It is my intention to deal most seriously with the statements he made on oath. Possibly Sir James Duke might disagree with them, or desire to contradict one or all of them. On these grounds the proprietors of the 'Winning Post' hereby hold themselves responsible, and guarantee that £1,000 shall be paid to the Queen's Unemployed Fund in the event of Sir James Duke satisfying a committee of three gentlemen that any statement I am about to make in regard to this evidence is untrue.

The proprietors of the 'Winning Post' are prepared to nominate a gentleman who is on the committee of one of the leading military clubs in London, for the membership of which Sir James Duke is not eligible. On the other hand, Sir James Duke is at liberty to nominate a gentleman on the committee of any recognised club, and the two to appoint a third, the hearing to take place in public, or with closed doors, at the option of Sir James Duke. In case of the latter being decided upon, the verdict of these three gentlemen, who need never be named if such a course be deemed advisable, to be published in the 'Winning Post' in brief, merely stating that I had failed to substantiate what I am about to state, or, on the other hand, that Sir James Duke had not succeeded in securing the £1,000 for the Queen's Unemployed Fund. This will give Sir James Duke not only the opportunity of stultifying myself and this paper in the eyes of the public, but also the chance of being a philanthropist to the extent of four figures without having to provide the money."

A part of the slander uttered by Sir James Duke to Major Sellar was that a man had been found murdered under the window of my house in Australia, and that there were ugly stories in connection with this, to the effect that I had played cards with him and then resorted to foul play with the result stated. This is untrue in every particular. I challenge Sir James Duke to produce a tittle of evidence to uphold this wanton fabrication. If there was a scintilla of truth to support this accusation, nothing would be easier than for Sir James Duke to obtain it. If a man is found murdered, or even let us suppose a case of suicide, it is inevitable that an inquest must be held, and the evidence can be produced. But Sir James Duke's difficulty in this instance is his total inability to prove that a certain thing has happened which has never occurred.

Sir James Duke left Eton in a hurry, and this may possibly account for his visiting Australia at the early age of seventeen, where he asserts that he saw me thrown from a boat into the sea for being suspected of cheating at cards. This accusation is on all fours with the foregoing, except that it is a degree worse when it is considered that Sir James Duke has falsely sworn that he was a spectator of this incident. In the early stages of the case Sir James Duke asserted that this happened at Adelaide, but in cross-examination he was asked the following question:

"Where did this boat incident happen?"

Answer: "At either Adelaide or Melbourne. I believe the latter."

This points to an extraordinary weakness in his memory, inasmuch that he could not remember within 500 miles where this incident had taken place, which had so much impressed him at the early age of seventeen.

He was then asked:

"Where were you standing at the time?"

Answer: "On the pier."

There is no pier at either Adelaide or Melbourne, neither city being on the sea-coast, yet it is recorded on the oath of Sir James Duke that he saw this happen from the pier! Furthermore, though he could distinctly remember it was a pier, he could not swear whether it was in South Australia or Victoria. There had never been a suggestion that this affair had happened in Melbourne until he was cross-examined; but in any event, as I have already stated, it would be impossible for it to have occurred in either place, for the only sea which borders either of these cities, exists solely in the imagination of Sir James Duke, for up to now the explorer has not discovered it, nor has the geographer recorded it.

But I do not hold Sir James Duke to the letter of his statements. I say that such an occurrence as detailed by him never happened in any part of the world whatever.

Continuing, the following question was put to Sir James Duke:

"Until you went to Australia again, you had no idea who had been pushed into the water?"

Answer: "No."

I think I am right in stating that few men have ever been better known throughout Australia than myself, and it being a thoroughly sporting country, my name was continually before the public; indeed, I might go so far as to say that I was as well known as the Governor of any one of the Australian colonies. Under these circumstances it is passing strange that when Sir James Duke, as he asserts, saw so prominent a person thrown into the sea, fished out of it, and dragged on to a pier, that he should not have known who that man was, and that in a subsequent conversation which he alleges took place at the club on that day, my name should never have been mentioned. Sir James Duke has asked the world to believe that this extraordinary story, which occupied the attention of the members of a certain unnamed club, in a town the name of which he cannot remember, merely referred to the incident as though it had happened to some strange person unknown, unheard of, and unrecognised. He further stated that he did not know it was I until he saw me on a subsequent visit to Australia! But he could not accurately fix this, as his answer, "It *may* have been on my next visit to Australia," implies.

For an instant let us take Sir James Duke's own words for the foundation of his story. In answer to a question as to whether he had inquired what the row was about, he replied:

"I was told by a bystander."

Therefore it is to be rightly assumed that whatever Sir James Duke hears from a bystander, of whom he is perfectly ignorant, he will repeat what that bystander says as being a fact, without any further inquiry.

He was then questioned as to the document which contained the particulars which the defence put in, in mitigation of damages. He was asked the following questions:

" Have you read it in the club? "

Answer: " No."

" Did that document contain accusations of a serious nature against Sievier? "

Answer: " Yes."

" Was one of the people to whom you showed it Mr. Arthur Chetwynd? "

Answer: " I should think not."

" Now, I ask you on your oath, did you ever show this document, or tell its contents to Mr. A. Chetwynd? "

Answer: " Yes."

Here in the last two answers is an absolute contradiction, and I accept the latter as being the truth. It is a fact that Sir James Duke had a copy of this document which contained accusations against me concerning the many false slanders he had uttered, and I assert, with a full appreciation of the contingency which the proprietors of the " Winning Post " guaranteed, that he read these particulars aloud in the Raleigh Club in the presence of Mr. Arthur Chetwynd and another gentleman whom I need not name, and within the hearing of any members who happened to come into the room. At this time Mr. John W. Taylor, a portion of whose career I have already dealt with, was present as a stranger, he not being a member.

In Sir James Duke's cross-examination he at one time stated:

" I never read them [these particulars] to anyone in the Raleigh Club."

And at a later stage contradicted this by swearing:

" I was in the club on the occasion when I read the paragraph from the particulars to Mr. Chetwynd."

It was under these circumstances that he met Mr. John W. Taylor, with whose experiences of club life and his career on the Stock Exchange my readers are familiar.

Thus it does not take a very intelligent man to discover that Sir James Duke's first answers in cross-examination did not tally with those which he gave when pressed by Mr. Eldon Bankes.

It may be matter of opinion, but I am inclined to think that it would have been more delicate if Sir James Duke deemed it advisable to read these allegations to anybody, that he should not have chosen the smoking-room of a club, where members and strangers were present. This possibly also occurred to him when he was first cross-examined on the subject and denied it, only to be compelled to admit it ultimately.

Another of the slanders was to the effect that I had been expelled from Boodle's Club. Had this been so, Sir James Duke was in a position to verify this with little or no trouble whatever. For this statement he again relied on the bare word of an individual, but in this case he assumed it was a friend. Had he chosen to make the most ordinary inquiry he would have found that his friend's story was false. This I proved in the box, while, on the other hand, the defendant failed entirely to substantiate his statement.

As if this were not enough for one·man seriously to tell another without any chance whatsoever of verifying his statements, Sir James Duke further said that I had been turned out of the Jockey Club Enclosure at Newmarket, and that it was through his instrumentality that I had been unmasked to the Stewards. This is as great an untruth as are the whole of the assertions which I have already disposed of. In the first place I was never in the Jockey Club Enclosure in my life, and had I been, and had the Stewards ordered my being turned out as stated, at least one of that body must have remembered the incident, and would have been available as a witness. Then Messrs. Weatherby must have either made a minute of this extraordinary matter or have had some recollection of it. To have "unmasked me to the Stewards" they must have held some inquiry, or at least a consultation; and bearing in mind that the defence alleged and called illegal and inadmissible evidence, and that this was permitted by the judge, why was not some corroboration of this episode, if it ever occurred, produced in court? Because, as in all these extraordinary accusations, there was none to be found.

Impossible as it appears, I will attempt to take Sir James Duke's evidence as seriously as my imagination will carry me. What does it come to? That a boy of seventeen, travelling in Australia, returns to England, and after a lapse, according to his own testimony, of something like twenty-two years, recognises that individual as the man he saw on the Flemington racecourse, and whom he had previously seen thrown into the water! Of that he was perfectly sure, but whether it was within 500 miles of any particular spot he could not definitely swear to. Nevertheless, a bystander had told him something, and in the fulness of time this formulated another something in his mind, which he repeated on a most serious occasion in connection with a series of other malignant accusations. And though he admitted that detectives had been employed throughout England and Australia, and all records of the courts searched, he could not call a solitary witness to confirm a single incident. There were plenty of men in England to whom my Australian career was well known. Mr. Joseph Thompson, Mr. J. D. Marks, Mr. B. S. Thompson, and a host of others were all available as witnesses, and Sir James Duke could have placed them in the box. The reason why he did not is obvious.

The defence had subpœnaed a valet of mine whom I discharged for drunkenness. They placed him in the box, and he appeared as a witness, though his evidence was immaterial. Again, the police-constable Drew, as we are aware, was put in the box. It would be interesting to know whether Sir James Duke first approached Drew, and if so, why? Or, on the other hand, whether Drew voluntarily tendered to Sir James Duke the irrelevant evidence he proposed giving? But I do not in any way wish to draw inferences, so will merely observe that it must be deemed ill-becoming that Sir James Duke and his partisans should have invited this police-constable into the Raleigh Club and entertained him as a guest after he had given his evidence in the box, which they did.*

Sir James Duke failed to make any response to the challenge I threw out. His enforced silence spoke for itself, releasing the reader from being compelled to draw his own deductions. It may be regretted by some that the chance, faint and remote though it must have appeared, of benefiting the Queen's Unemployed Fund to the extent of £1,000 was not persevered with by Sir James Duke, who, to succeed, had only to prove that a single fact I had stated was incorrect. I should be sorry to imagine that he would not be ready to place what would, in the event of it being decided that this sum should be paid over to this royal and deserving charity, substantially prove to be his valuable services to his Queen and the poor—and in cases the starving. But I never held out a thread of hope that he could ever make even the feeblest attempt to accomplish this.

---

* The whole of the questions and answers set out are taken verbatim from the report of the case as it appeared in "The Times" newspaper.

## CHAPTER XXXVII.

## THE SUMMING-UP!

R. LAWSON WALTON, K.C., addressed the jury before calling witnesses. It was a curious course for him to take, and was one of those legal tricks with which I had not been previously acquainted. Being confident of not being checked by the judge, he had a very fine opportunity of displaying that rhetorical power which he undoubtedly possesses. Mr. Eldon Bankes, K.C., replied, and at the close of his speech told the jury that his Lordship would explain to them the points of law. Then Mr. Justice Grantham commenced what is commonly known as the summing-up. *Had I been a blind man I should have pronounced this the final speech for the prosecution of the plaintiff!* Throughout I listened for the " points of law," but I listened in vain. Word by word, sentence by sentence, I waited for a single statement unaccompanied with dramatic gestures, which had played so prominent a part throughout the hearing.

Patiently I sat, denuded of a vestige of hope that one solitary fact which had been proved in my favour would be touched upon. It required no man of the world to discover which way the judge had inclined from the moment Major Sellar entered the witness-box—a child could not but have noticed it. Mr. Justice Grantham summed-up the case,

"Sievier v. Duke," and I will now proceed to sum-up his summing-up.

That one or two judges take very elastic views in their summing-up of a case, more especially when it is one which has aroused public curiosity, is common knowledge, and in this instance it has been generally agreed that Mr. Justice Grantham broke all records, even eclipsing his own reputation. Apart from those who were present in court, the consensus of opinion of those who merely read the newspaper reports fully confirms this.

As I have previously observed, my solicitors, counsel, and more especially myself, had been very anxious to get the hearing removed to another court. If for no other reason, Mr. Justice Grantham had previously convinced me that he was not a judge I should choose to try a case where any prejudice might possibly be introduced. So long as Mr. Justice Grantham lives it will never be forgotten that he, in his judicial capacity as one of his Majesty's Judges, publicly denounced Roman Catholics and their religion. This was a most unwarrantable and undignified pronouncement. Worse still, it was uncalled for, and therefore gratuitous. It is not the concern of a judge wantonly to take upon himself an authority not vested in him by dictating his unsolicited opinion of a religious sect of which he does not happen privately to approve.

The bare idea takes one back to mediæval ages, for if this kind of thing were tolerated the days of the Inquisition might be revived. For centuries it has been England's boast that a man is free to follow that religion in which he believes. It is not for any man to judge another's faith. Each and every man's religion should be reverently respected, and not sneered at and publicly scoffed at, no matter what our inmost views may be. There is a Higher Tribunal to judge these things, and all unbiassed men would safeguard their speech so as not to hurt the sensitive feelings of those who did not happen to think and believe as they. I should say that, with the exception of Mr. Justice Grantham, not one of his Majesty's judges would discredit a witness because he was not a member of the Church of England, let him be a Roman Catholic, a Hebrew, or even an idolater.    Has Mr. Justice Grantham forgotten that the late Lord Chief Justice, Lord Russell of Killowen, was a Roman Catholic?

That his sentences are at times severe in the extreme, as they are at other times light, is amply illustrated by two recent cases.    For firing a rick of straw recently, when the prisoner pleaded that "the devil was in him," Mr. Justice Grantham passed a sentence of seven years' imprisonment "to keep the devil out of him"; while a few weeks later, for a heinous offence, worse than actual cannibalism—an offence so revolting that it creates an indescribable feeling of horror and disgust—a blind clergyman who pleaded guilty to this terrible degradation, who had for ever ruined the lives of his victims, and had been the cause of his wife committing suicide, and for whom hanging was too good, was sentenced by Mr. Justice Grantham to *six months' imprisonment*    It is interesting to conjecture what punishment would have been meted out to him had he been a Roman Catholic.

Thus the incendiary is pronounced fourteen times as bad as the clergyman who is guilty of the foulest offence against the canons of nature.

Early in his remarks the judge repeated what he had previously stated as Sir James Duke left the witness-box, namely, that "he was very glad the jury had determined to hear Sir James's evidence."    Why was he glad?    Why should a judge be pleased that this or that evidence had been tendered?    In this instance it was at the request of the jury that the defendant entered the box, otherwise he would never have been heard.    It was not a voluntary act. And had I cross-examined him, instead of Mr. Eldon Bankes, I do not think the judge would have been so highly delighted.

Mr. Justice Grantham took up a line which I can only describe as defending the defendant.    If my layman's phraseology is not quite in accord with the ordinary legal term I must ask to be excused. He said " he thought he could ask the jury to say whether there was one single syllable in Sir James Duke's evidence to justify the observation that he had been guilty of ungenerous conduct in protecting his own pocket. *The only question that arose* was whether, in their opinion, the statements made by Sir James Duke were privileged by the circumstances under which they were uttered."

He did not once touch upon the bona-fides of those statements, nor did he for an instant refer to the absolute contradictions which the defendant had made in the box. He failed to point out that had I been thrown into the sea for cheating at cards, first at Adelaide, then possibly at Melbourne, it was not quite certain where, that it was highly improbable that I should have been elected, and remained, a member of the Victorian Club, proposed by Captain Standish, the chairman of the Victorian Racing Club, a position equivalent to the Senior Steward of the Jockey Club, and seconded by the Hon. William Pearson, a member of the Upper House, and vice-chairman of the V.R.C. He did not state that Sir James Duke had said that this allegation had been the subject of conversation at a club, and that, if so, it must have been common knowledge, and evidence of the fact must have been easily procurable. He ignored any reference to the age of the defendant at this period, who was then but a boy of seventeen, and who had been sent away from England, and had thus early attended race meetings at Flemington. What this youth of seventen did was to be looked upon as the act of a cherub, but my presence at Flemington was, by inference, referred to in the blackest manner possible. It was not put to the jury that as Sir James Duke had stated that he unmasked me before the Stewards of the Jockey Club in England, it might appear strange that he did not act in a similar manner in Australia, where the charge would have been ripe for investigation, and evidence, if there was any, at hand, nor did he refer to the fact that he had, on his own statement, nursed this incident, which he swore he witnessed with his own eyes, for twenty-two years before he made any statement or complaint whatever. Had he been in a position to substantiate any one of his accusations he could have done so on the spot where he alleges they happened, and my licence must have been at once cancelled by the Stewards who had granted it, the two foremost of whom had actually proposed and seconded me for the leading sporting club in Australia! The judge did not point out that it was extraordinary that the two principal men on the Australian Turf should never have heard of Sir James Duke's murder story, of the cheating at cards, or of my being thrown into the sea.

It will be noticed that the judge did not deal one by one with the unfounded and slanderous statements uttered by Sir James Duke; but the summing up resolved itself into an intemperate attack upon me from first to last, never once dealing with the merits or demerits of my statement of claim. The whole of the facts were ignored en bloc as far as the truth was concerned. The judge advocated that the occasion was a privileged one, and strongly impressed this upon the jury. I would be the last to say that a member of a club should not be privileged to warn a brother member against an undesirable stranger, but I also say, and most emphatically, that what is told in confidence by one member to another should be solely honest, straightforward fact, and not a tissue of lies. No circumstances, no matter how extraordinary, can be put forward as an excuse for a man solemnly stating to another that which is without a shred of foundation. Had one of Sir James Duke's allegations been true in substance and fact, that one would have been sufficient to satisfy any man that I was undesirable, and there would have been no need to have continued the string of accusations until they stretched to murder. When a man professes to know "too much" against another, it points to one of two things, possibly to both—weakness or malice. But the greater the length of the charges, and the more numerous they were, the judge implied, the greater the privilege.

Then the judge stated that "Major Sellar had introduced Mr. Sievier to this club."

Mr. Eldon Bankes rose, and, correcting him, said, "I think your Lordship will remember that Major Sellar stated that he did not introduce him."

Mr. Justice Grantham thought "it was a fair inference that Major Sellar had introduced Mr. Sievier. At any rate, there was no indication in the book as to who had introduced him, and he was Major Sellar's friend." A more biassed view than this it would be hard to imagine. I had sworn, and the evidence was before the court, that I had not even entered the club with Major Sellar, that I had driven up with another member, and that the whole of the members in the now notorious "gazing room" were acquaintances of mine. I had no idea that Major Sellar was even likely to come into the club, which he did some time after I had called. Major Sellar had also testified to this, but the visitors' book being unsigned, that was sufficient for the judge to set aside uncontradicted evidence and to introduce any inference he chose. It is a matter of no vital importance, except that it distinctly points to the judge's persistent attitude, which he clearly assumed throughout the hearing. Then he did not ask the question of the jury whether, in their opinion, it was so, but laid down that "the jury knew that Mr. Sievier had been in the company of gamblers, card-players, card-sharpers, and the greatest scoundrels on the earth." This was a monstrous misstatement for any judge to make in his summing up, when it was considered that, during a period of twenty-five years, evidence showed that I had only come into contact with one cheat, the man Cavanagh, whom I had myself denounced. Who were "the greatest scoundrels on earth"? There was nothing before the court to justify this. The judge

could not refer to a single fact to justify it.   That I had
been in the company of gamblers might be said of any man
who mixes with owners of racehorses.   Card-players there
are in the most respectable and exalted circles, and in spite
of the fact that I had played cards and betted over a period
of more than a quarter of a century, during which time
I had only once come into contact with a sharper, *to whom I
had that night been introduced*, and who within a few days had
been pronounced a swindler, the judge informed the jury that
they knew I kept the company of sharpers and scoundrels.
Bearing in mind that I have lived a great part of my life
in hotels, and that my career has been rather of a public than
of a private nature, I should have thought that any reasonable
judge would have said that I had shown no little astuteness
in only once having found myself playing in the company of
a cheat in the course of five-and-twenty years.

As to my being a gambler, this could only have been
introduced with a view of prejudicing me in the eyes of the
jury.   There is no doubt, generally speaking, a strong anti-
pathy in England amongst certain classes against gambling,
but, on the other hand, there are, taking an average, as many
honourable men who gamble as there are in any other walk
of life.   The judge did not inform the jury that there are more
solicitors annually struck off the Rolls for forgery, theft, and
criminal offences than there are defaulters declared on the
Turf; yet to belong to the one class is deemed reputable, to
be connected with the other a disgrace!   I submit it should
not be allowed, or for an instant tolerated, that a judge should
have the power to tell the jury that they know this or that to
be the case unless the evidence clearly establishes it, and is
dealt with by the judge in support of his statement.

So the summing-up continued.

Had the jury been composed of men with an open knowledge of the world, I am of opinion that the judge's " summing-
up " was so obviously biassed that their sense of justice would
have revolted.   But, as I have already shown, they were not.

Mr. Justice Grantham never once left the jury to form their own opinion, but dictated to them in the most emphatic, if not virulent, manner that I was everything the defence had by inference attempted to prove. Having blackened me in language which no one who heard it could describe as unbiassed, embellished with those dramatic gestures and expressions, of which Mr. Justice Grantham is a past-master; having besmeared me with filth and rolled me in the mud with a disregard of a tittle of evidence unique in the annals of any court (or the record of the most frenzied summing-up of modern times) he then proceeded to deal with the question of damages.

He said: "But supposing the jury were to say that Mr. Sievier was a man who might be introduced into this club, and that Sir James Duke was wrong, then the question arose as to what damages they should award. The plaintiff, if he had suffered any material damage, was entitled to those damages. If not, the damages would be judged by the character of the man. What damages did they think the plaintiff was entitled to receive because somebody had said he had no right to be in the Raleigh Club?"

The judge directed the jury that the issue resolved itself into whether I was "a man who might be introduced into the Raleigh Club," and this was not put to them until after I had been maligned by the judge in a manner calculated to influence ninety-nine jurymen out of a hundred. But, apart from this, I maintain the judge was wrong in so directing them. Surely the real issue in the case was whether Sir James Duke had spoken the truth or lied. Whether I was a fit person to enter the Raleigh Club, or, for that matter, a cabmen's shelter, had nothing whatever to do with the calumnies the defendant had uttered against me, and which were never proved or even supported. Police-constable Drew, as already stated, was entertained by Sir James Duke and his friends as a guest of the Raleigh Club, but he would have little or no prospect of being elected a member—at least,

22

as I remember the club in the old days.    Hence, according to Mr. Justice Grantham, any member could have slandered Drew to an unlimited extent, solely because he was not a man "who might be introduced to the club."

I never complained that anybody had said that "I had no right to be in the Raleigh Club."    My case was whether I was a murderer, a card-sharper, a puller of horses, a man who had been unmasked to the Stewards of the Jockey Club, &c., &c. The judge was monstrously in error in stating that the question of damages rested solely upon *somebody's opinion* as to my locus standi in regard to the club referred to.    He might as well have said that a man once blackballed for a club is *ipso facto* stamped a blackguard!

Nobody can possibly concur in these extraordinary notions of Mr. Justice Grantham, which he has publicly stated in open court.

Having, as it were, condescended to refer, in a contemptuous manner, to the question of damages, the judge continued :

"Now, who is this man?    They had heard of his career in Australia, how he had become the father of two illegitimate children in two years, and how he had been divorced for cruelty and adultery."

As to my having two illegitimate children in Australia, I denied this in the box, and no other evidence, documentary or otherwise, was put forward to rebut it.    But assuming I was the father of an army of illegitimates, what had that to do with the slander?    Take the opposite side of the case ; had my counsel asked Sir James Duke a similar question, would that have been sufficient to prove that all his accusations were lies?

In regard to my being divorced when I was twenty-five years of age (1885), it is quite correct.    I decline to deal with the affair as I might ; but I think, after the long space of time which has elapsed, it was not fair to harp on it, nor had it anything to do with the issue before the jury.

But the judge dwelt on this incident as though it had just happened, and as though there were extraordinary things connected with it which are not met with in the divorces which take place every day. Does the judge know how long the hearing of this "terrible divorce suit" took? Exactly twenty minutes. If the judge's inference possessed the slightest substance, the newspapers were defrauded of considerable copy! Then, I would ask, how long a time is supposed to pass before a man can expiate a mistake? If an unhappy matrimonial alliance, freedom from which can only be gained by divorce, is to be a matter of adverse comment in the eyes of Mr. Justice Grantham after twenty years, then a criminal offence must be inexpiable even by purgatory!

Mr. Justice Grantham then proceeded:— " Was it for those wretched people they were asked to give a verdict for this man?" He did not say that though these circumstances might not redound to a man's credit, yet they had no direct bearing on the legitimate points at issue, and that the introduction of this stale story might possibly suggest how weak were the props upon which Sir James Duke depended to support his slanders.

Then, inconceivable as it will appear—indeed, if I were not quoting from the shorthand notes I should not expect to be believed—the judge continued : " There was a lady to whom he had been engaged for four years. Was she the person for whom the jury were to find a verdict?"

More than sixteen years ago I had been engaged to be married to a lady, and the engagement had been broken off! What had this to do with the case—indeed, what had it to do with anything out of the ordinary common occurrences of everyday life? Such an observation as that of the judge was as ridiculous as it was preposterous; but the jury were gaping in astonishment, and were floundering in the slough of bewilderment.

Then he stated, " There was another lady, to whom he was married two days before she was to have been married to a gentleman with whom she would have lived all her life." On what grounds could he lay it down as an absolute fact that any woman would live all her life with any man? Yet the judge put it to the jury as an accomplished circumstance without any element of doubt. I would suggest that for an individual to be inflated with sufficient dangerous conceit to blindly lead him to pose as a matrimonial prophet is sufficient proof in itself that he is not fitted to uphold the dignity of the Bench.

He continued in the same vehement strain, cruelly and unjustifiably referring to my wife's private affairs : but he never once touched upon my children. Why should he so palpably have ignored any reference to them? Is it not crucially significant? He did not even suggest that it might be for them that the jury were asked for a verdict! No ; there would have been a true, legitimate ring about that ; so he left them unmentioned and unheeded.

"How did the case open?" he went on. "It opened with a wretched story of the plaintiff's career in Australia, of his wife, and about his trading as a bookmaker in a false name. Sir James Duke knew something of that story, and the question was whether he was justified in telling a member of his own club what he knew."

The judge did not once review Sir James Duke's evidence. He did not point out a single one of the discrepancies with which it teemed. The fact that the defendant had spoken, how or under what circumstances was immaterial, whether true or false, was no question for the jury. Had Sir James Duke told the truth to Major Sellar and others, is it conceivable that I should have been ignorant of the gravity of the situation if made public? Had his statements possessed even a grain of fact, were they not sufficiently stale and forgotten for me to forbear to reopen the chasm which time had filled up? Better stand on thin ice than not stand at all. But I took my action against Sir James Duke because his accusations were deliberate lies.

Mr. Justice Grantham avoided any reference to his evidence ; on the contrary, he laid it down, without expressing any doubt, that "Sir James Duke knew something of that (Australian) story." Something! Did he define that something? Did he remind the jury that the defendant was then a boy of seventeen, and that there was no evidence to support his statement, which vacillated, with regard to one specific charge, between towns and places covering an area larger than that of the United Kingdom? That on all the other charges he could make no coherent reply at all! Did he hint that it might be considered peculiar, that according to the evidence, Sir James Duke had allowed twenty-two years to elapse before publicly proclaiming me? Or, what was. perhaps equally vital, taking into consideration his age, did the judge even suggest that he might have made a mistake? He never even once referred to any of these statements ; had he done so, he knew the case must have been decided in my favour. Again, it was totally incorrect to say that my case opened with a wretched story of my career in Australia : and though the judge more than once introduced the subject of my wife, was this an episode which could permit of a judge describing a man's career as wretched? Certainly I had traded as a bookmaker, but I have yet to learn that the following of that occupation is illegal. A calling which the law permits is not one for Mr. Justice Grantham to decry in his official capacity. Then he solemnly stated that I carried on this business in a *false* name. The word *false* which he introduced clearly defines the temperament of his summing-up. Solicitors of the High Court trade in names other than their own. Would a judge define those as false? Many a large firm in the City has not a single partner in it bearing its name, and the same applies to banks and many other institutions. On the stage there are few actors or actresses who do not carry on their professional duties under "a false name," and many continue that name in their private life. I was but twenty-two years of age, and for business purposes—my own being a peculiar and very uncommon one—I adopted my mother's maiden name. On these grounds it was inferred I was engaged in something nefarious by the introduction of the word FALSE.

"There was no reason to go into the history of this man in all its particulars, and his relationship with the ' Jubilee Plunger,' Benzon ; but he should have thought that any honourable man would have been sorry to get money out of such as he." I have already referred to Mr. Benzon's letter, stating that all our transactions were honourable, written at a period when that gentleman had had ample time for reflection. I betted against horses with Mr. Benzon in the course of my business. One was Redpath, for the Grand National, who started at a third of the odds I had laid against him, and had he won I should have been in Mr. Benzon's debt, and not he in mine. We had only one settlement, running over a number of transactions, of which Redpath's was the last. Yet it was inferred by the defence that I had cheated him, and this was suggested by the judge's remarks. I might ask how many thousands Mr. Benzon lost in the Raleigh Club, of which Sir James Duke recently was one of the committee ?

The judge said that there was " no need to go into the history of this man " : but as I deal, item by item, with the subjects he dealt with, it will be seen that not a single stone which could be cast at me was unthrown. And of what were these missiles compounded ? Inference. What better instance than that I had traded under a *false name.* when I had only practised what was common custom ?

## CHAPTER XXXVIII.

### THE SUMMING-UP (*continued*).

HOUGH Mr. Justice Grantham promised that his summing-up would be brief, he waded on and on through the mire, and left one wondering if he was ever coming to an end. Wherever there was a stray scrap, no matter how insignificant, he threw out the scraper and heaped it up with a precision and professional finish which would have done credit to the most expert of the County Council's road cleaners. He continued:—

"Then there was the incident where the plaintiff played billiards up to two or three o'clock in the morning *with a young man*, and sat talking until six or seven doing nothing. If they were doing nothing, how was it he was found drugged or drunk hours afterwards?"

Mr. Eldon Bankes: "There is no evidence of that, my lord."

Again Mr. Eldon Bankes was forced to rise and object to the judge's summing-up because it was unsupported by any evidence. Mr. Bankes might as well have attempted to have invoked the gods as to have corrected the judge in any way whatsoever, no matter how crucial the point, evidence or no evidence. Seldom is a judge interrupted when addressing the final word to the jury, and it can be taken for granted that counsel is quite sure of himself

before he protests under such circumstances. There is no
judge on the bench or counsel at the Bar who will for an
instant believe that Mr. Eldon Bankes would attempt to
correct a judge unless he was convinced he was right in
doing so—not one except Mr. Justice Grantham.

What was Mr. Justice Grantham's answer to Mr. Eldon
Bankes's emphatic statement that "there is no evidence to
that effect"?

He said: "I hold that is a fair statement from evidence."
What evidence? I was the only one who gave any evidence on the point. I have the shorthand notes in front
of me, and there is no evidence whatever to support the
judge's audacious assertion that Horn was either a young
man or drugged. Before dealing at length with this point
I will give the whole of the judge's observations with regard
to this episode. After a pause he added: "They (the jury)
knew that the man had apparently tried to sign some
cheques, and that five or six cheques were missing from
his book. There was no explanation of the cheque for £600,
and no explanation that the plaintiff was at the bank as
soon as the doors were open, and he was able to cash it.
Then there was the incident of the *young man Horn*, 'Drunken
Horn.' The jury would be able to form their own opinion
of what happened from the plaintiff's evidence. The plaintiff had demonstrated how this foolish fellow had waved
his arms about, challenged him to play billiards, plaintiff
giving Horn 25 or 30 in 100, *and just winning;* then giving
him 40, *and just winning;* then giving him 50, *and letting him
get to 98, and winning again.*"

What could be more monstrous than these misstate-
ments? There was not a scintilla of evidence as to Horn's
age—the question had never been put—and it was a gross
misdirection to the jury when Mr. Justice Grantham in
his judicial position, solemnly described Horn as a young
man. Had Horn been alive he would have been exactly
twelve years younger than Mr. Justice Grantham, who is

seventy years old. If a person who had survived three
score years and ten can be fittingly described as an old man,
equally so a man of forty-five—which was Horn's actual
age at the time in question—could hardly be truthfully referred to as "a foolish young man," as the judge defined
him, with an almost incredible asperity considering *the
matter of Horn's age had never once been mentioned during the
case, and no evidence whatever on the subject had been tendered.*

If this was not misdirection it would be interesting to
the layman to learn what is. Nor did he end here, but,
warming to his subject, he reached the point of ebullition
when he described the games of billiards. It is difficult to
imagine that he could ever have hoped to have been taken
seriously. There was no evidence that I *just won* each
game, and his final remark, "then giving him 50 *and letting
him get to* 98 and winning again" was, in the face of his own
words, a gross misrepresentation by the judge. Moreover,
it was a misrepresentation of the game and rules of
billiards. As I have previously pointed out, any man
who knows how the game is scored—he need never
have handled a cue—is aware that when a player reaches 98
in a hundred up he is within two of game. He is then entitled to another stroke, and if he makes the minimum score
must win before his opponent can have a chance. But
assuming he fails to score. it is no certainty for his opponent to win the game on his next venture, even if he is a
Roberts or a Stevenson ; therefore, apart from Horn having
the command of the table when 98, on losing this by his
failing to make the winning stroke, he still had the possibility of his opponent not making the necessary number of
points. Then it must be remembered that on reaching 98
points Horn would bring all his ability into play so as to
leave, if possible, an easy hazard or cannon which would
win him the game. During this time my cue was dead. I
was, as it were, out of the game. In short, Horn had to
fail to score to have any chance of losing. Yet Mr. Justice

Grantham seriously stated that *I allowed* him to get to 98. He might as well have added: "The plaintiff very probably then hit this young man Horn over the head with the butt-end of his cue, and finished the game." There was no more evidence of the one allegation than the other.

As to a cheque of £600, there never was one for that sum given, but it was undisputed that Horn had lost this amount to me, and that he had given me a cheque for £100 and one for £500. The former was paid that morning, and the latter dishonoured. The statement that I had been able to cash it was utterly incorrect, for the dishonoured cheque was in the possession of my solicitors at the hearing of the case. As to some counterfoils not being filled up in Horn's cheque book, I could, and did, account for two of these, as he wanted to give me two post-dated cheques which I refused, and these were subsequently torn up and thrown into the waste-paper basket. But according to the judge there must have been something suspiciously wrong about that! What I cannot conceive. Mr. Justice Grantham said, and on this occasion the evidence supported his observation, that we sat talking in the hall of the hotel after the games were over until six or seven in the morning. Yet he instructed the jury that Horn had been drugged. When, and for what reason? The games were over, and we sat for some three or four hours in the company of perhaps half a dozen visitors chatting in the hall. There was no dispute. All this had been sworn to.

Even if the judge honestly thought Horn had been drugged, he did not point out it was impossible that this could have happened in the billiard-room during the progress of the games. In the first place, a drugged man could not play billiards, much less get within two points of game by scoring 98. Nor is it within the bounds of imagination that a large number of spectators would permit a "drunken or drugged young man" (aged 45) to play a game of billiards for a large stake of money without at least one dissentient voice being raised, even assuming they did not stop the game being played at all. As a matter of fact, it was sworn to that several present betted on the result, and at one time good odds were laid on Horn winning. Therefore, it would have been a reasonable deduction, assuming Horn was found "drunk or drugged," that it must have been *after* he had reached 98 and just missed winning the game by not again scoring. It was proved that he sat talking in the hall with several others for hours after this, so the drug, if administered, must have been a most impotent one, or have been a deuce of a time in taking effect!

And what were the servants of the hotel doing all this time to allow a drugged or drunken man to stagger about the place for some seven hours on end? Why was not even one of these men called to prove that Horn was in the state Mr. Justice Grantham assumed he was? Why, indeed?

What did really occur? The evidence is quite clear. Horn, when the company in the hall broke up, went to his bedroom on the third floor—a long way up if either drugged or drunk—and made out two post-dated cheques for the money he had lost, which I refused, and on my writing out two others he signed them, tearing the others up. I fail to see anything irrational in this. The reason for his giving two cheques was that he wanted a little time to enable him to find funds to meet the one for £500, which, as I have stated, was never honoured, and is in my possession at this moment, while the one for £100 was. It must appear clear that Horn could not have been drugged up to this period. But if ever he was, what possible motive could there have been? He would have been incapacitated from playing billiards, or writing a cheque afterwards.

Having lost, and, what is still more to the point, having slept on it, Horn then tried to get out of discharging his liabilities. This was no rare thing with him; it was a habit. It had been proved that he was expelled from the Badminton Club for much the same thing. Why did Mr. Justice Grantham burke this fact, recorded in the books of the club? He never failed to trot out skeleton after skeleton and dangle them in all their nakedness before the jury, while here he had some substance to deal with. Why stifle the truth? Echo answers. Nothing else could.

I regret being compelled to pursue this episode further, but the judge's inaccuracies increased to such a degree by his waving aside the whole of the facts sworn to, that I have no choice. Mr. Lawson-Walton had inferred on behalf of the defence that the Monte Carlo police had made an inquiry as to whether Horn had been drugged or not. But he failed to acquaint the court with the result of their inquiries. The reason is obvious. Had Horn been drugged the police could have given evidence on this point, and it would have been far more valuable and reliable than the mere opinion of a police-constable, which the judge welcomed. Such testimony would have been fatal to me. But it was not forthcoming—except when given by Mr. Justice Grantham.

Again, the judge absolutely ignored the facts which had been proved. What was the upshot of this scandal, made scandalous solely through Horn being a man who, by hook or by crook, habitually disputed and wriggled out of discharging his debts of honour? In the end, after the British Consul at Nice had come to Monte Carlo at the request of Lord Dufferin, to whom I had telegraphed, Horn left and never returned, while I, with my wife, remained.

As I sit following the shorthand notes of the evidence word for word, I drop my pen and wonder.

Having passed this "drugged or drunken" allegation, the judge then mumbled something to the effect that "the jury had heard what the inspector had said," but it was in a subdued tone, which gave me the impression that he had possibly been reminded of the inadmissible and false evidence he had permitted in the case, the admission of which was subsequently censured in the House of Commons. Some good has come out of evil, for such unwarrantable statements will never again be allowed to disgrace England's Courts of Justice. the highest authorities having pronounced that such a course is illegal and unjust.

Facts. and facts only have been dealt with by me, and so far as I have been able to restrain myself, I have attempted to record them dispassionately. I think I am entitled to say that so far not a single allegation was brought home to me, any more than a single one of the calumnious accusations with which Sir James Duke charged me, was proved. The defendant's own evidence showed them without the slightest foundation ; false to a letter. If I am wrong, Sir James Duke has a dual remedy. On the one hand he can be the means of securing £1,000 for the Queen's Unemployed Fund, and on the other he can take an action for libel against me and the proprietors of the WINNING POST.

Mr. Justice Grantham then touched upon the Braganza incident. The facts I have already dealt with, by publishing the Duke's letters to me and Mr. Guy Chetwynd's (son of Sir George Chetwynd) statement. I will briefly refer to them again. I had played cards in a public room of a hotel in Monte Carlo in the company of four other gentlemen. Some lost, others won, and among the former was the Duke of Braganza, who took the bank at baccarat. After the game was over not a reflection was cast. We sat smoking and chatting for some time, and then the party broke up. Subsequently a cocotte stated that Mr. Burns, one of the players, was a notorious cheat. No one had detected him cheating, nor had a breath of scandal been connected with the game prior to this. I saw Count Batthyany, with Mr. Ralph Sneyd, who introduced us, on the subject. Nothing definite beyond this cocotte's assertion could be discovered against Mr. Burns. The Duke thereupon discharged his debts of honour, and *I volunteered to return the money I had won* if it was ever discovered Mr. Burns was the man it had been so irresponsibly assumed he was. I have never been asked to return a penny ; but, on the other hand, about a week after, played baccarat

in the same room under almost exactly similar circumstances
with the Duke of Braganza's brother, who was present at
Monte Carlo during the whole of the time! Nevertheless, the
judge laid it down that I was doubtless in the company of a
cheat and in collusion with him! Count Batthyany, a gentleman whose honour has never once been impugned, and who is
a man of the world and was on the spot, decided the contrary.
Who on earth was in the better position to form an opinion,
or whose judgment in worldly affairs should carry more weight
—that of Count Batthyany, a member of the Austrian Jockey
Club, who was on the spot, or that of Mr Justice Grantham?

Going on, in face of his unfulfilled promise to be brief, Mr.
Justice Grantham continued : " Then there was the incident at
the Hotel Metropole, Brighton, where the plaintiff was again
accused of being in the company of a known card-sharper.
What would any of the jury have done if such an allegation had
been made against them? Would they not have spent the
last penny they possessed in clearing their character from
such a charge? What did the plaintiff do ? Withdrew his
action, and paid the whole of the costs."

This is a terrible distortion of the evidence.

It was quite true that a man who I believe was a card-
sharper was present, but I was introduced to him by Ernest
Renton that evening in the billiard-room of the hotel. Later,
we played cards, and Renton, *who had the bank at baccarat
throughout*, lost a good round sum to me. He breakfasted with
me the next morning, and it subsequently transpired that the
cardsharper was known to some of the hotel servants. Renton
had not the money to settle ; indeed, he was at this time a
defaulter on the Turf to several bookmakers, and what he
then owed has never been discharged to this day. Like the
majority of men in his impecunious position, he was ready
to seize any excuse for repudiating his debt. As regards a
cardsharper's presence during the game, I agree he was right,
and in fact I forewent my claim, but Renton, in his anxiety
to free himself through the only loophole open to him, con-

nected me with the man *he had himself introduced me to the previous evening.* I brought an action against him. Meeting him in the paddock at Epsom some time after this had been commenced, he came up to me and apologised. He withdrew everything, and so frank was he that I introduced him to my wife, and he lunched in our box at the races on this and the following day. My solicitors addressed a letter to Renton's solicitors, setting forth these facts, adding that as I had accepted Renton's apology the action would be withdrawn. A copy of the letter was produced in Court and put in in evidence. I paid the costs at a time when Renton was abroad, and he afterwards repaid me by handing me a cheque for £100. This was the evidence. Yet, in face of this, the judge made his misleading statement, never once stating that my solicitors' letter was the basis upon which this action was settled. Would it not have been fairer to have assumed that Renton was as much in the company of a cardsharper as I? And what grounds had the judge for saying I " was *again* accused of being in the company of a cardsharper "? This was the first time I had been accused of this, unless he, by a stretch of imagination, included the Burns "incident," which occurred years afterwards. There was no other case. Surely it was for me, in consultation with my solicitors, to decide whether I would accept Renton's ample apology or not, and their letter to his solicitors distinctly stated that they had advised, and agreed that I ought. By what right did Mr. Justice Grantham direct the jury that I had acted as none of that body would have done, with these facts and documents before him? And why did he not refer to this letter, and remind the jury of the true ending to the proceedings I had taken. No, the whole of the facts were concealed, and comment took their place.

Following on the lines palpably suggested by him to Mr. Lawson Walton. the judge retained the Volunteer "incident" for the last. It had nothing to do with the case, but the judge made what I can only describe as a dramatic appeal to the national feelings of the jury. I have dealt with the matter previously, as indeed I have with all the other "incidents," but this one is so far outside the question which was at issue— or rather which in justice should have been at issue—that I feel there is no reason to refer again to this irrelevant topic of which the judge made so much.

The jury retired. What verdict could they possibly be expected to find when subjected to the influence of such a "summing-up"? They would have had to be men of intellect and education to have withstood such a lengthy and drawn-out misrepresentation of the true facts. They decided as they were dramatically directed, and returned a verdict that the occasion was privileged.

## CHAPTER XXXIX.

## MR. JUSTICE GRANTHAM SUMMED UP.

O sooner was the case over than Sir James Duke delivered his bill of costs with electrical haste, and I believe in this respect broke all records. I at once instructed my solicitors to have them taxed, and made arrangements to secure the defendant his costs with the same promptitude that they had been got together and delivered. Hence I was pretty busy. Before the taxing master I was faced with as much opposition as I had experienced during the hearing of the case, and when I mention that £500 was allowed by him for getting up the Brief, and only three witnesses were called, this will probably astonish lawyers more than the man in the street, who is unacquainted with the procedure of taxing costs. Though I only had one K.C. and was the Plaintiff, the cost of two K.C.'s were allowed the defendant. I need say no more upon this subject except that a firm such as Messrs. Lewis and Lewis did not succeed in reducing this bill of costs, which they described as excessive, to within many hundreds of their estimate. The pronounced prejudice against me amounted to as great an injustice before the taxing master as before the jury.

23

After the verdict, before leaving the court, I asked Mr. Eldon Bankes forthwith to appeal. This he did not do, possibly he did not hear me in the excitement which prevailed. It was on the eve of the Whitsuntide Vacation, and Sir George Lewis was away. In his absence I consulted Mr. Griffiths, his managing and confidential clerk, who I believe is himself a solicitor. I had often seen him in place of Sir George in regard to the case. He informed me we had three months in which to appeal. Shortly after this he advised me we had only twenty-one days. Then it was discovered that the appeal should have been lodged within eight days! This was a thunderbolt. I then saw Mr. Eldon Bankes, K.C., in consultation with Mr. Norman Craig, my junior counsel, and it was decided that an application should be made to the Court of Appeal, praying that I should, under the extraordinary circumstances, be given leave to appeal. This is a recognised practice in the High Court, and leave is invariably given when the occasion has arisen through no fault of the applicant. It was refused. Possibly the hearing of the appeal would have created a scandal, the Drew incident alone being sufficient to assure this. With the case standing where it did, I was the only sufferer, and with all respect, I feel that the refusal to grant me the justice I asked for, merely on the grounds that I was a few days out of time, appeared to me to be a harsh and arbitrary decision, more especially when it is remembered that the defendant's costs had been amply secured. Beyond this I make no comment.

Since then I have heard many varied opinions as to the manner in which Mr. Eldon Bankes conducted my case. If I have no fault to find with my counsel it is not for others to attempt to change my opinion, more especially when these gratuitous criticisms emanate from those who merely read the garbled and distorted reports which appeared in the Press. All I complain of is that I had not a fair trial. Mr. Eldon Bankes fought on the lines of a gentleman. Notwithstanding the methods of my opponents, and I use this word in the plural advisedly, for I had not only the defendant but also the judge as my adversaries. I nevertheless uphold his attitude. We were in a Court of Justice—presumably! The utter hopelessness of my counsel being able to convince the jury on any point in my favour was vividly apparent from the attitude which Mr. Justice Grantham took up from the very moment the case opened. The ear of the Court was deaf to my counsel. Had he been Cicero and Demosthenes rolled into one he might as well have addressed the desert air. Realising, as I do, the almost tragic position in which Mr. Eldon Bankes was placed by the judge, I feel no other counsel could have done more than he did. One might as well have expected a man in the stocks to run!

The hypnotising effects of the result of this case—I again repeat I can never style it a trial—had not subsided when Sir James Duke, directly or indirectly, through the agency of the Raleigh Club, advertised in the public Press for subscriptions to assist him to defray the costs, by far the greater part of which I had paid. Though this appeal was most urgently made by his small coterie of followers, the result was a dire failure as far as the public were concerned.

I do not think it will be considered out of place if I depart from strict autobiography, to which I have hitherto confined myself, and devote a few words to summing up Mr. Justice Grantham, which I will endeavour to do briefly, without exaggerating the truth or distorting facts.

Sir William Grantham appears to be a compound of two extremes—severity and leniency. Unfortunately, I am afraid that if his various and varying sentences were reviewed, they would generally include the former, while the latter commendable qualification has been too often applied to those cases which were undeserving of any mercy whatever. Take as an instance the recent sentence, to which I have referred, of only six months which he gave to a blind clergyman who was found guilty of the most heinous offence against Nature, and who had been the cause of his wife committing suicide. On

the other hand, a woman who shot at a man and his son—
both of whom she accused of having treated her in a manner
I need not describe—Sir William Grantham sentenced to seven
years' penal servitude. The merits of this case I am not
dealing with ; I merely compare the two offences and the
sentences. Had I the space or the desire, similar comparisons
could be continued *ad infinitum*.

In a few words, I should sum up Sir William Grantham by
pronouncing him as severe a judge as he is a weak one. His
stoical attitude in all criminal cases is in contradistinction to
his demeanour as a witness. He has sentenced men to death,
as was his bounden duty, without a quiver ; he has sent law-
breakers to gaol for long terms of imprisonment; but on an
occasion when he himself broke the law and gave evidence
in support of his case, a mere civil one, he wept in the box!
He wept, as others had wept when pleading for mercy before
him. What a contrast! On the one side a deaf ear to the
plea of the poor wretch in the dock, the starving man or the
homeless woman, in some cases hardened wretches, but here
and there a stray one with a touch of nature not yet made
callous by the harshness of reverses and the worldly
struggle of life : on the one side Mr. Justice Grantham.
as a judge, tenaciously holding the conviction that to check
crime first offenders should be punished the more severely ;
that the mercy of a ministering angel is wrong, that prolonged
punishment, no matter whether it throws the first sinner into
contact with hardened criminals or not, is the only remedy :
on the one side inflexibility, a total disregard of the possibility that one of these wretched prisoners, man or woman,
might be contrite, whose heart-strings might be breaking to
reach that goal, the opportunity of doing right : on the other
side, Tears! An extraordinary combination.

When Sir William Grantham was prosecuted by the Urban
Council of his district he had broken the law in a most flagrant
manner. He treated the laws of this country in a manner
which would have landed the ordinary individual who pays

rates and taxes with a heavy fine and a long bill of costs. What was the result? Beyond that he shed tears in the box, nobody knows.

With the public for my jury, I ask, is this not an inexplicable state of things? That a judge does not always know the law requires no stretch of imagination to believe, or there would be no need for a Court of Appeal and so on ; but for a judge to be ignorant of an Act of Parliament, he is fully aware is no plea to justify him in breaking it. But Sir William Grantham could not, even if he had so desired, have pleaded ignorance, for he had been served with notices, in face of which he continued, possibly with renewed vigour, to build workmen's cottages which had been condemned as insanitary by His Majesty's officers.

Though we may not all respect the individuality of this or that judge, we all hold a profound regard for the dignity of the bench, and it is more than a pity that indirectly it received such a rude shock as the result of those proceedings. For a judge to pose as immaculate in his ordinary private life is to hold himself up to ridicule, and in this instance I submit, Gentlemen of the Jury, Sir William Grantham scored one of his principal successes. It almost suggests the groundwork for a psychological story, "Tears Which Failed," with a sequel, "Tears Which Succeeded."

The majority of people entering a court for the first time, look upon a judge with such profound awe that they appear to be lost in bewilderment, wondering if he was not born on the bench, wig and robes complete. As a matter of fact, judges are appointed through so many different channels that it would be difficult actually to state, in some instances, why they were ever elevated to the bench at all.

It is to be deprecated that the political hand, upon which is the finger of party promotion, plays all too prominent a part in this respect. Sir William Grantham owes his judicial position first to the electors of East Surrey and Croydon, then to the late "St. Stephen's Review," and finally to the

Conservative Party, of which he was a unit in the House of Commons. Would it not be a refreshing reform if the lawyers, by ballot, selected those to be elevated to the bench, the successful candidates to be finally approved of by the presiding judges? If the House of Commons was not a back stair-case to the Bench, then the legal profession would not be so anxious to obtain seats in Parliament.

Late in the '70's and in the early '80's Sir William, then Mr. William Grantham, was closely identified with the "St. Stephen's Review," in its day a powerful Conservative organ. In this connection he held a unique position, almost reaching the ambitious altitude of a Gilbertian Pooh-Bah. On the one hand a director of the company, and on the other advisory and consulting counsel. Whether as counsel for the company he refused to accept the emoluments of a director, or vice versâ, I cannot say; but in dealing with the dual positions, I submit, Gentlemen of the Jury, they smack of clashing interests. The layman director might endeavour to avoid an action at law, but this would hardly be the "advice" of an ambitious rising barrister. Nor is it beyond the pale of criticism that a counsel should act as a director on any company, for if it is correct that he should do so, why not go a step further, and, amongst other outside lucrative jobs, become a company promoter right away? Though no doubt the "St. Stephen's Review," with its numerous libel and other actions, was a source of income to him, it had far greater attractions in those days for Mr. William Grantham, who took silk and became a Q.C. in 1877. As I have pointed out, the back staircase to promotion is up the political steps, and supported by the then powerful "St. Stephen's Review," Mr. William Grantham had a very rosy chance of reaching the landing.

At this time Gladstone and the Liberal Party were paramount. John Bright sat in the House under a Quaker halo, Joseph Chamberlain was budding into a Fiscal Orchid of the Empire, and Lord Rosebery, arm-in-arm with Lord Hartington, now the Duke of Devonshire, was making himself felt throughout the land. This gave the journal I have mentioned a great scope for attack, and the cartoons by Phil May and Tom Merry were as excellent as those of The Snark to-day. This furnished the director-counsel of the " St. Stephen's Review " with a brilliant inspiration. In anticipation of what a Conservative Cabinet would be, it was proposed that a cartoon should appear in the " St. Stephen's Review " depicting the different Ministers. Mr. William Grantham voluntarily suggested, without a tear or a blush, that he should appear as the Attorney-General, and, Gentlemen of the Jury, under the peculiar circumstances, I respectfully submit this was a legitimate business proposal. Possibly it was more ambitious than after results warranted, but it was no less cute for all that. Nor were this young man's pushing proclivities, for a second checked ; indeed, they appear to have been encouraged, for at a later period he promoted himself, in his mind's eye, by proposing that he should be depicted in a subsequent cartoon as the Lord Chancellor. So attached was he to these caricatures that he took many of the originals away with him from the offices of the paper, and probably is the happy possessor of them at this moment. Possibly they are now heirlooms.

Nor did the predominating influence of the " St. Stephen's Review " end here, for its columns continuously, almost regularly, contained notices in fulsome praise of Mr. William Grantham, Q.C. Naturally directors, or in this case one of their number, would help to encourage their consulting counsel ! This might be passed by without severe reflection if the subject always emanated from, or was inspired by, the Editorial staff. But such was not the case. At times many of the puffs were written by Mr. William Grantham himself, and these eulogistic paragraphs duly appeared in the " St. Stephen's Review." I submit, Gentlemen of the Jury, that this was playing the political game somewhat strongly. Was it not juggling with the electors, who would read the state-

ments with the confidence inspired by honest criticism? If
Sir William Grantham's memory fails him, I refer him to the
late Editorial Staff, either singly or collectively.   I undertook
to be brief.   I hope I have fulfilled my promise.

## CHAPTER XL.

## THE AFTERMATH.

T is not my desire—though I admit it has frequently been a great temptation—to diverge from the practice I have observed throughout my auto-biography of recapitulating the facts to the very letter, and as far as possible without comment. But where the surroundings are of common know-ledge and of recent occurrence, I feel I shall be pardoned if I here and there make a critical observation, which my reader is, of his own knowledge, in a position to concur in or dissent from.

Under these circumstances, I strongly maintain that the verdict in my action for slander was in truth the ukase of Mr. Justice Grantham, to which the jury were compelled to bow. I have already stated that at least two of "my fellow-country-men" were aliens, who kept "lodging" houses in a most notorious street off Tottenham Court Road. That "such" should follow as sheep the bell wether is not surprising ; but it was astounding, I feel sure, to the great majority that, after this verdict, without calling upon me for any ex-planation, or giving me any notice directly or indirectly, officially or unofficially, the Stewards of the Jockey Club should have warned me off Newmarket Heath. I am left to conjecture a reason—none has been vouchsafed me. Though I was one of the most prominent owners of recent years, who had never once been called before the Stewards of any

meeting the world over, in regard to the running of my horses
during a period of close on a quarter of a century, I received,
without a shadow of warning, that formal notice, which carries
with it the most severe sentence the Stewards of the Jockey
Club have in their power to pronounce.  I have always main-
tained, and do so to-day, that an owner who enters into the
sport, at once places himself in the hands of the Jockey
Club, and that any decision of its Stewards, no matter how
it may be resented, must be accepted as final.  There is no
appeal that I am aware of.  And it is obvious that, unless an
appeal were heard by the members at one of the club's
meetings, any other course would be futile.  Even assuming
this was permissible, it is by no means probable that the club
would stultify its Stewards.  Yet against this, where a man's
honour, his social existence, is at stake, I submit he should
at least have an opportunity given him of vindicating his
character if it lies in his power.  True, he can appeal to the
law of the country ; but in England, and I say so deliberately,
with a full knowledge of the force of my words, in our Courts
of Justice an ounce of prejudice will outweigh a ton of fact.
Yet I maintain that no owner, without the gravest possible
reason, should appeal to anybody outside the Turf tribunal ;
but even if these were not my views, I was struck when
I was down, and had no opportunity of appealing for help,
alien or otherwise.

There is one crucial point which must not be overlooked,
and it is that Mr. Charles Gill is the advisory counsel of the
Jockey Club.  He appeared against me in the action for
slander.  During the progress of the case I had grave cause
to charge Mr. Gill with what I consider, and what every man
I have consulted, including many of the legal profession, also
considers, a gross breach of confidence.  Though it is in my
power to adversely criticise him outside these particular
matters, I refrain from so doing, having not the least desire
to create a prejudice against him.  Hence it is with some
disinclination that I say I believe, and have very strong

grounds for my statement, that Mr. Gill, as counsel to the Jockey Club, used his utmost influence against me. It would take a very strong contradiction from a high quarter to convince me to the contrary. To hope I am wrong would cause me to feel I was hoping against hope.

On this point my information is so trustworthy that a review of some of the surroundings cannot fail to be interesting. Some time before my action against Sir James Duke commenced both Mr. Gill stated and the defendant boasted that, no matter what the issue might be, I should afterwards be prosecuted for perjury. This is edifying, having regard to subsequent events, which I shall deal with later. It was as much common comment at the Garrick Club, which, I believe, claims Mr. Gill as a member, as it was at the Raleigh—a club Sir James Duke does not patronise with such regularity as was his wont prior to my autobiography reaching a certain stage, which placed him on the public platform in the searching rays of the limelight. Therefore that secrecy which usually covers most cases before they are heard was not observed on this occasion, and the possibility that considerable prejudice might affect the result by the aid of open boasting is the only reason I can assign for this extraordinary state of things. As consulting counsel of the Jockey Club, Mr. Gill could hardly be expected to have an unbiassed and unprejudiced opinion of me. On my side I can unhesitatingly declare I have no prejudiced opinion of him, for I have no opinion of him at all. Hence I hope, even if I do not trust, that he will accept what I am going publicly to put to him in as fair and open a spirit as he can conjure up.

It will not be surprising if I have a very pronounced feeling that as the Stewards are strong, so should they be merciful—within reasonable limits of their laws always granted. Anomalous as it is, on the one hand a man is visited with the extreme penalty without being given a hearing or a shadow of intimation of the reason ; on the other, if a man is a cheat, and commits the vilest offence against the canons of racing by causing his horse to be pulled, he is given an opportunity of answering the accusation, and no obstacles are put in the way of his defence. I may be wrong, but, with all respect, I do not think the creation of this precedent can commend itself to men generally, and to say that the Jockey Club is unanimous on this point would be totally incorrect. At the time, my legal case created great excitement in racing circles, and I am rather inclined to think that to this I owe the extreme sufferings I have been compelled to experience. The calm deliberations which would prevail to-day might award me a different fate. Is any verdict of Mr. Justice Grantham immaculate?

I think I have a right to attempt to discover, if possible, where undesirability on the Turf begins, and how far an owner can go without reaching the limits which would declare him "an undesirable." On these grounds I addressed an open letter in the columns of the "Winning Post" to Mr. J. B. Joel, of Grosvenor Square. I proved beyond doubt that his name was Isaac Joel and that John Barnato were assumed names. How far the laws of racing apply to this it is not for me to dictate. I also proved that he was an illicit diamond buyer, a thief's accomplice, and a fugitive from justice, having estreated his bail in one of His Majesty's Colonies for many thousands of pounds. I further proved that he incited and engaged a man to beat and maim me, offering this desperado a minimum of £200 as a reward, with an increasing scale according to the limbs he broke, and that it was even suggested that vitriol should be thrown over me as I passed through Lewes Station on my way to Eastbourne, where I then resided. I published the numbers of the bank-notes he gave to the man to commit these deeds, which were worse in every criminal degree than the charges brought against Hugh Watt, who is now undergoing five years' imprisonment. I also published the letter he sent to the ruffian he employed, and every detail. *Every word I caused to be made public was supported by documentary evidence,* and the papers substantiating these statements are in the custody of my solicitors, Messrs. Wontner and Sons, and if further proof were needed the "Police Gazette" at Scotland Yard will bear testimony to the fact that this owner of racehorses. a member of the majority of the racing clubs around the metropolis, is a thief of the worst kind.

In reply to my publishing these facts what did this man. Ike Joel, do? He consulted Mr. Charles Gill, K.C.; and it must be surmised that he advised him he could take no action. But did Mr. Charles Gill report him to the Stewards of the Jockey Club as being an undesirable? If not, then a man who commits a felony, and has been concerned in crimes of the blackest kind, is either not undesirable in Mr. Gill's opinion, or, for some reason best known to himself, in this instance he extended to Joel the hand of clemency!

On these grounds may I not ask where undesirability begins?

Whether Isaac Joel, of Grosvenor Square, should be arrested to-day and conveyed to South Africa to stand his trial, or whether the boasted equal justice of the laws of England has been tarnished and disgraced is no concern of mine; but I should not be human if I did not express myself as feeling that I have been dealt with precipitately in regard to the laws of racing—I may say, mistakenly so. Yet I would sooner have never written a line of my life if one of my thousands of readers is led to imagine that. generally speaking, I do not thoroughly uphold the authorities of the Turf. The Jockey Club is the foundation and the pillars which support the Turf. It controls its honour, and that one word defines the Alpha and Omega of its duties. The one solace I have— and having been a sportsman all my life it is a great one—is that I believe I have suffered only through the adverse verdict in a case where I had not a fair trial, on the contrary, no trial at all.

The contagion—I can call it nothing else—spread among the credulous and the enemy's camp with all the virulence of

an infectious disease, and I received as many as twenty-two
writs, or summonses, for outstanding accounts in one day.
The fever reached a high temperature ; but on the other hand,
I discovered who were my real friends, and that, if anything,
their number had increased in the time of need. I was the
recipient of hundreds of letters and telegrams from all parts
of the United Kingdom, and from all classes of people—a
strange contrast truly! Several, and among them some whom
I hardly knew as acquaintances, offered to, and did, put their
hands in their pockets to help me to stave off the dead set
which was being prosecuted to its bitterest end against me.

The local tradesmen at Shrewton made no rush at me,
and I desire here to express my great gratification for the
courtesy they have always shown me. Not quite the same
were those of the Cathedral city of Salisbury. From their
number, however, I must except Messrs. Foreman, tailors and
livery makers, and Messrs. Hart, the fishmongers. Strange
as it may appear, some of the first to join in the scramble
to get their money were those who had received hundreds and
hundreds of pounds from me. One of the early birds to issue
a writ was the Carlton Hotel, where I had had a running
account for years, the total of which now causes me to reflect
on my folly. In the face of the large accounts which the
proprietors had been paid, they joined in the chase of the
quarry, which was being hunted by a pack of all sorts, from
the sleek greyhound to the gutter mongrel, and they wrenched
for the comparatively small sum of about £70. Then came
Mr. Douglas Baird, a member of the Jockey Club, who caused
a bankruptcy petition to be served on me for a sum of about
£80 due for a stallion's fee, at a time 1 was lying dangerously
ill, and in such a serious state that my medical adviser had
to call in two specialists. This was the reply I received to a
letter stating how seriously ill 1 was and asking for time. I
was between two extremes—I was either shown no mercy ; or,
on the other hand, every sympathy. Messrs. Fieldings,
the money-lenders, were most generous towards me,

and have extended to me that leniency which has enabled me
to secure my indebtedness to them. I especially mention
this firm, for, as a rule, their calling is erroneously abused.
To say my West End tradesmen did not extend to me the
credit I desired would be to say that the traditions which
have surrounded their old-established businesses had ceased
to exist. Had it not been for this the evil designs of my
enemies would have been accomplished, and the hidden hand
which has pursued me would have completed its work. Who
has guided this hidden hand, and to whose arm it belongs, I
cannot say ; but I have more than a shrewd suspicion that it
is connected with one whose name appears in the pages of
" Burke."

What my enemies could not understand was my not going
under and sinking once and for ever beneath the surface until I
touched the bottomless quicksands. They could not imagine
why my hair did not turn grey, or fall off altogether, how my
eye retained its normal state, and why a hump did not protrude
on my back ! They declared, if anything, I looked fitter than
usual—I believe I did. I had through all their malicious
attacks one mainstay—*I was innocent of the charges brought
against me.* If a man cannot show fight under these circumstances, no matter how he may be pressed into a corner, then
he is a coward, unworthy of the title of "man." I do not say
I have led that life which the hypocrite professes ; it is fairly
before my readers, and they can judge for themselves. An
angel may pass muster in his own sphere, but a man who poses
as one upon earth, and who has never been proved to have
fallen into temptation, is either a man who has been a schemer
and a cheat, or nature has tragically incapacitated him from
the enjoyments of this life—the latter are as scarce as the
former are plentiful.

Knowing the true state of things as I did, this was the
incentive which caused me to set my teeth and face the false-
hoods of my tormentors, who, for the moment, had been transformed into little saviours of society. Where are they to-day ?

Not one. not even the Ali Baba of the gang, dare come forward.

My excommunication from the Turf meant much more than the casual observer might imagine. I had laid out thousands of pounds in bloodstock, and a compulsory and hurried sale carries with it a loss hardly realisable by any except the professional. I had also spent large sums on my establishment at Shrewton, and it now has the deserved reputation of being the best of its kind in England. This had to be closed immediately, but labour has had to be employed to keep the rust away. With a stroke of the pen the whole of this money was sunk, except what the horses might realise at a hurried auction.

A racecourse was the only place to sell them. and I was debarred from being present. So useful a horse as Colonel Wozac went for 280 guineas, Sophron 250, Brother Bill 400, Cherry Ripe the same, and so on. The stud, which I had only just succeeded in getting together, and in which I took an enthusiastic pride, fared even worse. Brood mares with foals at foot, and covered by stallions whose fees were from 200 to 300 guineas, fetched small prices, and as an instance one of the foals realised, as a yearling, one hundred guineas more than he and his dam, covered by Persimmon, fetched when I was compelled to sell! Thus, apart from being cut off from a sport with which I have been associated all my life, and which as an owner I never abused, I lost a very large sum of money, which it would be difficult to estimate, though it runs into thousands of pounds, while the establishment at Shrewton, which will for ever be associated with the name of Sceptre, remained on my hands—empty!

## CHAPTER XLI.

## PERSECUTION.

AVING been ruthlessly condemned by the subtle influence of the " hidden hand," I retired to my home at Shrewton, where I hoped, after a brief rest, to determine on the future. Everything had been suddenly taken from me. My property had been reduced to rubbish-heap value, and I was left a scarecrow—a thing of tatters. This estimation of me by my enemies was hardly, however, realised, for I found I had not lost a friend. but, on the contrary, received much sympathy—expressed and practical —from all kinds of people, many of whom I had never met. But the hunger of my tormentors was not appeased, and the threats which were made before the civil action commenced were being put into operation. The Treasury had been communicated with, and every possible unfair influence was being used against me. Not contented with my being struck down by a foul blow, and afterwards cut aloof from a sport which I upheld as honourably and traditionally as any man now running horses, underhanded, or, at least, unprofessional means were resorted to, and a ridiculous charge, reeking with vindictiveness and malice, was got up against me and laid before the Public Prosecutor. The almost unanimous feeling of sympathy which the large majority of sportsmen extended to me had to be met in some way ! Down, and kicked when down, not alone did my enemies make every possible effort to

24

keep me there, but they attempted by cunning trickery to go to extremes, and if possible dishonour my children, and for ever ostracise them from that society which by birth they have a right to claim.

As I have already stated, in different words, if an ounce of prejudice lurks in the corridors of the Courts of Justice it creates a Satanic influence against its victim. In my case a weighty quantity must have been introduced into the offices of the Treasury. Its officials were forced, rather than encouraged, by the merits of the legal aspect of the charge, to do something. It was suggested that I had given false evidence in an inquiry held in Chambers in connection with my estate. In other words, that I had cheated my creditors. The sole grounds for this allegation were that, in an affidavit which I made to gain a right-of-way across a property I had subsequently rented, my statements did not exactly tally with those which I had sworn to when I was examined, and to show the skimble-skamble way in which the case was got up against me, dates had not been considered, or if they had been then the disgrace which redounds on those responsible for the prosecution is increased. Though the document and my evidence were before the Treasury, it appears it did not deem these sufficient, and they therefore put Scotland Yard in motion to make inquiries, and get up evidence against me by scouring Bedfordshire, where I had resided. In the course of these operations several of the witnesses who were subsequently called for the Crown were intimidated by being told terrible stories about me, even to saying that my children were illegitimate. Many of the witnesses are ready to come forward to-day and swear on oath to the truth of this. One of their number has since been made a Justice of the Peace. Was the hidden hand not still at work?

To say I was absolutely ignorant of what was going on would be incorrect, for I had received an anonymous letter, which on inquiry I discovered proved to contain the true facts of the situation. What did I do? Nothing. I could only wonder when I should be left in peace, when the carrion would satisfy itself, and leave my torn and beaten flesh alone. Metaphorically I had been reduced to a skeleton. But my spirit had not been broken. My courage, if I ever had any, had been redoubled. The occasion demanded it.

When the Treasury take up a prosecution a man is at once half condemned. Rightly or wrongly, it is assumed that the Public Prosecutor would not take upon himself the grave responsibility of applying for a warrant for anyone's arrest unless he was fully satisfied that there was at least a primâ facie case to go on. Therefore, assuming that this public servant carries out his duties in a just and capable manner, the presumption that a culprit has already one leg in prison, as soon as this official points his finger at him, is not an exaggeration.

No matter how independently strong a magistrate may be, it would be unreasonable to assume that he would, at least in the early stages of the hearing, for an instant imagine that the Public Prosecutor had made an egregious blunder, any more than, with these influential surroundings, he would look upon the accused as possibly being innocent. Apart from the great facilities which the Treasury have at their disposal by setting in motion the whole of the machinery known as Scotland Yard, it has all the power of the law and its myrmidons, from the Attorney-General downwards, to call to its assistance, and when once it decides to take action the result depends not so much on the case for the prosecution as on *the accused being able to prove his innocence.* As a comparison, let one bring a civil action against the Government for damages in regard to an accident for which it is responsible, and, if successful, compare them to those which would have been assessed had the action been brought against a railway company or an employer of labour.

It must not be overlooked that immediately the Treasury calls in the assistance of the police it means that the detective, generally speaking, will only report that which will assist in the condemnation of the accused, and anything in his favour will probably be smothered. This is dubbed "getting up the case." During its progress nothing except a miracle would cause the police to relinquish their exertions. Where is there any justice in this system, carried on without a vestige of a desire to help a man to prove his innocence? Only his guilt will suffice. When the cases are being "got up," there is no more independent justice dispensed than one may expect in Hades; on the contrary, the more difficult it becomes to gather evidence against a suspected person, especially if that person is a public man, the keener becomes the detective's nose, and if there is no scent he will, if possible, create a stink. I am writing from experience, calmly and with full deliberation, and I assert that the general practice of the police in only offering evidence which will condemn a man, and stifling points which might prove the charge to be false, is a crying scandal. Take the very last day of my case. I asked one of the detectives what witnesses they were going to call. What was his reply?

"We are not going to call any more *witnesses for the defence.*" Was this not a monstrous thing to say? If so, how much more monstrous was it to put it into force?

And what happened after the charge had been heard, and I was acquitted? I had, under the dramatic circumstances which involved me, been courteously treated by Inspector Arrow. He had not caused me to suffer the indignity of being thrown into a cell and subjected to unnecessary pain and annoyance. Before leaving the court I crossed over to him and thanked him for the consideration he had displayed. His reply astounded me. He said, "You have nothing to thank me for, Mr. Sievier; if I could have got you convicted I should have."

If the Public Prosecutor does not belie his responsibility to the public, and if Scotland Yard is to hold its head up, I submit it should be a greater satisfaction to either and both to be in a position publicly to state they had made a mistake rather than to be able to prove a man's guilt. What does it imply when the Treasury refuses to call evidence which would bring this much-desired ending about? It means that the Crown insists on a man's guilt, and demands his incarceration, though it holds in its grasp the Key of Freedom to which the victim is entitled.

And the innocent victim probably pays rates and taxes, which go to make up the salaries and wages of his prosecutors!

As I have remarked, I was not totally ignorant of what was going on, and after five or six weeks' "consideration," during which period I feel convinced considerable influence was brought to bear on the Treasury, a warrant for my arrest was applied for and granted. It may be a peculiar coincidence that a Sunday should be the time chosen for its execution. This would at least have entailed one day's imprisonment, as bail could not have been granted until the Monday, when I appeared before the magistrate. But as the officers of the law were driving towards Shrewton to put this into effect, I received a telegram, which acquainted me with the fact that something was wrong, and when my little girl came running towards me in the garden, telling me two gentlemen were in the house and wished to see me, my suspicions were aroused. A friend was with me, and, after consulting him, it was decided he should interview them. This he did, while I remained — well, elsewhere. The "two gentlemen" attempted to conceal their identity by stating they had called with the hope that I would show them over the stables, one giving the name of Captain Robinson. Their demeanour did not deceive my friend, who returned to me. Not being inclined to spend a solitary Sunday, I sent him back to say I would meet them at Scotland Yard on the following day at one o'clock punctually, and, jumping into the saddle, I rode off across country, making arrangements that my friend should meet me later with the aid of a motor-car. On his return to the visitors Inspector Arrow ceased to conceal the reason of his call, and, finally accepting my friend's undertaking for my giving myself up as agreed, returned to London with his *confrère*. I am only too glad to state that Inspector Arrow displayed every courtesy towards my friend, and that he in no way made himself offensive or obtrusive to my guests, being evidently satisfied that he had been told the truth. Naturally, and it was his duty, he took all precautionary measures for my arrest if I was seen, and he called on the local police all along the line, and sent messages to various railway stations. From a small plantation about a mile off, mounted on horseback, I saw him drive away.

I then rode leisurely across the downs until I reached the house of a brother trainer. I had no secrets, and told him the facts. He telegraphed to Salisbury for a motor-car, and before long my friend arrived with a change of clothes, for I had been playing tennis but a few minutes before "the visitors" paid me their call, and had ridden away as I stood. On my friend's return, I sent a message to my wife that I should be back about midnight, and then continue my journey. catching a train at Swindon which would land me at Paddington about five in the morning.

On my return I took every precaution not to run into the arms of the local sergeant, and, taking a back road, made my way to the house through the pleasure grounds, hidden by shrubs and laurels. A few cheery words, and I went upstairs to bid "good-night" to my children as they slept, and once more leaving my home, made my way to the motor-car, which was hidden in a clump of trees, and set off full speed towards Swindon with an old friend of mine. On reaching London, I went to his chambers, and after performing my ablutions and having had breakfast, I drove to a friend's to arrange for bail, and then to my solicitors, instructing them to appear for me.

As Big Ben struck one I walked into Scotland Yard with my friend, who had made himself responsible for me. Inspector Arrow stood at the door to give us "welcome." I again have pleasure in remarking that I was treated in a most courteous manner. After being detained in one of the spacious offices, I was driven in a cab to Bow Street. Formal evidence of arrest was given, and then the question of bail arose. Mr. Blanchard Wontner, who had assured me this would be nominal, explained that I was charged with having committed perjury some five years previously. He stated that it was a stale charge, and in the whole course of his experience he had never heard of anyone being charged with such an offence after so long a lapse of time. In fact, it was a record in the annals of the criminal law. He proposed myself in £200, and another surety in the same amount. Mr. Bodkin, who appeared for the Public Prosecutor, made no observation. Now comes what I have always looked upon as the most extraordinary incident of this case. The magistrate, Mr. Marsham, with little or no argument or comment, fixed the bail at £12,000, myself in £6,000 and two sureties in £3,000 each. Such bail has seldom been demanded, and only in such celebrated cases as that of Whittaker Wright has it been heard of. But it was no good ; there was that indefinable something behind it all, and I had to suddenly find this or go to prison, pending the hearing. I say unhesitatingly that requiring enormous bail was unfair, and out of all proportion to the reasonable discretion which is vested in a magistrate, and was significant of a premeditated arrangement between the Treasury and him. At the very same court and time, before Mr. Fenwick, a man was charged with perjury, he having attempted · to defraud a railway company by swearing that he had sustained injuries which was untrue. He was liberated on £200 bail, and was granted his freedom on these recognisances up to the day he was sentenced to nine months' hard labour! I leave my readers to draw their own comparisons.

The bail was forthcoming at once, Mr. Robert Topping and Mr. Clarke-Frost being my sureties.

To go through the evidence of each individual witness for the Crown would be monotonous and futile, but among the early ones was a Mr. Marchant, who swore that he had played two or three cricket matches at Toddington, and had cold beef and shandy-gaff for lunch. He knew nothing else, nor was he asked anything further by Mr. Bodkin. Mr. Avory, K.C., who, with Mr. Elliott, defended me, rose to cross-examine him. I give the colloquy in full:

"What are you here for?"

Answer: "I don't know."

"Nor I either," and Mr. Avory sat down.

And so the case went on. There was not a single witness called who did not help to prove that my statements when I was examined in Chambers were true. Indeed, as the inspector said on the last day, "We are not going to call any more witnesses for the defence." But I must draw attention to one fact, and that is the attempted suppression of the evidence of the under-manager of the City and Midland Bank. A clerk, who was not engaged at this particular branch at the time in question, was subpœnaed by the Crown in place of the previously subpœnaed sub-manager. The latter's evidence we knew would be a satisfactory answer to the suggestion the Crown wished to make, while the clerk's thorough want of knowledge of the facts would leave a stigma behind. It was not until Mr. Avory made an appeal to the magistrate that the Public Prosecutor should be compelled to call the sub-manager that this course was agreed upon. Yet his evidence had been taken by the Crown, and was in the offices of the Treasury; and it was this witness who admitted that he knew Mr. Sawyer apart from me, as I have before mentioned.

Then Lloyds Bank were subpœnaed; but for what reason I cannot imagine. Their representative merely proved that I had won £35,000 when The Grafter won the City and Suburban, and £40,000 when Diamond Jubilee won the Derby, and that I regularly allowed my wife over £1,000 a year. Being a customer of Lloyds Bank, I think the latter should have informed me of what was going on, for they were not to know it might not be serious to me; and I state this more strongly when I remember that the manager, Mr. Mackworth Praed, had been my guest at Toddington Park on more than one occasion.

After five tedious remands, which ran over as many weeks, the Crown offered no more evidence. The magistrate then invited Mr. Bodkin to make the usual speech for the prosecution; but in response he only shook his head negatively. The Public Prosecutor, after his witnesses had been heard, was left in the helpless position of not being able to even ask for my being committed for trial! Then why did he not rise and ask for my acquittal? Why did he not fearlessly announce that the officers of the Crown regretted they had made a mistake? Are they infallible?

The innocent victim has no recourse against the Treasury. He can get no damages; he is not even allowed costs—costs the outcome of its mistakes! Mr. Avory went through the evidence and my examination under oath. Each witness in turn had corroborated what I had stated. Had I been called on to put in a defence, the witnesses called for the prosecution would have established my case. Why was the case ever brought? Why? The magistrate dismissed it as being one in which a jury would never convict. It is, indeed, rare that a Treasury prosecution so utterly collapses, and a man's innocence must be clearly and wholly proved before a magistrate refuses to send a case for trial. The Treasury had not even shown a primâ facie case against me.

Apart from the anxiety which these five weeks brought with them, and the tedious delays of seven days' adjournment, it cost me over £1,000, without any legal claim to be able to recover a penny of that sum. Why, with all the machinery and power at its command, should Government officials be exonerated from liability? Had they carefully, or in the ordinary way of business, compared dates the action would never have been brought. Yet perhaps the most significant thing of all is that the three persons who should have been the principal witnesses had the prosecution been sincere were never called, nor was their testimony taken in any way whatever, while the fixing of my bail at £12,000 is a scandal. Again echo answers. Why?

I must thank Mr. Avory, and no less Mr. Elliott, for the able way in which they defended me ; nor can I let the opportunity pass without acknowledging the good service Mr. Blanchard Wontner rendered, and the personal sympathy he extended to me.

After the case of Sievier v. Duke, certain papers published long articles about me, and I denounce them and their writers as cowardly. But when I was pronounced innocent not one of them had a word to say. So much for a minority of the Press. Yet I had no little consolation, for when the verdict reached Shrewton my friends there rallied, and the village band paraded the streets playing various airs. If my detractors would not own they were beaten, at least my friends and neighbours rose to the occasion.

What was I to do?

I had been faced with this perplexing question before, as my readers may have observed.

I decided upon starting a newspaper, made the necessary arrangements, named it the "Winning Post," and its history is common knowledge. I thank my friends and the public generally who have so heartily come forward and supported me, with the result that I can now claim more than 100,000 readers weekly. It will always be a great gratification for me to remember that in the hour of need an unbiassed public joined hands and pulled me out of the slough of despond into which I had been unfairly cast.

Retaining a strong affection for all sports, and clinging to old associations, I was impelled one day last winter (1904-05) once more to visit my old home at Shrewton. As I walked up the deserted drive all seemed so lonely as compared with the days not so very long ago. A lifeless house, which but a few months earlier was full of life, made merry with children's laughter and the gaiety of an open door, was a melancholy contrast. I rang the bell. I listened to the grating noise which the caretaker made in unbolting the door, the chain fell with a clank, and I entered the empty hall. The only welcome I received was her curtsey, but it was a welcome nevertheless. Reminiscences passed through my mind, the whole of the time of my residence flashed before me, and I stood looking out of a window on to the terrace which runs in front of Elston House. With the exception of two gardeners, not a man was on the place. Before I had left I had kept over fifty people in employment. Opening the window, I went through the gardens, and wended my way to the stables —stables which have earned for themselves a name in Turf History, and will live long after we have all passed the Winning Post of life. I went through the boxes, picturing in my mind's eye the different horses that once stood there— mine, and trained by me. Last of all I entered Sceptre's box. The winter leaves blew about my feet, my eyes became a little dim, and with a lump in my throat I went out into the open.

FINIS.

CPSIA information can be obtained at www.ICGtesting.com
Printed in the USA
LVOW041953200912

299644LV00001B/293/A